AMERICAN FIGHTS & FIGHTERS SERIES

Border Fights & Fighters

"THEY CAME ON WITH FIXED BAYONETS WITHOUT FIRING."

AMERICAN FIGHTS & FIGHTERS SERIES

Border Fights & Fighters

The Conflicts on the Eastern Frontiers
With Indian Tribes and the British
During the 18th Century

Cyrus Townsend Brady

LEONAUR

Border Fights & Fighters
The Conflicts on the Eastern Frontiers
With Indian Tribes and the British
During the 18th Century
by Cyrus Townsend Brady

First published under the title
Border Fights & Fighters

Leonaur is an imprint of Oakpast Ltd

ISBN: 978-0-85706-763-0 (hardcover)
ISBN: 978-0-85706-764-7 (softcover)

http://www.leonaur.com

Publisher's Notes

Contents

I DEDICATE THIS BOOK IN THE BONDS OF AN OLD AFFECTION
TO THAT VENERATED AND ADMIRED SCHOLAR & GENTLEMAN
EDWARD BROOKES, A.M., PH.D., LL.D., ETC.,
SUPERINTENDENT OF PUBLIC EDUCATION,
PHILADELPHIA, PENNSYLVANIA,
WHOSE VARIED LEARNING, PHILOSOPHIC CULTURE,
WIDE EXPERIENCE, AND MOST OF ALL,
UNFAILING CHRISTIAN COURTESY AND KINDLINESS OF HEART,
HAVE SO ENDEARED HIM TO ALL THOSE WHO, LIKE MYSELF,
ARE PRIVILEGED TO CALL HIM FRIEND.

Prefatory Note

From De Soto, who opens the first book of this *Fights and Fighters Series*, to Houston, who closes the third, is just three centuries. The salient incidents of these three hundred years, from the Conquistador to the Pioneer, have engaged the greater part of my attention for a long time, and with the completion of this book they are set before the reader. To me this last book of the series has been the most interesting. It is more thoroughly American and the men come more closely home to us therefore. Two of them come especially close to me, since Captain John Brady was my great-great-grandfather, and Captain Samuel Brady my great-granduncle. It has been a pleasure and pride to me to find them worthy of inclusion in this category of heroes.

As I look back upon the history of America through my studies therein, I seem to catch a glimpse of the great purpose and plan back of it all. The story of our land has been the story of a struggle for the possession of a continent, a story of the rise to domination of that branch of the Germanic Race known as the Anglo-Saxon. Whatever be the continental affiliation of the early or late settler, whether Irish, Dutch, Scots, German, or Latin, he has been modified, changed, absorbed by the dominant racial solvent, primarily into a Germano-Anglo-Saxon, latterly into an American—the new racial type. Our social habits and political practices, like our language, law, and religion, are English, with just enough modification to differentiate us and give us an originality of our own.

The struggle by which this has been brought about is the true meaning of our history, and that is the story told in these books. Alien races were compelled either to affiliate or go out; absorption or destruction were the unconscious alternatives, and if they could not be absorbed they had to disappear in one way or another. The French, the Spanish, the Indians, have gone, and so jealous of control have we been that even the ties that bound us to older civilizations of Europe had to be ruthlessly broken.

To anticipate a little, the dominant idea of America for the free Americans persisted through a Civil War of appalling magnitude, and until we had driven the Spanish flag from Cuba and the Antilles; and if I dare venture a prophecy, though I personally am called an Anti-Imperialist, this supreme idea of American Continental Domination will not reach its limit until there is but one flag from the Isthmus of Panama to the Arctic Circle, and that the Stars and Stripes.

One of the greatest questions that troubles the American mind is the ultimate solution of what is known as the race problem. How far modern ethics may modify ancient habit cannot be said, yet the experience of the past presented but two possibilities to the alien, assimilation or disappearance—*and we cannot assimilate the negro!*

As to the particular volume in which this note appears let me say that to these unfamiliar subjects I have given more thought, study, and investigation, than to both the preceding books. Again, I admit the free use of all authentic printed authorities,—among them only citing by name Roosevelt's great Epic, *The Winning of the West,*—much old manuscript unprinted and some personal recollections of ancient men, together with family traditions. Many of the incidents depicted, while more or less familiar, are not easy to come at in detail, even in the larger histories accessible to the people.

The period treated of was a most important one in our history, and its masters must be judged according to their tasks. The president in a recent speech well said:

> To conquer a continent is rough work. All really great work is rough in the doing, though it may seem smooth enough to those who look back upon it or gaze upon it from afar. The roughness is an unavoidable part of the doing of the deed. We need display but scant patience with those, who, sitting at ease in their own homes, delight to exercise a querulous and censorious spirit of judgment upon their brethren who, whatever their shortcomings, are doing strong men's work as they bring the light of civilization into the world's darkest places.

And Stuart Edward White, a welcome young apostle of the west, in a recent clever novel writes:

> When history has granted him the justice of perspective, we will know the American Pioneer as one of the most picturesque of

her many figures. Resourceful, self-reliant, bold; adapting himself with fluidity to diverse circumstances and conditions; meeting with equal cheerfulness of confidence and completeness of capability both unknown dangers and the perils by which he has been educated; seizing the useful in the lives of the beasts and men nearest him, and assimilating it with marvellous rapidity; he presents to the world a picture of complete adequacy which it would be difficult to match in any other walk of life.

In this book I have striven to do the Pioneer justice, as I have striven to lay aside prejudice all through the series and to write fairly even of the enemy, be he Briton, or Indian, or Mexican, or whatever he may. And in addition to a mere recital of heroic incidents I have endeavoured to depict the characters of men like Boone, Houston, Crockett, Brady, Sevier, Tecumseh, Bouquet, Santa Anna, and the rest.

More pressing literary engagements will probably prevent the issuance of the fourth volume of the series in 1903, as I had wished, but the next book is already planned under the title of *Beyond the Mississippi Fights and Fighters*, and I hope to have it ready in 1904.

C. T. B.

The Normandie,
Philadelphia, Penna.,
June, 1902.

1

How Henry Bouquet Saved Pennsylvania

At once there rose so wild a yell
Within that dark and narrow dell.
As all the fiends, from heaven that fell
Had peal'd the banner-cry of hell!

1. A VETERAN SOLDIER AND HIS PROBLEM

In the far western part of the province of Pennsylvania on the night of the 5th of August, 1763, a little party of English soldiers found themselves confronted by as desperate a situation as ever menaced a military expedition. They were encamped upon a low barren hill with a few stunted trees upon it, which was surrounded on all sides by a thick dense forest. Not a fire was burning on the hill, not a light of any kind could be shown. The sky was overcast and no star sparkled like a beacon of heaven above them.

The troops, numbering four hundred and fifty, were posted on the slopes of the hill in a large circle. Within this circle some three hundred pack-horses were tethered. On the very crest of the elevation, in the centre of the cordon of soldiery, a temporary breastwork had been made by piling in a circle bags of flour and meal which had been the burden of the pack-horses. Within the meagre shelter afforded by the enclosure so formed, some thirty-five desperately wounded officers and men were lying. What slight attention the suffering soldiers received was given them in the darkness. There was not a drop of water on the hill.

At irregular intervals a flash of light would lance the darkness of the mass of trees enclosing them like a wall, and the report of a musket, followed by a terrifying war-cry, would break the stillness of the

13

night, apprizing the anxious soldiers that their 'watchful enemies were still there. The pickets crouching down on the slopes and peering into the blackness about them, kept fearful watch while the rest of the exhausted soldiers lay upon their arms full of dismal forebodings for the morrow, vainly endeavouring to stifle the pangs of thirst or to get a little sleep. Across a little ravine in front of the position they held, upon the slopes of a similar hill, the bodies of some twenty-five of their fellow-soldiers lay still and ghastly under the trees. The well-aimed bullet, the brutal *tomahawk*, and the terrible scalping-knife had done their fell work. There were no wounded there.

The soldiers on the hill were alone in the wilderness. Back at Fort Ligonier, some fifty miles away, there was a little garrison, the major part composed of sixty invalids too weak to accompany their comrades on the expedition. About twenty miles before them another small body of English soldiers, hopefully awaiting for the arrival of the very party in such sore straits, were tenaciously defending Fort Pitt, situated at the confluence of the Monongahela and Allegheny rivers. On all sides of them extended the unbroken wilderness, virgin woods, forests primeval, covering mountain range and valley. The soldiers on the hill, therefore, could hope for no assistance and must depend upon their own endeavours to extricate themselves from their desperate position.

The locality in which they found themselves was pregnant with menacing history. A few miles away, a few years before, twice their number of English troops had been utterly defeated with dreadful loss, and some of the same Indians who had overwhelmed Braddock with such terrible success, lay encamped about these men that night. Still nearer in time as the place was closer in distance, these same red men could recall the disastrous beating they had given Major Grant and his Highlanders. They had never been conquered by the white men—they did not mean to be then.

Every military post on the western Pennsylvania border, except those two mentioned, had been captured by these selfsame savages during the spring; their garrisons had been first tortured and then murdered and the forts themselves burned and destroyed. All over the northwest the Indians had risen, animated by the genius and inspired by the enthusiasm of Pontiac, and they had fed fat their ancient grudge against the hapless English. Not yet glutted by their successes and the ensuing slaughter, they were slowly making their way eastward into the populous and well-settled portions of Pennsylvania.

Such a scene of rapine and murder as had followed the destruction of the military posts has never been equalled. The frontier was left entirely unprotected. In every clearing, where, a few months before, had dwelt the settler in comparative peace and security, tilling the soil, planting his crops and wresting from the wilderness his hard-earned livelihood; and with his wife and children devoting himself to the conquest of the country to the arts of peace and to the spirit of civilization, now stood the tottering remnants of a chimney amid the ashes of a home. Unburied bodies by hundreds, the prey of the wild beasts of the forest, the wolves and the vultures, aye, of the very swine that ranged the wilderness, gave mute attestation to the thoroughness with which the border had been swept by the desolating Indian.

The struggling little towns clustering about the walls of some feeble fort, such as Shippensburg, Carlisle, and Bedford, were crowded with terrified fugitives. With their limited accommodations they were able to afford a shelter to but few of those who sought their protection. Their already depleted stocks of provisions were soon exhausted, and famine and privation added their pangs to the troubles of the people. And there were many wounded and ill, some who had been tortured, shot, even scalped, who yet lived, for whom nothing could be done, who must needs suffer without any alleviation of their anguish.

Distracted wives who had been bereft of their husbands gathered their children about them and lay house-less in the fields. Starving children who had lost their parents wandered from group to group, their pitiful wailings almost unnoticed in the general misery. Here a mother mourned a son, there a friend longed for a friend. And there were many haggard desperate men, too, who had seen their dear ones taken from them and submitted to a fate too horrible to mention. These kept watch and ward over the huddled fugitives; and, as they grasped their rifles with nervous hands, with breaking hearts they swore eternal vengeance against the red man.

And the colony of Pennsylvania did nothing to protect its children!

Fortunately, however, there happened to be at the time an officer named Henry Bouquet[1] in command of the king's forces at Philadelphia. He was one of the most accomplished soldiers and gentlemen of his time; an officer, the variety of whose talents was only equalled by

1. *Bouquet & the Ohio Indian War* by Cyrus Cort & William Smith, two accounts of the campaigns of 1763-1764 *Bouquet's Campaigns* by Cyrus Cort and *The History of Bouquet's Expeditions* by William Smith also published by Leonaur.

his bravery and sagacity. He had for some seven years held a command in America. During this time he had so mastered the tactics of the savage foeman, against whom he most often warred, that in address and cunning he proved himself able to give even the wiliest Indian chief a bitter lesson. Though the service he rendered America was of the utmost importance, though he manifested in the performance of it the steadiest courage, and exhibited the highest skill; though he fought, all things considered, the most brilliant and effective battle which was probably ever waged against the Indians—certainly the most notable engagement in which a British officer commanded—he is a forgotten hero and his services are now but little remembered.

This great and gallant soldier was born in 1719, at Rolle in Switzerland, on the north shore of the beautiful lake of Geneva. Springing from an humble family and possessed of little fortune, he made his way upward by sheer force of natural ability and talent. As did many Swiss, he chose to follow a military career, and entered the Dutch service as a cadet when only seventeen years of age. Shifting his allegiance, as was the habit of soldiers of fortune, he later became adjutant to the King of Sardinia, in whose employ he saw much hard service, in which he greatly distinguished himself. The Prince of Orange made him lieutenant-colonel of the Swiss Guards of Holland in 1748.

After the peace of Aix-la-Chapelle he spent his time in mastering not merely military art but the polite learning of his day as well. In 1756 he was appointed lieutenant-colonel commanding one of the four battalions of the regiment called the "Royal Americans" which King George III had directed should be raised in America for service in the French and Indian War. This was a regiment composed mainly of Pennsylvania Germans, and it was necessary, as the majority of the men spoke little or no English, that officers who should be conversant with their language should be appointed to command them. A special act of Parliament had been required in order that Bouquet and other foreigners could be commissioned by the English king, a most fortunate act indeed. The regiment performed superb service on many hard-fought battlefields in the French War; and various detachments, since the Peace of Paris had ended that conflict, had made up most of the garrisons of the different posts in the west and northwest which had just been overwhelmed by the savage onslaught.

2. The March Over the Mountains

Sir Jeffrey Amherst, who commanded all the English forces in

America, when he received news of the Indian outbreak, immediately directed Colonel Bouquet to advance to relieve Fort Pitt, and to afford some protection to the distressed inhabitants of western Pennsylvania with whatever forces he could assemble without delay. Bouquet could only gather up about six hundred men and this he did by ordering the remnants of two regiments, the Forty Second Highlanders and the Seventy Seventh infantry, which had just been invalided home from the West Indies, to the front. The men were so broken by their arduous and wearing service in the tropics that they were really fit for nothing but garrison duty. Some of them had to be carried along on the march in wagons on account of their weakness. There were no other troops available, however, and they had to go. They cheerfully undertook the campaign for the relief of the suffering people.

On the 3rd of July, 1763, the expedition arrived at Carlisle, to which point orders had been sent that supplies and transportation should be in readiness. Nothing had been done, owing to the panic of the inhabitants. In fact, so far from finding any supplies, Bouquet, who was a man of extreme sensibility, felt obliged to share the meagre provisions of his little army with the starving women and children. The situation was apparently hopeless, but such was the energy, ability, and tact of the commander that eighteen days after his arrival the expedition left Carlisle with a large number of wagons fully provided. Fort Ligonier, the most westerly post, except Fort Pitt, which still held out, was relieved by a party of thirty of the strongest men, who were sent ahead on forced march and succeeded in breaking through the besieging Indians and gaining the fort.

Bouquet arrived at Fort Bedford on the 25th and on the 28th he reached Fort Ligonier. There, putting what supplies he could on pack-horses, and leaving his wagons and heavy baggage he pushed forward toward Fort Pitt in much apprehension. The little army followed Forbes' road,[2] which, through neglect, had become almost impassable; and their progress led them through such scenes of desolation that the hearts of the men were inflamed with an ever-growing desire for vengeance upon the red authors of the ruin.

The army marched with the greatest care. A little body of back-woodsmen scouted before them, followed by a strong advance party, then came the main body, then the baggage train, then the rear-guard, while another party of frontiersmen covered the rear and the flanks.

---

2. See my book *Colonial Fights and Fighters*: The Struggle for the Valley of the Ohio, (also published by Leonaur.)

There were only thirty of these valuable adjuncts, however, and the protection they could give and the scouting they could do, was limited. Bouquet had left the weakest of his men in the forts and his force now amounted to about five hundred men all told.

On the 5th of August they had arrived in the vicinity of a little creek called Bushy Run, about twenty-five miles from their goal. Their advance had been subjected to desultory firing from time to time, so that it was perfectly well known that savages were marking their progress.

Early in the afternoon, in a dense wood, they came in touch with the Indians. The firing, which began with startling suddenness, was too heavy for a mere skirmish. The Indians were in great force and had determined to intercept them, having temporarily raised the siege of Fort Pitt for that purpose. The continual rattle of arms and the wild yells which rang through the wood, apprized the experienced leader that the engagement was fast becoming serious. In fact twelve out of the eighteen men who led the advance were shot down almost instantly. Ordering the baggage and convoy to halt where they were on the top of the hill mentioned, and leaving the rear company to look after it. Bouquet hurried to the front followed by the main body of his soldiery. Advancing his troops and deploying them into such a line as the forest growth permitted, Bouquet charged through the woods with the bayonet. The Indians at once gave way before the onrush of the Highlanders and the light infantry, but when Bouquet halted the charge and recalled his men lest they should become scattered, and he lose control of them, the savages crept back through the trees and resumed the engagement.

As they had done years before to Braddock's men, so now they extended themselves through the wood on either side and endeavoured to attack the British on the flanks. But whatever they did the soldiers met them. There was no panic this time on the part of those weak and feeble half-invalid soldiers. Bouquet was an entirely different man from Braddock and he had won the confidence of his men. They trusted him entirely and they had seen and heard too much of the Indian customs on their march not to know that to break and run meant destruction.

Bouquet carefully manoeuvred his men through the trees, skilfully checking and driving back the advancing Indians from time to time by well-delivered volleys or short rushes with the bayonet. The battle was going favourably when firing in the rear told him that the Indians, who much outnumbered the English, had engaged the rear-guard. Still keeping his front to the enemy Bouquet withdrew his troops and posted them around the hill in rear of the first position, thus affording protection to the convoy and the baggage.

It was late in the afternoon now and until night fell the battle was kept up. The Indians surrounded the camp and fought from behind the trees. There was no more volley firing by the British, but they lay on the ground availing themselves of all possible cover, firing slowly and endeavouring to make every shot tell. Whenever the impatient Indians, growing bolder as they apparently saw their prey within their grasp, left cover and advanced they were driven back to the woods with the deadly bayonet.

Presently the welcome night came and the attack ceased. The situation of the British was indeed deplorable. A line of dead men from the first hill where the first onset had been met, back to the camp, showed how faithfully they had fought and how resolutely they had been attacked. There were no wounded out in the forest glades either. The Indians ruthlessly butchered and scalped all who fell. Some sixty of the English had been killed or wounded.

They were surrounded by a large force of savages and it appeared likely that the terrible experiences of the past would be repeated upon them on the morrow. Bouquet wrote to Amherst that night, commending in brief soldier-like words, the steadiness and valour of his men, but preparing him for the worst possible results of the expected action, which he realized would take place on the morrow. He was too good a soldier not to recognize the peril of their situation and too brave a man not to admit it.

With almost any other commander in the English service in a similar situation, the result would have been certain. Bouquet, however, was in himself a host. He knew that his only chance of escaping annihilation would be in bringing the savages to a stand, where he could deliver with his veterans such a decisive blow as would completely defeat them, otherwise he was doomed. The Indians could keep him on that hill picking off his men until they died of hunger or thirst, if nothing else. To retreat was impossible.

3. The Battle of Bushy Run

There was no sleep for the anxious commander that night. As he walked around the circle among his exhausted men lying on their arms, as he passed the heavy cordon of sentries who kept watch over those who sought to snatch a few moments of needed rest, as he thought of the helpless wounded stifling their groans with heroic resolution in the little enclosure on the crest of the hill, as he recalled the wretched women and children, the terrified inhabitants of the forts and towns who were looking to him for protection, and praying God for the success of his expedition which was the only barrier interposed between them and the red scourge sweeping through the forests from the westward, he sustained a weight of responsibility which would have crushed a man less stout of heart. In his desperation he concocted a plan whereby he fondly hoped he could extricate his forces from their deadly peril, and at the same time deliver a crushing blow upon the Indians.

It was a plan worthy of the keenest warrior that ever endeavoured to conquer his foe by savage subtlety and woodland stratagem. Feverishly he waited for the morning and prayed for a favourable time and opportunity to put the plan from which he hoped so much, upon which so much depended, into execution.

The night was marked by one instance of conspicuous heroism. From a little brook hard by the hill, practically gone dry in the summer weather and therefore neglected by the besieging Indians, one of the frontiersmen named Byerly, unobserved by the savages, succeeded in the darkness in bringing in his hat from a hidden pool which he had discovered, a few mouthfuls of precious water which was given to the most severely wounded. A slight rain which fell toward morning also refreshed them somewhat, but most of the men suffered greatly from thirst during the night; they had had no water since noon of the day before.

When the day broke over the haggard but desperate and determined band, the Indians resumed the attack. As soon as it was light enough to see, the firing began again. Steadily the men fought on, lying crouched behind such shelter or cover as they were able to come by, while the slow hours of the hot morning dragged away. The Indians, having learned by the experience of the preceding day, at first took great care not to expose themselves and the British sustained their fire as best they could. The savage warriors at once marked their commander from his brilliant uniform, and fired at him so constantly that upon the insistence of his officers he changed his clothing to render himself less conspicuous. The small tree behind which he took shelter while he did this was hit by no less than fourteen bullets during the time.

Many of the soldiers were struck down, and of the pack-horses numbers were killed and others broke through the lines, plunging upon the men, especially the wounded, and creating wild confusion in the camp. Their drivers as a rule proved cowardly and left the terrified animals to their own devices. Still Bouquet did not dare to drive the horses away. He would need them when he had won the battle.

So he clung tenaciously to his position and his heroic men fought on uncomplainingly while he waited for the favourable opportunity to display the stratagem he had planned. For four hours the men lay on that open hill in the hot sun of August, without food or water, and kept up the engagement. The Indians, as Bouquet had foreseen, grew bolder from their immunity, being adepts at fighting under cover, and as the certainty of success grew upon them, they began creeping nearer and fighting more recklessly. At last the colonel determined that the moment for striking had arrived.

Fortunately one side of the hill was cleft by a ravine which gave entrance upon the surrounding valley. The front of the English line where the main attack was being made, was held by two companies of the Highlanders. Explaining clearly to all his men what he proposed doing, and why, so there would be no panic and they would carry out his orders intelligently, Bouquet ordered these two companies suddenly to withdraw from the line and retreat rapidly across the hill until they reached the ravine, which they were to enter, advance down it, and hold themselves in readiness to attack from it. At the same time the companies on either side of the gap they left were ordered to extend across it in open order to keep the circle intact.

At the word, the Highlanders immediately ran to the rear and plunged into the ravine, where their movements were sheltered from the view of the Indians by its depth and by the bushes growing on its edge. The movement was carried out perfectly. As the Scots rushed away from the field the men of the companies to the right and left closed the opening.

The Indians of course saw the manoeuvre. Imagining, naturally, that it was the beginning of a retreat, they abandoned their cover and came swarming out into the open. Pouring a furious fire upon the weakened line, with most unusual courage they charged deliberately at it, tomahawk and scalping-knife in hand. The thin line of soldiers could not stand the massed onset of the horde of the braves, and, although they fought heroically hand to hand for a moment, they were about to give way. In the very nick of time the Highlanders in the

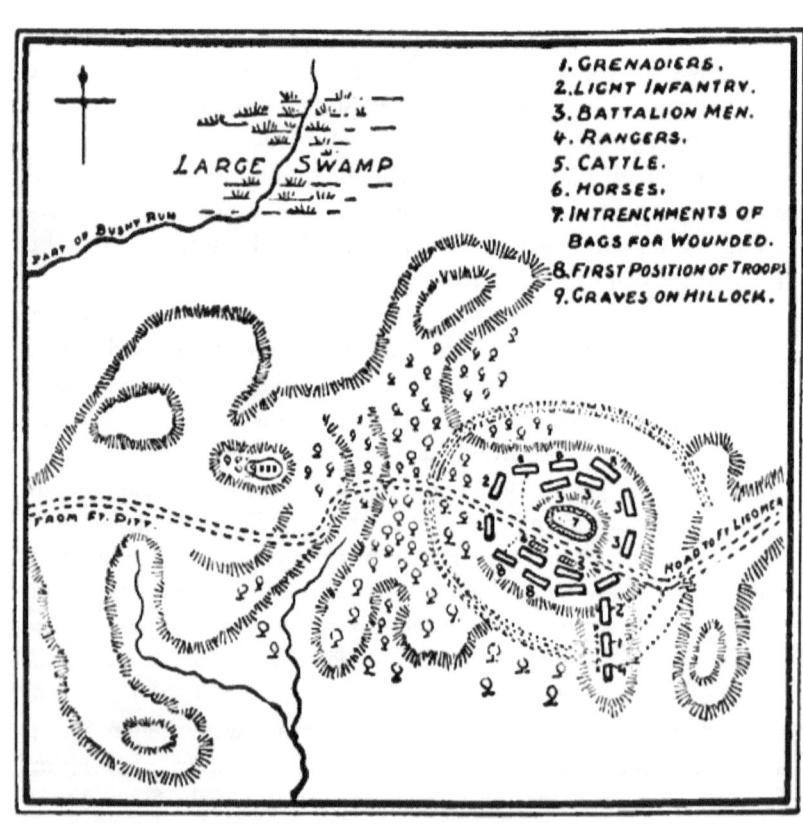

1. GRENADIERS.
2. LIGHT INFANTRY.
3. BATTALION MEN.
4. RANGERS.
5. CATTLE.
6. HORSES.
7. INTRENCHMENTS OF
   BAGS FOR WOUNDED.
8. FIRST POSITION OF TROOPS
9. GRAVES ON HILLOCK.

LARGE SWAMP

PART OF BUSHY RUN

FROM FT. PITT

ROAD TO FT LIGONIER

PLAN OF THE BATTLE OF BUSHY RUN.

ravine, came running out into the open. As they appeared on the right flank of the Indians, without halting they poured in a volley at point-blank range. Though they were greatly surprised by this unexpected discharge; the savages, who displayed the most astonishing resolution in this battle, at once faced about and returned the fire, but when they saw through the smoke the fierce Highlanders springing upon them, bayonet in hand, revenge and triumph in their stern faces, they gave way and fled.

> For life! For life! they plight their ply—
> And shriek, and shout, and battle-cry.
> And plaids and bonnets waving high.
> And broadswords flashing to the sky.
> Are maddening in the rear!

Staking everything on this manoeuvre. Bouquet, when he saw the Highlanders advance, broke his line again and threw two companies of Light Infantry out of the circle on the other flank. The flying Indians ran right into them and a final volley swept them from the field. The Indians in the rear of the camp had advanced to attack at the same time those in the front had endeavoured to break the weakened line, but, witnessing the repulse of those in front, they gave way on all sides before a general advance and abandoned the field.

More than sixty dead Indians lay upon the ground where the Highlanders and Light Infantry had charged, and bloody trails through the woods in the direction of their retreat, showed how many men had been wounded. They had been beaten by an inferior force in a pitched battle, in a fair field and an open fight. On the English side the loss had been very heavy. One hundred and fifteen, or nearly one fourth of the troops, had been killed or wounded. The loss of the Indians was probably equally as great, if not greater. But one Indian prisoner was taken and the men, with the memory of the scenes through which they had passed to animate them, shot him to death as he had been a mad dog.

Tactically this engagement, called the Battle of Bushy Run, was one of the most brilliant fights against Indians which ever took place on the continent, and it was rendered memorable by the fact that the savages had exhibited a willingness to join in hand to hand fighting which was as remarkable as it was unusual. During Forsyth's defence of the Arickaree in western Kansas, a hundred years later, the Indians there made a charge in the open and endeavoured by close fighting to

23

win the day, but that is about the only similar instance I recall.

The expedition had been saved from destruction by Bouquet's brilliant tactics alone. The English were still, however, in a desperate state. Many of the pack-horses had been shot and most of the precious supplies had to be destroyed or abandoned. It was with the greatest difficulty that the wounded could be transported, yet Bouquet, making such dispositions for their comfort as he could, resumed their march. Camped on the bank of Little Turtle Creek that same evening, they were again attacked, but the Indians manifested little disposition to fight after the decisive and costly defeat they had sustained in the morning, and they were easily driven away.

On account of the condition of his men it took Bouquet five days to march the twenty miles between him and Fort Pitt. He reached it, at last, however, and relieved the garrison. The Indians crushed and broken by their defeat and seeing no prospect of making head against the combined forces, withdrew from that section of Pennsylvania. As the various posts were re-established and garrisoned when re-enforcements were forwarded from the east, many of the old settlers, and some new ones, reoccupied their deserted clearings.

4. The End of Bouquet

The Indians were eventually defeated everywhere in the general conflict which was raging through the northwest; and the year after his splendid fight, Bouquet led a brilliantly successful expedition through the country west of the Ohio, which brought about their complete submission and which resulted in the restoration of hundreds of captives to those who thought they had lost them forever.[3]

For his extraordinary skill and courage and for the success of his expedition, Bouquet was thanked by the king and promoted to be brigadier-general. He died in the service at Pensacola three years afterward while still in the prime of life. In addition to his other claims

---

3. There is a touching little story of a mother with this expedition whose child had forgotten her and who had vainly endeavoured to awaken her recollection, which illustrates one phase of Bouquet's character. "Sing her the song with which you put her to sleep as a baby," he said to the agonized woman, with a touch of inspiration. And the woman sang this hymn:—

"*Alone yet not alone am I*
Though in this solitude so drear,
I feel my Saviour always nigh,
He comes my weary hours to cheer."

When the little girl heard the familiar strain of her infancy, memory came back to her with the first verse, and at last she knew her mother.

upon our consideration, romance appropriates him, since he was the victim of an unrequited passion for a beautiful Philadelphian. Anne Willing refused to accept him because he was a soldier, and she married another and less noted man! Poor, lonely Henry Bouquet, it almost broke his heart.

It seems a heartless thing to say, but the bullet that struck down Wolfe on the Plains of Abraham, and the fever that carried Bouquet away at Pensacola, did good service to the country destined to become the United States of America; for they were such accomplished soldiers, men of such talent and genius, that had they been in command of the British forces in the War of the Revolution, that struggle might have been shorter and its results possibly vastly different. They were both young enough men when they died to have been available for service in 1775.

We do not find such another Indian fighter as this gallant Swiss in the colonial records, and it is noteworthy that the same sort of troops as were found entirely inadequate to the situation when led by Braddock, proved themselves heroes indeed when under the command of a greater and abler man.

Captain Samuel Brady, Chief of the Rangers

1. A FAMILY OF FIGHTERS

As a typical pioneer and Indian fighter I have chosen to include in this series some account of a few of the exploits and adventures of Captain Samuel Brady, whose name for cool daring, unremitting vigilance, unsparing energy, fertility of resource, and successful enterprise, was a household word in western Pennsylvania during the beginnings of the nation.

Few families among our early settlers contributed more generously and freely of their best to the service of their country than that from which Brady sprang. His father, Captain John Brady—son of Hugh, the *Praepositus* of the family in America, who was descended from that famous Irish family of which the noted versifier of the Psalms was a member—like Washington and George Rogers Clark, was a surveyor.

He was commissioned captain in the 2nd Pennsylvania Battalion in 1764 in Bouquet's expedition. He was a noted frontiersman prior to the Revolution, and when that war broke out was appointed a captain in the 12th Pennsylvania Continental Line. At the Battle of the Brandy Wine his regiment was cut to pieces in the desperate fighting near the Birmingham Meeting House. He was badly wounded and his son John, a lad of fifteen who had come like David of old with supplies for the camp, and had remained for the battle, was also wounded, and only saved from capture by the act of his colonel in throwing the boy upon a horse when the troops retreated. So fierce was the fighting that every officer in Captain Brady's company was killed or wounded, together with most of his men.

In 1778, Captain Brady was ordered to Fort Pitt and attached to the regiment of Colonel Brodhead, who was charged by Washington personally with the duty of protecting the western Pennsylvania frontier from the incursions of the savages. It is estimated that there were at one time or another more than twelve thousand Indians in arms in the pay of the British. Campbell states that four hundred Seneca warriors in three years on the border, took more than one thousand scalps, two hundred and ninety-nine of them having belonged to women and twenty-nine to children! They were sent by the Indians to the Governor of Canada, to be by him sent as a present to the King of England.

As most of the able-bodied men west of the mountains had enlisted in the Continental Line the valleys were without protection until Washington sent Brodhead thither. One of the frontier posts by which it was hoped to protect the country was located near Muncy and called Fort Brady in honour of its commander.

James Brady, Captain John's second son, who was himself a militia captain, was killed near there by the Indians. A small party of men were reaping in one of the fields a short distance from Loyalsock, in the fall of 1778. Captain James Brady was in command of them. Four men watched while the others worked. A large party of the Indians stole upon them unperceived and opened fire, whereupon the most of them fled. Captain Brady ran for his gun. According to one account, he secured it, shot one of the Indians dead, seized another gun, was shot himself, then stabbed by a spear, *tomahawked*, and scalped. He had long red hair. It is related that one of his frontier friends a week before his death, watching him dress and plait it in the queue, which was the fashion of the day, remarked to him:

"Jim, the Indians will get that red scalp of yours yet."

The young captain, who was only twenty at the time, laughingly replied that if they did they would have something to lighten their darkness for them! The red hair was characteristic of the family and has persisted in many members to the present day. Young Brady survived his frightful wound for five days and died at Fort Brady in the arms of his mother, an heroic pioneer woman.

A year after this, Captain John was shot and instantly killed by Indians, who fled from the scene of the murder with such precipitation that they did not scalp him, and his body with his watch, seals, and weapons, was recovered intact. His son, Hugh, too young to fight

27

in the Revolution, rose to be a Major-General in the United States Army. As commander of the 22nd Infantry, he was shot through the body in the first charge at Lundy's Lane. A letter from Hugh's nephew. Captain John's grandson, who was an officer in his uncle's regiment, tells how the general fell and fainted from loss of blood but was lifted to his horse and continued in command until nearly the close of the action. He had two horses killed under him in this battle and only gave up the command when he was unable to sit or stand from loss of blood.[1] Another of Captain John's grandsons, William, volunteered for service in Perry's squadron and fought in the Battle of Lake Erie.

There were thirteen children born to this old Pioneer Captain, of whom five were girls. Two boys died in infancy and another just before the War of 1812. The other five fought in every war which took place while they were alive.

The most distinguished of them all, however, unless it be General Hugh, was the oldest, Captain Samuel Brady, Chief of the Rangers. On August 3rd, 1775, he enlisted, being then only nineteen years of age, as a private soldier, and was ordered to Massachusetts. He participated in the operations around Boston, and in the Battle of Long Island, where he so distinguished himself for bravery that he was promoted to a lieutenancy, skipping the grade of ensign. He fought at White Plains and was one of that ragged starved little band of men who clung to Washington and with which he made that desperate strike back at Trenton and Princeton in the darkest hour of the Revolution.[2] As one of Hand's riflemen at Princeton, he barely escaped capture on account of his impetuous gallantry.

He was brevetted a captain for gallant service at the Brandywine and Germantown. At the Massacre of Paoli, he was surrounded, pursued, and narrowly escaped with his life. So close were the British to him that as he leaped a fence they pinned him to it by thrusting bayonets through his blanket-coat. He tore himself away, shot dead a cavalryman who had overtaken him and ordered him to surrender, found safety in a swamp, where he gathered up some fifty-five men who had escaped and led them safely to the army in the morning. He, too, was ordered to western Pennsylvania with his regiment, in which he appears at first as a captain-lieutenant. He was borne on the rolls successively of the Third, Sixth, and Eighth Pennsylvania Line until

1. See my book *American Fights and Fighters*. Niagara Campaign, (Published by Leonaur).
2. See my book *American Fights and Fighters*. Washington's Greatest Campaign.

the termination of the Revolution.

2. THE FIRST OF THE BORDERERS

It was his services as a borderer, however, that especially entitle him to attention. What Boone was to Kentucky and Kenton to Ohio, that Sam Brady was to western Pennsylvania. His services were so great that Colonel Brodhead successfully urged his promotion to a full captaincy and commended him specifically in a personal letter to General Washington. Indeed, on more than one occasion, he was selected by Washington, through Colonel Brodhead, for certain specific and important duties; and there is a letter of Colonel Brodhead's extant, which is published in the Pennsylvania archives, in which the colonel states that he has just received a special letter of commendation for Captain Brady from the great commander-in-chief himself. Although he was only twenty-seven years old when the war closed he was by universal consent regarded as the chief ranger, hunter, scout, and frontiersman on the Pennsylvania border.

The Allegheny and Ohio Rivers constituted the western and northern boundaries of the colonies. George Rogers Clark, Boone, and others ranged over the northern Kentucky line to protect the settlements, Poe and Wetzel around Wheeling, and Brady and his men from Fort Pitt to Lake Erie. His services were well-nigh continuous. He was always in the woods. No enterprise was too dangerous for him to undertake. No danger was so great as to deter him. He was constantly employed until the war was over, and when General Wayne mustered an army to avenge St. Clair's defeat and crush the Indians, Brady was given command of all his scouts, rangers, and pioneers.

Captain Brady died on Christmas Day, 1795, leaving a name which is still remembered in western Pennsylvania, and which has been much referred to by those who have written the annals of the west. Indeed the old settlers in their letters, reminiscences, and early records, do not hesitate to compare him—and not to his disadvantage—to the great Daniel Boone himself.

Partly from these records and partly from family traditions and old letters, some of his exploits have been preserved. I shall not attempt to give them in chronological order. Indeed it is impossible to date some of them. Like every other famous borderer he has been made the subject of myth and legend, and heroic tale has grown about him, but there is good authority for the adventures here set down.

On one occasion he was ordered by Colonel Brodhead upon a scouting expedition. He took with him two tried comrades named Biggs and Bevington. Ranging northward from Fort Pitt, at a place above the mouth of the Beaver, near the present village of Fallston, where there was a clearing, they came upon the ruins of the cabin of a settler named Gray. The Indians had just visited the cabin, the walls and chimney of which were still blazing from the torch which they had applied.

There was not a living person to be seen. They were carefully reconnoitring the place when the keen ears of the captain detected the sound of a horse approaching. Fearful lest the Indians who had committed the depredation might not have departed, Brady and his men scattered and concealed themselves. The horseman proved to be Gray, the master of the cabin, who had been away some distance on that morning.

Brady and his companions, as was the usual custom on such expeditions, were dressed to resemble Indians and had painted their faces further to disguise themselves. The captain knew if he showed himself to Gray in that guise the settler would probably shoot him before he could explain, so he waited concealed until Gray passed him, leaped upon the horse, seized the settler in his arms and whispered, "Don't struggle. I'm Sam Brady."

When the man became quiet he told him of the catastrophe at his cabin. Summoning Bevington and Biggs the whole party cautiously made their way to the ruined home. Gray's state of mind may well be imagined, for he had left in the cabin that morning his wife, her sister, and five children. A careful search of the ruins satisfied them that there were no charred remains among the ashes. They were confident, therefore, that the Indians had taken the women and children away with them.

The experienced woodsmen soon picked up the trail, which they cautiously but rapidly followed. The Indians, who seemed to be in some force, made not the slightest effort at concealment. Brady's men had wanted to return to Fort McIntosh and get assistance before they pursued. The captain of the rangers pointed out that to do that would cause them to lose so much time that they could not hope to overtake the Indians, so the four men resolved to press on and do the best they could. They swore to follow Brady's leadership and he promised not to desert Gray, who would have gone on alone if the others had failed him.

Brady's knowledge of the country enabled him to foresee the path the Indians would probably take and by making short cuts, toward evening the party caught a glimpse of the Indians they were pursuing, trailing over a mountain a mile away. They counted thirteen Indians, eight of them on horseback, together with the two women and five children. Bringing his woodcraft again into play, Brady concluded that the Indians would stop for the night in a deeply secluded dell in a ravine in the mountains where there was a famous spring. The configuration of the ground made it possible to light a fire there without betraying the whereabouts of the fire-builders to the surrounding country.

He therefore led his party up a little creek, which thereafter was known as Brady's Run, until about seven o'clock they reached a spur of the mountain from which they could look down upon the spring. Sure enough, there were the Indians. There, too, were the weary, dejected women, and the children too exhausted and too frightened to cry. Utterly unsuspicious of observation the savages made camp, built a fire and prepared their evening meal.

For three mortal hours the four woodsmen lay concealed watching the camp. Finally the Indians disposed themselves in a semicircle, surrounding the women and children, with the fire in the centre. The muskets, rifles, and tomahawks were piled at the foot of a tree some fifteen feet from the right point of the circle. One by one the Indians sank into slumber, as did the poor dejected prisoners.

Brady had long since made his plan. There was only one way to kill those Indians, and that was without waking them. If they had fired on them they might have killed four, yet the odds would have been still more than two to one, besides which the rangers could hardly have fired without killing some of the women and children. He decided that the Indians should be knifed while they slept.

Appointing Gray to take the right of the semicircle, Bevington the left, choosing the centre himself, and directing Biggs to secure the guns and tomahawks, the three men approached to within three hundred yards of the sleeping camp and then crept on their knees toward the Indians. They were forced to leave their guns behind them and trust only to scalping-knife and tomahawk. It was a frightful risk, but their only chance.

With snake-like caution and in absolute silence they crawled over the ground. When within fifty feet of the camp a dead twig cracked and broke under Biggs' hand. The sound woke an Indian, who lifted himself on his hands and stared sleepily over the fire. The four men were as still as death. Hearing nothing further the Indian sank back again. They waited fifteen minutes for him to get sound asleep and once more began their stealthy and terrible advance. They so timed their manoeuvres that they reached the line simultaneously.

Three knives quietly rose and fell. Frontier knowledge of anatomy was sufficient to enable them to strike accurately, and three Indians died. Again they struck. And yet again.

The third Indian that Gray struck was not instantly killed. He partially rose, whereupon Gray finished him with his tomahawk. The body of the Indian fell across the legs of the man next him. He opened his mouth to cry out, but before he could make a sound Brady's ready knife struck him in the heart. There were now only three Indians left alive.

The women and children were awakened at the same time and the woods rang with their frightened screams. As they saw the supposed Indians, bloody knife in hand, looking horribly in the flickering light of the fire, the women and children fled to the woods. Gray pursued them calling their names.

The three remaining Indians, now wide awake, attempted to rise. Brady's terrible knife accounted for one, his tomahawk did for the other, and Biggs, who had at last reached the rifles, shot the last one dead. Brady had killed six, Bevington and Gray each three, and Biggs one. That war party was annihilated.

The women and children were soon found. The horses, arms, and other plunder of the Indians were secured, every one of the savages was scalped, and the party returned in safety to Fort McIntosh. The place bears the name of Bloody Spring to this day, (as at time of first publication).

It was the constant practice of frontiersmen to scalp the Indians whenever they could. It is impossible for us to enter into the spirit prevalent at that time, but it is evident that the settlers thought no more of killing an Indian than they would of killing a rattlesnake, or a panther; and indeed the horrors they witnessed and which every one of them had felt, either in his own person, or in the persons of those near and dear to them—as Brady's father and brother—had rendered them absolutely ruthless so far as Indians were concerned. Besides, the scalp of an Indian had a commercial value. In the Colonial Records of Pennsylvania, under date of Monday, February 19, 1781, Philadelphia,

"THAT WAR PARTY WAS ANNIHILATED."

in the Minutes of the Supreme Executive Council of Pennsylvania, of which Joseph Reed was President, I find the following:

> An order was drawn in favour of Colonel Archibald Lochry Lieutenant of the County of Westmoreland, for the sum of 12 lbs, 10s. state money, equal to 2500 dollars, Continental money, to be by him paid to Captain Samuel Brady, as a reward for an Indian scalp, *agreeable to a late proclamation of this board.* (Italics mine.)

This interesting document is signed by his Excellency Joseph Reed. He, with his associates, therefore, is *particeps criminis* in the scalp-taking business! It was a government affair.

4. Brady's Famous Leap

On another occasion Brady led a party of rangers into what is now Ohio, in pursuit of some of the Sandusky Indians. He ambushed them at a small lake in Portage County, which was known thereafter as Brady's Lake. The ambush was successful in that the party they were pursuing were most of them killed, but unfortunately a second and larger war party of Indians unexpectedly appeared on the scene in the middle of the action. Brady was captured after a desperate fight. Most of his men were killed and scalped and but few escaped.

Rejoicing at the importance of their capture, the Indians deferred his torture until they could take him to the Sandusky Towns which were the headquarters for all the Indians in that part of the country. They resolved to make his burning a memorable one and kept him in confinement until they could communicate with the surrounding tribes.

The day of his punishment finally arrived. He was bound to a stake and the fires were kindled around him. They were in no hurry to kill him and the fires were kept rather low while different bodies of Indians arrived on the scene. In the confusion attendant upon these arrivals the watch upon Brady was somewhat relaxed. He was a man of great physical strength. He cautiously strained at the withes with which he was bound and finally succeeded in loosing them. According to some accounts the heat of the fire enabled him to break them.

Although he was badly scorched, for he had been stripped of his clothing when he was tied to the stake, he leaped across the barrier of flame, seized, according to one account, an Indian squaw, the wife of the principal chief, according to another, her child, pitched her into the fire, and in the alarm caused by his bold action, broke away.

He had kept himself in as good physical condition as possible, taking what exercise he could though confined, and he dashed madly for his life through the woods with several hundred Indians upon his heels. He actually made good his escape. He had no arms, no clothing, nothing to eat. The Indians pursued him with implacable persistence. Yet, sustained by his dauntless resolution, he managed to keep ahead of them. For over a hundred miles he plunged through the woods, subsisting upon roots, berries or whatever he could get, until finally he came to the Cuyahoga River, near what is now Kent in Portage County.

He had intended to cross the river at Standing Rock, a noted ford, but found that the Indians had intercepted him. The river at the point where he struck it, flowed between steep rocky banks rising some twenty-five feet from the water's edge. It was a deep roaring torrent. At the narrowest point, at that time, it was between twenty-five and thirty feet across to the opposite bank, which was not quite so precipitous as that upon which he stood, being rough and somewhat broken.

Having cut him off from the ford, the Indians believed that they could take him without fail in the *cul de sac* formed by the river. There was no other ford for miles up and down. Running back into the woods toward the approaching Indians whose shouts he could hear to get a start, Brady desperately jumped from the bank. He cleared the river and struck the bank on the other side a few feet below the edge and scrambled up it just as the first pursuer appeared.

"Brady," said the man, "make damn good jump. Indian no try."

The Indians, however, shot at Brady and wounded him in the leg before the captain could escape. Without waiting he resumed his flight, but his wounded leg so hampered him that the Indians who had crossed the ford were again hard upon his heels. In this extremity he plunged into the water at Brady's Lake, where he had been captured, stooped beneath the surface, and concealed himself among the lilies, breathing through a hollow reed. The Indians followed his bloody trail to the lake, around which they searched for some time and seeing no sign of his exit concluded that he had plunged in and was drowned. He afterward succeeded in getting safely back to the fort.

5. An expedition with Wetzel and other adventures

The year 1782 was a remarkable one for savage Indian outbreaks.

It was known in local border history as "The Bloody year," or "The Bloody '82." Rumours of a grand alliance between the western tribes to descend upon the settlements and finally wipe them out, reached Washington, and the general requested Colonel Brodhead to send reliable persons to spy on the Indians and if possible find out what they were about to do. The choice, as usual, fell upon Brady. He asked but for one companion, who was the famous Lewis Wetzel.

Brady and Wetzel were familiar with the Indian tongue. They could speak Shawnese or Delaware like the natives themselves. Contrary to the family habit Brady was a swarthy man, with long black hair and bright blue Irish eyes, taking after his mother in that.

The two men disguised themselves as Indians, deliberately repaired to the grand council at Sandusky,, representing themselves to be a deputation from a distant *sept* of Shawnees, which was desirous of joining in the projected conspiracy. They moved freely about among the Indians at first entirely unsuspected. They participated in the council and obtained a complete knowledge of the plans and purposes of the Indians.

One veteran chief, however, finally became suspicious. Perhaps he detected the white man through the guttural syllables, or the white faces under the war paint. The two men whose every nerve had been pressed into service and whom nothing escaped, caught the suspicious glances of the old man. Consequently when he sprang to his feet and seizing a tomahawk started toward them, it was the work of a second for Brady to shoot him dead.

Concealment being no longer possible, Wetzel shot a prominent chief, the men clubbed their rifles, beat down, opposition, sprang away from the council fires, dashed through the lines, seized two of the best horses—Kentucky stock which had been captured in a raid—and rode for their lives. They were pursued, of course, by a great body of Indians, and had many hairbreadth escapes.

Wetzel's horse finally gave out and thereafter the two men, one riding the other running, pressed madly on. Finally the second horse, fairly ridden to death, gave way, but reaching a village of some friendly Delawares, they got another horse and dashed on. Several times they doubled on their trail and shot down the nearest pursuers, checking them temporarily.

Finally they reached the Ohio. It was bank full, a roaring torrent. It was early in March, and the weather was bitterly cold. They forced their horse into the water, Brady on its back, Wetzel, who was the better swimmer, holding its tail and swimming as best he could. They had a terrible struggle but reached the other bank at last. The water froze on their bodies. Wetzel was entirely exhausted and almost perished with the cold. Brady killed the horse, disembowelled it and thrust his companion's body into the animal, hoping that the animal heat remaining in it might keep Wetzel alive while he built a fire, which he recklessly proceeded to do.

As soon as the fire was kindled he took Wetzel out of the body of the horse and brought him to the fire where he chafed his limbs until the circulation was restored. The Indians gave over the pursuit at the Ohio, and the two men escaped.

The plans of the Indians being discovered by this daring exploit, the settlements prepared for them, the conspiracy fell to pieces, and the projected incursion came to naught.

Words fail to tell of the many incidents in which this dashing young pioneer bore a prominent part. The enterprise for which he was commended by Washington was similar to the one just described. He went alone to the Sandusky Towns in 1780 and made a map of the region, located the towns, crept near enough to the principal village to learn the plans of the Indians, captured two squaws, mounted them on captured horses and made good his escape.

Near the Ohio one of the squaws escaped. With the other, ranging through the forest, he came across an Indian on horseback with a woman on the pommel of the saddle and two children running alongside. Recognizing the woman as the wife of a frontiersman named Stupes, Brady, by a wonderful exhibition of marksmanship, shot the Indian dead without injuring the woman.

"Why," said Jenny Stupes, as she saw the painted figure of the captain, for he was still in his disguise, dashing toward her scalping-knife in hand, "did you shoot your brother?"

"Don't you know me, Jenny? I am Sam Brady," said the captain, grasping the terrified woman by the hand.

Taking Jenny and her children and still retaining his prisoner, he rapidly retreated toward the settlements. The Indian he had shot had been separated from a small band which happened to have retained Jenny Stupes' little dog. By the aid of the animal, which naturally ran after its mistress, the fugitives were trailed.

At the time he shot the Indian Brady had but three loads for his rifle. He could not afford to expend one of them on the dog yet it had to be killed or it would betray its mistress. They sat down and waited until the dog came running up to them, when he was speedily despatched with a tomahawk, and Brady succeeded in bringing the party safely to Fort Pitt.

He was several times captured. On one occasion he rolled to a fire in the night, burnt his bonds, brained one of the Indians with a stake and got away.

At another time, after a long scouting expedition, he suddenly came upon two Indians near a huge tree. One was standing on the shoulders of the other cutting bark for a canoe. Brady had but one load for his rifle. Quickly deciding what to do he shot the lower Indian through the heart, whereupon the other one came tumbling heavily to the ground. He was partially stunned. Brady ran toward him knife in hand but the Indian staggered to his feet and fled, by which the captain came in possession of two guns and a supply of ammunition and was enabled to proceed on his expedition.

Whenever there was danger or loss his services were at command. Not only did he serve his country in several of the battles in which he commanded his company both in the east against the British, and in several expeditions against the Indians in the west, but he did more to guard the helpless settlers, rescue captured women and children, and to discover and thwart the Indian plans than any man in Pennsylvania. The women and children loved him and the men swore by him, for he was the protector of the frontier.

From these gruesome tales it must not be imagined that he was only a bloodthirsty and reckless borderer. On the contrary, like most of his family, he was a devout Presbyterian, and a marvellous student of the Bible. His grandnephews and nieces tell how he used to arrive at the cabin in which they lived, after some expedition, and when the evening meal was over and the lesson of Scripture with which these simple people prepared for rest, was read, Captain Sam Brady would suggest that they read it "varse about;" and they relate that when his turn came he generally recited his verse without the aid of the book, such was his mastery of the Bible! To his family and friends he was as kind and gentle as a woman. A family tradition says that he was the model for Cooper's famous Leatherstocking.

His brother, General Hugh, says that James Brady, who was killed by the Indians, was six feet one inch in height and that there was scarcely an inch difference in height among all the brethren. Sam was a man of great personal strength and activity. His favourite resting-place when at home was on the floor by the open fireplace. There he would lie and tell stories to the children who adored him. There he slept rolled in his blanket.

He was a singular mixture of the Puritan and Cavalier. He could pray like an old Covenanter and fight with all the dash and spirit of Prince Rupert. Pennsylvania owes him a debt of gratitude which should never be forgotten.

1

On the Eve of the Revolution

1. ANDREW LEWIS AND HIS BORDERERS

Around the pedestal of Crawford's Equestrian Statue of Washington in Richmond, among those of Jefferson, Patrick Henry, John Marshall, and other worthies, is carved the figure of a huge man dressed in a fringed hunting-shirt and carrying a rifle. It is the effigy of General Andrew Lewis, one of the greatest of the borderers.

Lewis was born in Ireland in 1720. His father was a Huguenot, who came to America after a quarrel when Andrew was a child. The family settled on the western border of Virginia near what is now Staunton, and speedily became prominent. Andrew was the oldest of four brothers, all of whom did good service in the colonies and in the Revolution. Three of them were soldiers, one of whom died in battle, and the last, prevented from active campaigning by physical disabilities, shone as statesman, was an associate of Patrick Henry, afterward a member of the Virginia Constitutional Convention, and in every way possible did what he could for the cause of liberty.

Andrew was the most conspicuous member of the family. He was one of the little band under Washington that fought off Coulon de Villiers at Fort Necessity in the Great Meadows, at the breaking out of the French and Indian War. Lieutenant Lewis was wounded on this occasion. As captain he formed part of Braddock's army in 1756, where, although he was not in the actual battle on the Monongahela, he did good service under Washington in endeavouring to protect the ravaged border after the overwhelming defeat of the British.[1]

In 1759 he was major of Washington's regiment under General John Forbes. He participated in Grant's foray against Fort Duquesne,

---

1. See my book *Colonial Fights and Fighters: The Struggle for the Valley of the Ohio,* (published by Leonaur.)

where he was involved in the defeat of that rash officer's foolish enterprise. He was there captured after a desperate hand to hand tight in which he was wounded again. When Grant, seeking a scapegoat, strove to cast upon Lewis the odium of his defeat, the Virginian in a towering rage at the false accusation, spat in his face and knocked him down. Grant did not press the charge thereafter.

Promoted a colonel in 1759 he led an expedition against the Shawnees which, through no fault of his, was without decisive results, and which is known as the "Sandy Creek Voyage," or campaign. He was a commissioner from Virginia at the celebrated treaty at Fort Stanwix in 1768. Lewis was six feet two in height, and of Herculean proportions and strength otherwise, although he carried himself with great activity. "His countenance was stern and forbidding—his deportment distant and reserved; this rendered his person more awful than engaging." So writes a contemporary, who further relates that the Governor of New York, one of his fellow commissioners at Fort Stanwix, wrote of him, "that the earth seemed to tremble at his tread."

In 1774 there was a little war with the Indians at first known as Cresap's War, but latterly as Lord Dunmore's War, the importance of which was so overshadowed by the Revolution that followed hard upon it that, but for one incident, it would be quite forgotten today. Yet the student now sees it was quite essential to the prosecution of the greater war, to the first success of which it contributed in no small degree.

The treaty consequent upon Bouquet's expedition in 1764, was not rigidly observed by the Indians. There was constant trouble on the border, although nothing like what had before obtained. The Indians continued restless and active; there was a continual clashing of arms everywhere and, in this instance decidedly, the savages were mainly the aggressors. That is not saying that the settlers were blameless. Far from it, but the balance of wrong-doing was against the Indians.

To these unsettled conditions the unseemly strife between Virginia and Pennsylvania for the possession of the lands west of the Blue Ridge and Alleghenies largely contributed. In 1774 matters had reached such a state that it was felt that an open war must soon break out. Active hostilities were begun, under great provocation, in the spring by a certain Captain Cresap, who led a party of frontiersmen to the wilderness surveying, etc. Some Indians were fired upon by Cresap's party and killed, and the action, though small, was known as the "Captina Affair."

Some forty miles west of Pittsburg on the Ohio, there lived among the Mingos, or Shawnees, a Cayugan—that is, an Iroquois—warrior, named Tah-gah-jute, who is more commonly known to posterity by the name given him by the settlers, Logan. Among the warring tribes, Logan had exercised a strict neutrality. Rather more. He had befriended the white men on many occasions.

The most serious happening, which finally put an end to possibilities of even the quasi-peace which might have been maintained, was the unprovoked murder of Logan's entire family, including women and children, by a ruffianly trader named Greathouse, on April 30th, 1774. These Indians were first made drunk and then ruthlessly butchered without opportunity of defence, and for no occasion whatsoever.

The cruel murder turned the peaceable Logan into a fiend. With a few companions he declared war on his own account at once. Thinking that Cresap had ordered the massacre, although he was entirely innocent of it, and was, as frontiersmen go, too honourable a man to have done it, Logan sent him a defiance and began to raid the border. As usual, the vengeance fell on the innocent. No less than thirty people were killed by him before the authorities were awakened.

Lord Dunmore, the Royal Governor of Virginia, acted with commendable promptness. He embodied the militia of the counties west of the Blue Ridge and called for volunteers. The left wing was ordered to rendezvous at the Great Levels of the Greenbriar, now Lewisburg, and was placed under the command of General Andrew Lewis. The other division, under the command of Dunmore himself, assembled at Frederick. Lewis was ordered to lead his men over the mountains until he struck the Kanawha, down which he was to march until he came to the place where it flowed into the Ohio. There Dunmore, who was to march through Potomac Gap to the Ohio, was to meet him, and the two divisions conjoined were to march up the Scioto to the Shawanee Indian towns, which they were to destroy.

The movement was vastly agreeable to the old backwoodsman, and the sturdy pioneers of western Virginia were embodied under their local officers and repaired to his standard at Camp Union with joyous alacrity. Colonel Charles Lewis, the brother of the general, led some four hundred men from Augusta; Colonel William Flemming an equal number from Botetourt. From over the mountains came the settlers from the Holston and the Watagua in Fincastle County, led by Colonel William Christian. There was also an independent company led by Colonel John Field.

Among the subordinate officers were men destined afterward to achieve a wide reputation. Captain Evan Shelby commanded a company in which his son Isaac was first lieutenant. Isaac was afterward one of that dauntless band which wiped out Ferguson, and when he was a very old man and the Governor of Kentucky, he led his volunteers to the assistance of William Henry Harrison, and participated in the defeat of Tecumseh at the Battle of the Thames—"Old King's Mountain" they called him. Another captain was Benjamin Harrison, one of the signers of the Declaration of Independence from Virginia, and the ancestor of two of our presidents. Valentine Sevier, brother of the great pioneer of Tennessee, was with the force. A humble sergeant in the ranks was one James Robertson, whose name is held in the highest esteem in western Tennessee.

Others who participated in the war, although not with Lewis' command, were George Rogers Clark, Simon Kenton, Daniel Morgan, and the afterward infamous renegade Simon Girty. In one way or another nearly everyone of prominence afterward in the then far west, served in the war. Daniel Boone commanded three small frontier forts. John Sevier was a captain, and among the officers and soldiers were many men like General George Matthews, the hero of Germantown, General Andrew Moore, the first and only man ever elected to the United States Senate by Virginia from the west of the Blue Ridge, and many others of importance, although most of them are now more or less forgotten. In quality Lewis' force was remarkably high. They were in the main an undisciplined lot, who submitted grudgingly to his rule and would probably have utterly refused to obey anybody else. They knew nothing of the tactics of soldiers, but they were an unsurpassed body of border fighters.

2. THE BATTLE OF POINT PLEASANT

The assemblage began about the first of September and was nearly completed on the seventh.

On the eighth, the first division started accompanied by four hundred pack-horses loaded with flour and driving one hundred and eight beef cattle. Field and his company followed them and soon joined them. A few days afterward the second division marched out with two hundred pack-horses and the balance of the cattle. The march led straight across the mountains. There was no road; not even a trail. The men had to cut their way through the timber. Such a thing as wagon transportation was absurd and unheard of. They made good time, however, all things considered, and their progress was greatly facilitated when they reached the Kanawha at the mouth of the Elk, and marched down its banks.

They arrived at the mouth of the river on the 6th of October, having traversed one hundred and sixty-five miles of primeval forest and rugged mountain range. Colonel Christian, with some two hundred men, had been left behind at the camp to bring up the rearguard and the balance of the supplies. The pack-horses were unloaded when they reached the Kanawha and the supplies were floated down the river in canoes or on rafts. The horses were then sent back to the Greenbriar to bring up the remainder of supplies under the direction of Colonel Christian, who was very unwilling to delay his advance to take the part assigned.

Arrived at the mouth of the Kanawha, according to one account they found a note in a hollow tree which had been put there by Kenton and Girty; according to another, they were met by these men with letters from Dunmore ordering Lewis to march up the Ohio to join Dunmore's force. Lewis' men were greatly exhausted by their terrible march. They were not yet all assembled, and it would not be safe to leave Colonel Christian and his three hundred men alone in the wilderness, so he determined to delay his departure until the rearguard had joined him.

The ninth was Sunday. The assemblage was by no means the godless, reckless crowd which we naturally imagine it might have been, for it is related that they had services conducted by a chaplain in which the hardy Scotch-Irish Presbyterians lustily took part, Lewis setting the example, although personally he was an Episcopalian. On the morning of the tenth two young men started out before daybreak on a hunting expedition. Some four or five miles from the camp they ran into a large body of Indians. One was shot dead before he could get away and the other killed an Indian, made his escape, and ran posthaste to the camp bearing the alarm.

The chief of the Shawnees, who were to the middle west what the Iroquois were to the north and the Creeks to the south, was a veteran warrior named Cornstalk. In every war on the border he had borne a prominent part. Ruthless and ferocious, as all the Indians were, he was not without redeeming qualities. He was a man of the greatest courage and capacity. Indeed he showed a grasp of military science and tactics unusual in one of his race. The Indians were perfectly aware of the advance of the Virginians. They knew they were coming in two widely separated armies, and Cornstalk determined to fall upon the weaker body and crush it before it had time to effect a junction with the other, with which he could then deal. It was sound strategy.

Massing his warriors, whose number about equalled the Americans—say eleven hundred on each side—he led them down the river designing to fall upon Lewis' camp in the night and annihilate his force. The fortunate discovery by the two hunters in a measure frustrated his plans. Realizing that the escaping fugitive would give the alarm. Cornstalk at once put his band in motion.. They were ferried across the Ohio in rafts and came tearing through the woods close on the heels of the fugitive, thinking, as they phrased it, to drive the borderers "like bullocks into the river."

As soon as the alarming message had been delivered Lewis ordered the long roll to be beaten. Some of the men were not yet awake when the first rattle of the drum echoed through the forest. They sprang to their arms instantly, however, and fell into such line as their undisciplined condition permitted.

The camp had been made at the confluence of, and between, the two rivers. On the left lay the Ohio, on the right the Kanawha. There was little chance, therefore, of either flank being turned. It was a good place for defence, although if the American line were thoroughly broken the troops would be annihilated, for there would be no way of escape, being penned in between the Indians and the river.

No one at the time believed that the Indians were more than a scouting party; they never dreamed that the whole hostile force was upon them. Colonel Charles Lewis with one hundred and fifty men was ordered to march up the right flank along the Kanawha, Colonel Flemming with a like force was ordered up the left flank. Colonel Field was ordered to hold himself in readiness to advance in the centre with another party. The rest of the men were put in a state of preparation and kept in hand by Lewis himself until he could determine what was to happen.

The time was not long in coming. First one musket- shot, then another and another, then a roaring fusillade, apprized the listeners that here was no skirmishing party but an attack in heavy force, and not three quarters of a mile from the main camp. It was evident that the Indians were in sufficient numbers to cover the whole line between the rivers.

Back with the main body Lewis was calmly waiting. He had just taken out his pipe when the first rifle-shot rang out. Coolly waiting until he had completed the lighting of his pipe, the sturdy backwoods-man quickly sent Field's column forward to connect the two columns led by Charles Lewis and Flemming. The men dashed eagerly and gallantly through the woods until they reached the battle line.

The Americans had taken to the trees as the Indians had done and the battle was raging fiercely. Colonel Charles Lewis, a veteran of the French and Indian War, with a brilliant record for courage and skill, disdained the use of cover and walked about through his command encouraging his men. He was shot and mortally wounded. On the other flank Colonel Flemming, another veteran, while holding his men bravely up to the battle, was shot through the lung so severely that his life was despaired of.

The Indians were massed in force in front of these two bodies. There were probably three Indians to one white man at the point of contact and their firing was terrible. The trees offered little or no protection. Disheartened by the loss of the two commanding officers the Virginians began to give ground. One moment more would have turned their withdrawal into a disastrous retreat, which would have ruined the whole command, when Colonel Field arrived on the ground with his column and restored the line.

Captain Evan Shelby, who had succeeded to the command of the right flank after the wounding of Charles Lewis, managed to rally his men and the line held; Seeing now that the battle was general, leaving a small force to protect the camp and watch the river flanks. General Lewis led his force forward into the battle, the men extending in a long line which reached from river to river for a distance of a mile and a quarter. He got to the front just in time; Colonel Field had been killed and the line was wavering again.

The Indians exhibited a most desperate and gallant offence. They made charge after charge upon the Virginians, hurling themselves on the lines again and again; and many a grim, hand-to-hand conflict was fought out in the depths of woods between white and red man. The forest was full of smoke and fire, and rang with shots, yells, and cheers. Tomahawks and knives were freely used. Lewis was everywhere in the thick of the fray, cool and calm, encouraging his men and doing everything that a brave commander could do to ensure a victory, but what the end was to be was not easy to foresee.

The Indians were brilliantly led by old Cornstalk, who showed himself a hero. His voice could be heard above the din of the battle exhorting his braves to stand like men, to fight it out, to be strong. The suddenness of his attack and the tactics employed, which consisted in alternate advance and retreat, made the battle the most fiercely contested of any the Indians had ever taken part in on the continent. During the heat of the action Cornstalk was seen to cut down a cowardly savage with his tomahawk.

All day long the battle raged, but toward the late afternoon the superior steadiness of the Americans began to tell. Cautiously covering themselves, they advanced from tree to tree, slowly forcing the stubborn Indians to retreat. There was no rout, however, on the part of the savages, and Cornstalk managed his retreat in a way that would have done credit to a veteran European captain. His tactics were masterly. He would hurl a body of his Indians on the American advance, throw them into confusion for a moment, and before they could rally he would withdraw his attacking party, and when the Americans came on again they would be confronted by a new line. The loss among the Americans was fearful.

Finally toward evening the Indians reached a heavily wooded rise of ground from which they could not be driven. The battle so far was a drawn one, the advantage if anything, being with the Americans, except in the matter of loss.

Lewis, finding that Cornstalk had at last definitely stopped the advance of his army, detached three companies with Isaac Shelby in the lead, to march up the Kanawha until they came to Crooked Creek, up which they were to proceed until they got in rear of the Indian line, which they were immediately to assault. The movement was a brilliant one, and as soon as the crack of muskets and rifles apprized the general that Shelby's detachment had engaged, he ordered a final advance on the Indian line, which, however, did not wait the American attack.

Mistaking Shelby's party for the re-enforcements under Colonel Christian, which they knew were due, the Indians withdrew in good order, carrying most of their dead with them, and the battle ended leaving the Americans in possession of the field. They had paid a heavy price for their victory. Seventy-five officers and men had been killed and one hundred and forty wounded, over half of them very seriously. The loss among the officers was unusually severe. The Indian loss has never, been ascertained, but it was very heavy, although not so great as that of the Americans, which was over twenty *per cent*. Logan was not present at this battle.

Colonel Christian, to whom expresses had been sent, arrived on the field that night. Waiting several days to bury the dead, attend to the wounded, and erect a fort for their protection, Lewis left three hundred men on the battlefield at Point Pleasant—so the place was called—crossed the Ohio and marched up the Pickaway plains to join Dunmore. His men were filled with wrath against that commander. They thought he had betrayed them to the Indians, that he had placed them in a position subject to attack, and then had left them without succour; that he never intended to meet them.

It was charged afterward that Dunmore would not have been disappointed if the Virginians had been wiped out on this occasion. The disaffection which culminated in the Revolution six months later, was already widely prevalent in Virginia, and the men thought that Dunmore, as Royal Governor, would have been glad to have weakened the forces of the colonies by the annihilation of this large detachment.

There is not much to admire in the character of Dunmore. When the Revolution came, it is plain that he endeavoured to incite not only a servile insurrection among the slaves but also to throw the savages upon the border; but there is absolutely no foundation for the assertion that he played false in this instance, and we must acquit him of the charges made which have remained current for many years.

Indeed he seems to have acted with considerable capacity as well as courage, for he adroitly took advantage of the victory to make a treaty with the Indians, to which they assented in spite of the strenuous efforts of Cornstalk and others to constrain them to continue the war. And the peace was of lasting benefit to the rebellious colonies, for the remembrance of their defeat kept the Indians quiet during the early years of the Revolution; just at the time, in fact, when their antagonism would have been most serious in the colonies.

None of these things were then realized, and when Dunmore and Lewis met, such was the state of affairs that a guard of fifty men was required to prevent the undisciplined pioneers from taking summary vengeance for the supposed treachery of Dunmore by putting him to death. Lewis himself cherished great animosity to Dunmore.

3. The Fate of the Participants in the Campaign

When the chiefs met at Camp Charlotte to sign the treaty, Logan was not with them. He had refused to be present, professing that he would be unable to control himself in the presence of the race which had so bitterly wronged him. Knowing that no peace could be permanent or valid without Logan's assent to it, an envoy, a veteran frontiersman, was sent to him to secure his ratification.

To him Logan made a speech, very famous indeed, and much quoted in history and in reading books, and which used to be a great favourite with the youthful declaimers of the public schools, though now fallen into disuse and neglect. It is this speech which, in a measure, has kept alive the remembrance of the war and of Logan himself. It is undoubtedly the finest specimen of savage eloquence extant, and compares with any effort of the kind, civilized or otherwise.

Although its authenticity has been questioned, it may be fairly considered as a faithful report of the old chieftain's impassioned words. Most investigators now accept it as genuine. The messenger took it down in writing and translated it literally at the first opportunity, and it was immediately given to the world. Several versions of it exist. Although it does an injustice, unwittingly, to the brave Cresap, a soldier in the Revolution until he died—he is buried in Trinity churchyard, New York, by the way—it is here subjoined in its approved form :

I appeal to any white man if he ever entered Logan's cabin hungry and he gave him no meat; if ever he came cold and naked and he clothed him not? During the course of the long and bloody war, Logan remained idle in his camp, an advocate for peace. Such was my love for the whites that my countrymen pointed as I passed and said, 'Logan is the friend of the white man.' I had even thought to have lived with you, but for the injuries of one man.

Colonel Cresap, the last spring, in cold blood and unprovoked, murdered all the relations of Logan, not even sparing my women and children. There runs not a drop of my blood in the veins of any living creature. This called on me for revenge. I have sought it. I have killed many. I have fully glutted my vengeance.

For my country I rejoice at the beams of peace; but do not harbour a thought that mine is the joy of fear. Logan never felt fear. He will not turn on his heel to save his life.

Who is there to mourn for Logan? Not one.

Roosevelt aptly calls it "no message of peace, nor an acknowledgment of defeat, but instead, a strangely pathetic recital of his wrongs, and a fierce and exultant justification of the vengeance he had taken."

Logan afterward fell into bad habits; he drank to excess, and constantly. He participated in the attacks on the Kentucky settlements during the Revolution, particularly in the massacres at Martin's and

Ruddle's Stations. He was killed by another Indian in a drunken brawl—a melancholy end indeed.

Lewis' conduct in the battle has been called in question by no less an historian than Bancroft, but unjustly, and most modern investigators give him full credit for undaunted courage and devotion. That Washington continued to be his warm personal friend and that he recommended him for a major-generalcy at the outbreak of the Revolution, and privately implored him to continue in the service when his merits were passed over and he was given only a brigadier's commission, is evidence enough of his efficiency and the esteem in which his contemporaries held him.

Singularly enough to Lewis in the Revolution was committed the task of finally expelling Dunmore from the state of Virginia. He accomplished this in his usual thoroughgoing manner. He did not make much of a mark in the war subsequently, however. The fact that he had been passed over unjustly rankled in his mind and at last he resigned his command as John Stark and many others had done. His health, too, gave way; he had been subjected to much exposure in his many hard campaigns, and he died in 1780.

The fate of Cornstalk is a melancholy example frequently met with in our records, of our dealings with the Indian. In 1777, the old chief came to the commander of Point Pleasant, Captain Matthew Arbuckle, to warn him that the Shawnees were contemplating going on the warpath; that he was endeavouring to restrain them, but he feared his success would be slight. He also said that if they declared war he should be forced to join them as they were his people. With a fatuity which can hardly be understood, for he was removing the sole check upon the Shawnees, the American captain thereupon immediately made Cornstalk a prisoner, in defiance of every law or custom of civilized nations.

The old chief seems to have had a premonition that his race was run and for himself he did not greatly care. He had warred enough to satisfy even the heart of a savage and was ready for his end. After he had been a captive for some time his son Ellinipsico came to visit him accompanied by two or three other Indians. The day after their arrival two soldiers ranging the woods were fired upon by a party of Indians and one was killed. Charging that the Indians who had committed this offence had been brought there by Ellinipsico, the enraged soldiers proceeded to mob the fort shouting in their fury, "Death to the Indians!"

"CORNSTALK RECEIVED THEM WITH WIDE OPEN ARMS."

Old Cornstalk heard the cries and realized what they meant. Although Ellinipsico was in no way privy to the attack by which the soldier had been killed, and the murder it was learned afterward was not committed by any of his tribe, there was no use in remonstrating. The officers were powerless to restrain the men—indeed they manifested little desire to interfere. The soldiers burst into the hut where the Indians had been confined. Cornstalk received them standing with wide open arms. He was pierced by seven bullets and instantly killed. Ellinipsico was also shot, as was Red Hawk, another famous chief who had been at Point Pleasant battle, and there was still a fourth Indian left, who was brutally tortured.

Cornstalk had been a dreadful scourge on the border. He had ravaged and burned and murdered in his time, as few other Indians had ever done. In the French and Indian War, in Pontiac's War,[1] and in Dunmore's War, he had taken the prominent part. All that, however, does not make it right to have detained him as a prisoner when he came on a peaceable, helpful errand, nor to have allowed him to be shot for an action with which he had no possible connection.

---

1. *The Pontiac Uprising* by Thomas Guthrie, Edson L. Whitney and Robert Rogers, *Journals of the Siege of Detroit* by Robert Rodgers and *Wacousta*: (a novel of the Pontiac uprising & the Siege of Detroit-3 volumes within one special edition) by John Richardson also published by Leonaur.

2

The Pioneers of East Tennessee

1. JOHN SEVIER AND THE WATAUGA MEN

Upon a pleasant spring morning in the year 1772, three horsemen dressed in hunting shirts, the most convenient garb ever devised for wood ranging, rode up to the cabin of James Robertson, the principal man of the little settlement of North Carolina pioneers in the valley of the Watauga, in what is now eastern Tennessee. All three of them were destined to play important parts in the building of the nation, and one of them especially was to tower far above his contemporaries in character and achievement.

That man was John Sevier, the organizer of the first free and independent democratic government upon the continent, the leader of a great commonwealth; an Indian fighter whom few have ever equalled; a soldier who could meet the finest troops on the continent in the field, and with inferior numbers win success from adverse circumstances; an administrator who could conduct the affairs of his fellow-men under circumstances of the greatest difficulty; a statesman who takes rank not far behind those colossal men who watched the travail pains and facilitated the delivery of the new nation to be. Yet in the long roll of books telling of our national heroes I find singularly few which adequately treat of the character and career of this remarkable man. And the one series which professes to discuss his achievements with authority is interesting but highly traditional and little to be depended upon.

Save perhaps in the great state of Tennessee he is more or less unknown or forgotten. Even his decisive connection with one of the most notable battles of our Revolution is obscured by the reflection cast by men of less fame. To the trio of great Tennesseans, Crockett,

Houston, and Jackson, with whose career the world is familiar, must be added the name of Sevier. He may dispute pre-eminence fairly enough with all but a man of such colossal characteristics as Andrew Jackson.

Crockett and Jackson came from the same people. Their origin was humble, their opportunities limited, and the success they achieved the more creditable. Houston was a man of fairly good family of the middle class, Sevier, in the original sense of the term, when the word specified degree instead of character, was a gentleman; yes, a gentleman in modern sense, as well. His family, it is claimed, was an ancient one in France and his name was derived from the town of Xavier in Navarre at the foot of the French Pyrenees, where his family had an considerable estate and an old chateau. Possibly, as is sometimes urged, the name may have been originally de Xavier.

Sevier came naturally by his love for the mountains, for his people had for centuries dwelt on the slopes of that forbidding range. It is alleged that there was a relationship between his family and that of the great Jesuit St. Francis Xavier, than whom no more heroic soul ever lived; but be that as it may, unlike their Spanish namesake the French Xaviers were Huguenots, who fled the country when Louis XIV perpetrated that atrocious blunder—nay, that ineffable crime—known as the Revocation of the Edict of Nantes.

Abandoning their home the family went first to London and then migrated to America, seeking freedom in the land across the sea. The Old Dominion opened hospitable arms to people of their gentle blood, and as they had saved something from the wreck of their fortunes they presently became people of prominence among the planters of Virginia. There in 1745 young John Sevier, for so the family name became anglicized, was born. He was given the best education which it was possible to receive in Virginia, and of which, with his usual ambition, he made the most of in his life.

He was twenty-seven years of age, therefore, when he rode up to Robertson's house on the Watauga. He had been married some years at that time and was the father of two promising sons. While a mere boy he had made a name for himself as a hunter, trader, and pioneer, and now held a commission as captain in the Virginia line, the same corps in which Washington was afterward a colonel. He had come across the Alleghenies to the settlement on the Watauga to build himself a new home in this recently opened country.

I cannot doubt but that God led him across the hills, for charmed by what he saw, he determined to cast his lot with the people there, of whom he speedily became the idol and leader. His two companions, the elder a grizzly veteran, who also held the rank of captain in the Virginia line, were Evan and Isaac Shelby, father and son, two sterling patriots of Welsh descent. Evan Shelby rose to the rank of general in the Revolution and although he had a distinguished career, may be dismissed from our consideration. Isaac Shelby, the son, however, reappears again in this narrative, and was associated with Sevier in many heroic undertakings.

When Daniel Boone, redoubtable hunter, explorer, adventurer, man of heroic mould, first toiled over the tree-crested summits of the Alleghenies and surveyed the vast expanse of mountain and valley and river stretching inimitably before him toward the setting sun, country which no white man had ever trod, a doubtful legend says that he gave vent to his feelings in an outburst of enthusiasm to his comrades, in these words: "I am richer than the man in Scripture, who owned cattle on a thousand hills. I own the wild beasts in a thousand valleys!" Whether he said it or no, he probably thought it.

It is characteristic of the genius of the white race, that to see a place, to set foot upon it, was sufficient to establish a claim to any domain, any aboriginal inhabitants to the contrary, notwithstanding. The great waste of territory between the Ohio and the Tennessee, which the English claimed had been ceded to the king in the famous treaty of Fort Stanwix by the Iroquois,—who had no more right nor title to it than Germany has to France, for instance,—was the hunting ground, the place of resort, of great tribes of the most enlightened and warlike savages south of the Six Nations, upon the continent.

De Soto had visited it in 1540, and an Irish trader, named Dougherty, had settled within its confines within the latter part of the seventeenth century, but no one had ever presumed to attempt to colonize, or hold it, not even the Cherokees, whose country lay adjacent to the beautiful valley of the Watauga.

2. "The Rear Guard of the Revolution"

The first actual settlement was made in 1769-70 by Robertson and a party of North Carolinians, who climbed the mountains and built their huts in the fertile valley on the other side. There in a well-watered plateau, some two thousand feet above the level of the sea, in a country which was remarkable for the fertility of its soil and the salubrity of its climate, they purchased land from the Cherokees, erected cabins, and endeavoured to make the place a home. Thither Sevier resorted. Possessed of ample means, indeed, being a man of wealth for the time and place, his house became the resort of the hardy settlers, whom he received with true Virginia hospitality.

A man of urbane and charming disposition, gay and debonair, yet of inflexible resolution and matchless daring, he became the idol of the settlers. Thenceforward for forty-three years he led them in all their enterprises and undertakings; he conducted thirty-four battles against the Indians and met no defeat; he participated as the animating spirit in one great expedition against the British, with overwhelming success. In 1772, he and his associates in the trans-mountain settlements, organized the first free and independent government on this continent, administering the laws of their agreement and dealing justice in the vast region across the Alleghenies.

During the Revolutionary War many times he broke up the plans of the British for launching the savages upon the borders and thus overwhelming the American colonists; plans which, had they succeeded, might have been as fatal to American hopes of independence as would have been the success of Burgoyne's expedition. He and his men—Gilmore felicitously calls them "The Rear Guard of the Revolution"—kept the Indians in check, dauntlessly interposing their scanty numbers between the fierce warriors and the unprotected settlements on the hither side of the Alleghenies, performing service incalculable thereby. The borders were free, the patriots could leave their families without fear of savage foray because they were watched over by Sevier and his men. It was given to him at one of the turning points of the Revolution to inspire, and in large measure to strike the blow which determined that the south land should be free.

3. The State of Franklin and its Governor

After the Revolution, under Sevier's leadership, North Carolina having cast them off, the mountaineers organized within the limits of the present commonwealth of Tennessee, the state of Franklin,[2] named for the wise old philosopher, and Sevier was its first governor.

He administered its financial affairs with a currency of coon skins! When North Carolina withdrew the act of cession, by which she had turned the territory over to Congress and sought to assume her state rights again, Sevier conducted himself in the trying crisis with

---

2. Commonly and erroneously called the state of Frankland, *i.e.,* land of the Franks or Freemen!

discretion and firmness, and had it not been for the machinations of some bitter enemies—this is the penalty of greatness, always to make enemies—he might have succeeded in preserving the integrity of the state he had founded.

It is interesting to note that North Carolina, which was quick to follow the lead of her southern sisters in seceding from the Union in 1861, pointed out at this ancient date that if different communities were permitted to withdraw from a mother state and organize states of their own, at their own volition, the result would be the disintegration of the Republic. North Carolina was right in this instance, and Sevier was wrong in attempting to maintain his commonwealth.

He was treacherously betrayed, captured, and afterward tried at Morgantown, North Carolina, for high treason. Fifteen hundred men of the trans-Allegheny region, assembled to take him back, and a war between the sections was imminent. Aided by some of his old comrades in arms he made a romantic escape from the custody of the officers; whereupon the people of the Watauga district, having submitted to the inevitable, promptly elected him to the North Carolina legislature, in which, after some feeble protests, he took his seat.

When the state ratified the constitution and became thereby a member of the Federal Union, one congress- man was apportioned to the district across the Alleghenies. Sevier was unanimously elected and was the first man to sit in Congress from that great region beyond the mountains.

He was made general of the militia when Tennessee was a territory, and when she became a state he was chosen governor without opposition. For three successive terms he was elected, and then being ineligible constitutionally, for a period of two years, he was thereafter elected for three more successive terms, after which he was sent back to Congress and thrice re-elected!

He died in harness and in the field, in 1815, in a tent on a surveying expedition for the government, surrounded as he had lived, by his soldiers.

He lost his first wife in 1774 and was living at his home on the Nolichucky, from which, by the way, he was sometimes called in border parlance, "Nolichucky Jack," or "Chucky Jack," in 1775, when the Revolutionary War broke out. One of the first of the British attempts was to assemble the savages on the Watauga frontier, especially in the southern territory, sweep inland and ravage the settlements, while Sir Peter Parker and his fleet attempted to capture Charleston, thus placing the colonists between two fires and making their downfall apparently certain.

Moultrie and his little handful beat off Parker, and Sevier and a still smaller handful broke up the plan in the west by routing the Indians in a brilliant campaign terminating in the siege at Fort Lee, a rude timber enclosure which had been erected on the banks of the Watauga. The fort was closely beleaguered by the savages for some forty days without a casualty among the defenders, the Indians losing so severely in their attacks that old Oconostota. their head war chief, the inveterate enemy of the Americans so long as he lived, finally withdrew his force in dismay and abandoned the campaign.

It was at this siege that there occurred a romantic episode in the life of the young woman who became the second wife of Sevier. In defiance of warnings some of the people of the fort, irked by the confinement, had gone beyond the limits of the walls. A party of savages suddenly appeared and attempted their capture. The people fled to gain the stockade, which was crowded with women and children.

It would have risked everything to have left the gate open, indeed there was no time for it. Sevier sent his men to the walls to cover the escaping fugitives by a smart rifle fire, and drive back the Indians till the settlers could be taken in. One young girl, Katharine Sherrill, in her terror actually leaped to the top of the palisade and fell over the wall into the arms of the commander. She leaped into his heart at the same time and they were soon married. Bonny Kate is reported to have said,

> I would take a leap like that every day to fall into the arms of a man like my gallant husband.

The handsomest man in Tennessee, they called him, and the bravest and best; tall, just under six feet, blue-eyed, sunny-haired, graceful, he was a man to win any woman's heart, and his qualities were equally attractive to men. He was a glutton for work, a giant for endurance, a very paladin of courage.

After twenty-eight days of marching and fighting in the King's Mountain expedition, with scarcely any rest he set out for another campaign in the wilds of the mountains against the restless Cherokees. Another inveterate enemy of the white settlers was the chief of the Chickamaugas, named Dragging Canoe. When the British attempted a second time to combine the savages and hurl them upon the backs of the colonists, it was Sevier's brilliant expedition in the heart of the

Indian country which broke the spirit of the Cherokees, "Sons of Fire," and their allies. They smouldered thereafter and until the state of Franklin was organized gave but little trouble.

Such was the personal courage of Sevier that in this expedition he slew Dragging Canoe with his own hand, in a terrific hand-to-hand conflict. In thirty-four encounters with the Indians he was invariably successful.

It is difficult to describe any of these actions. They did not rise to the dignity of pitched battles, but generally consisted of a swift, noiseless approach, a surprise, a wild desperate charge upon the Indians, driving them into headlong rout, a destruction of their villages and crops and then a quick withdrawal to the settlements. Again and again were these tactics pursued.

Sevier had many qualities of Francis Marion, another great American of French descent, who fought in the Revolution. Instead of the slow, stealthy concealed advance, the hidden ambush, which the Indians made use of, Sevier adopted other tactics and depended upon audacity and speed. The Napoleonic idea of the value of a small mobile concentrated body hurled swiftly upon a slow-moving scattered if superior force, was exemplified in his attempts before the Corsican was born. It was exemplified nowhere so strikingly as in that most remarkable battle of King's Mountain, which, for originality of conception, boldness of execution, success in completion, stands among the most picturesque battles of the world; and with the story of that battle in which he won so many of his laurels, we will leave the old hero.

4. THE ASSEMBLING OF THE MOUNTAINEERS

One of the most distinguished officers of the king in America during the Revolution was Major Patrick Ferguson of the Seventy-first Foot, the Royal Americans. He was a brother of Adam Ferguson, the celebrated Scottish philosopher, and in his own way quite as gifted. To a reputation for bravery earned in Europe, he had added new laurels, notably at the Brandywine, receiving there a wound which permanently deprived him of the full use of an arm thereafter, and at the Battle of Camden, where the Seventy-first under his leadership, displayed such splendid courage and where he was again wounded.

He was a man of an ingenious turn of mind and had invented a breech-loading rifle, in the use of which he became very expert. Upon one occasion it is claimed that he had a reconnoitring party of Americans headed by a general officer within range of his rifle, and that from motives of humanity he refrained from killing the unsuspecting officer, which he could easily have done. He afterward learned that the man he had spared was George Washington.

For a time, after the overwhelming and disgraceful defeat of Gates at Camden, South Carolina, August 16, 1780, Cornwallis virtually had the whole south at his mercy. He moved slowly northward with the main body of his army, sending out columns on either flank, and in all directions in fact, endeavouring to occupy and pacify the country he fondly considered permanently subdued.

To Ferguson was given command of the various operations upon the left of the main advance. To him were assigned one hundred and twenty of his own regular regiment, and he was given power to embody and take command of all the Tory volunteers he could win to his following.

The Carolinas, be it remembered, with the exception of New Jersey—and New York in part—were the only states which were entirely swept from border to border by the besom of war. There was scarcely a nook or a corner in either one in which the rifle shot was not heard, the torch was not lighted, in which the passions of Hell were not let loose. The rancorous hatreds of civil strife in no section were more in evidence than in these two brave little southern colonies. Even the animosities engendered in central New York between the Whigs and Tories were not so persistent, so rigorous, so bitter, or so desolating in their effects.

Cornwallis soon awoke from his dream; for, while partisan bands sprang up on either side and attacked each other without mercy, success generally inclined to the Americans. The British found they could only hold the ground occupied by their armies. In their exasperation, they and the Tories resorted to ferocious cruelties, which were promptly met by reprisals in kind. Many of Cornwallis' parties and bodies of Tories were cut off without mercy. In fact, except under Cruger, Tarleton, and Ferguson, the British were defeated again and again by Sumter, Marion, Pickens, Davie, McDowell, and Williams.

Ferguson had experienced some reverses, but on the whole had been very successful. He succeeded in embodying some two thousand Tories, whom he organized into regiments, which he trained and drilled in British tactics with energy and success.

He had been brought in contact with a few of the trans-Allegheny men, the first settlers of Virginia west, of the mountains and the pioneers of Tennessee; the "Back Water Men," he called them on several occasions and knew their quality, especially from one bloody skirmish at Musgrove's Mills. Seeking to keep them quiet he released a prisoner and sent him across the range to inform the people there that if they did not "desist from their opposition to British arms, he would march his army across the mountains, hang the leaders, and lay the country waste with fire and sword."

In Ferguson's army, which was then about sixty miles from the Watauga, where was the principal settlement in East Tennessee, were several Tories, who had been expelled from the mountain region and who were thoroughly conversant with the passes through the mountains. It was possible for him to have made the attempt, although it is extremely doubtful that he ever had the slightest idea of doing so; for, as he well knew, his chances of success would have been of the very smallest. It is probable that the threat was merely intended to frighten the mountaineers into keeping quiet. They were not the kind to be frightened by idle threats, and Ferguson was to learn that it was a dangerous thing to threaten to do the impossible, or at least he would have learned it if the mountaineers had not killed him trying to teach him the lesson.

"Never was threat so impotent, and yet so powerful." Ferguson's messenger went first to Shelby, who acted with instant promptitude. Sixty miles to the south was the residence of Sevier on the Nolichucky. Throwing himself upon his horse, Shelby tore down the valley to apprize his friend and colleague of the news and to concert as to the best course of action.

The "tall Watauga boys," as they were called, were having a jollification at the time at Sevier's; oxen were being roasted for a barbecue, horse-racing was going on, and rustic sports were being enjoyed. Sevier was keeping open house to all comers. One authority says that the occasion was the marriage of the great pioneer to the girl of the stockade episode, but other investigators claim that the marriage occurred in the stockade during the siege, or shortly after, and it is probable that this was a rustic gathering to celebrate the garnering of the harvest. But from whatever cause, a great many of the inhabitants, men, women, and children, were assembled there having a good time, when Shelby dashed up on his sweat-lathered horse and stopped the merriment instantly by the sight of his grim, anxious, and troubled face.

The two leaders retired at once for consultation, while the people suspended their sports and with deepening anxiety awaited the results of the deliberation. What was to be done? Should they bid defiance to Ferguson, occupy the mountain passes, and await attack there? This was believed to be Shelby's idea. Sevier was more audacious. They should not wait to be attacked, they should assemble the men, cross the range and fall upon the unsuspecting partisan before he realized that they had more than received his message. His bold counsels prevailed. The news was immediately circulated, and the men and women assembled for the merrymaking received the decision with shouts of approval. A rendezvous was appointed at Sycamore Shoals on the Watauga, on the 25th of September.

Taking a fresh horse Shelby rode north to enlist for the enterprise Campbell and his Virginians, settled about the head waters of the Holston. Sevier sent messengers to McDowell, who, with a small band of North Carolinians, had been chased over the mountains by Ferguson. Sevier was to assemble the Watauga men as well.

Campbell at first refused to participate in the expedition, but upon being further approached by argument and appeal, finally consented. Expresses were despatched over the mountains and one of the most celebrated partisans of North Carolina, Colonel Benjamin Cleaveland, promised to join the assemblage with such men as he could secure. On the 25th of September, Campbell, Shelby, and Sevier, reached the rendezvous at the appointed time.

The situation was peculiar. On one side of the little settlement were hordes of savages who had only been kept in check by severe campaigning and constant watchfulness, and who wanted but an opportunity to fall upon the settlements. On the other side, with the mountains between, were over two thousand well-trained British troops, under a veteran officer. Yet so eager were the men to go on the expedition that they resorted to a draft to see who should stay behind to protect the women and children from the red peril so dangerously near.

Four hundred and eighty of the Watauga men were selected and divided into two regiments, commanded by Sevier and Shelby. In Sevier's regiment were no less than six persons who bore his name, including his two sons. Two of his brothers were captains. The Watauga boys were joined by one hundred and sixty of McDowell's men and two hundred Back Water Presbyterians under stout old William Campbell, presently re-enforced by two hundred more of the same sort under Arthur Campbell, his brother.

The assemblage, though small, was remarkable for its quality; tall, sinewy, powerful, brave, dead shots, accustomed to the fatigues and hardships of frontier life, it would be hard to match this body of borderers on the continent. The little army was without baggage, without equipment, without provisions, without everything but arms. Most of the men had no horses, although all were provided with the Deckhard rifle, a piece remarkable in that day for the precision of its shot and the length of its range.

Sevier and Shelby had long since exhausted their private resources, and they were hard put to know where to find money to buy horses and equipments for those who were without them, for they had determined that the expedition should consist only of mounted riflemen. There was one officer of North Carolina, however, on their side of the mountains, who had money. This was John Adair, the entry taker, whose business it was to receive the payments of the settlers for the land which they took up.

Sevier and Shelby went to him and asked him for the money in his hands, some twelve thousand dollars, pledging their personal honour and credit that thereafter he should be paid back every farthing—a pledge they scrupulously redeemed. Adair rose to the measure of the situation with true patriotism, as may be seen by his splendid answer to the demand:

> Colonel Sevier, I have no right to make any such disposition of this money; it belongs to the impoverished treasury of North Carolina. But, if the country is overrun by the British, liberty is gone. Let the money go too. Take it. If by its use the enemy is driven from the country, I can trust that country to justify and vindicate my conduct. Take it!

With this money the men were promptly provided with horses and powder. Even the women entered into the spirit of the occasion, and it is related that some of the powder which was afterward used with such deadly effect was made by their assistance, for they burned the charcoal on the family hearthstones.

5. The Dash to Catch Ferguson

Early on the morning of the 26th of September was the hour appointed for the march. Old Parson Doak, stern Presbyterian, black-gowned, stood in the midst of the one thousand rugged riflemen in their hunting shirts, who doffed their coon-skin caps, or buck-tail hats, and ringed themselves about him, leaning upon their arms, while he invoked the Divine blessing upon the expedition, bidding them to go forth and strike with the sword of the Lord and of Gideon. After this impressive ceremony, the men, speeded by the cheers of those unwillingly left behind, and followed by the prayers of the women, immediately took up the march. With them, rifle in hand, went another clergyman, the Reverend Stephen Foster.

Being well mounted, they made great progress. Unencumbered by baggage train of any sort, they were able to take short cuts and traverse apparently impracticable paths over the range, which they found covered with deep snow. There was no commissariat, a few beeves were driven on the march and slaughtered for the first day's rations, but the men depended upon what they could pick up on the way, or shoot with the rifle, to eke out the supply of parched corn which every man carried for himself. It is not too much to say that the west was won by parched corn and the powder horn.

They marched with great swiftness for several days, being joined at the foot of the mountains by Cleaveland, a redoubtable, if merciless and ferocious fighter, with three hundred and fifty men from Wilkes and Surrey Counties, on the 30th of September. On Monday, the 1st of October, they marched eighteen miles, but were stopped by the rain. On the 2nd they determined to select one of the various colonels who should command the expedition, pending the arrival of an officer of rank.

Choice fell upon William Campbell of Virginia, who had the largest regiment. McDowell of North Carolina, who was senior, had the smallest regiment, and was not thought sufficiently vigorous for such an undertaking. He relieved the dilemma regarding him, by volunteering to ride express to General Gates and ask him to send an officer of merit to take charge. Campbell hesitated to assume the command, and earnestly urged Sevier, Shelby, or other officers to take it, but they insisted that he should undertake the duty which they had devolved upon him, and at last he consented.

On the 3rd of October, while still in the gap at South Mountain, before the march was taken up, Cleaveland, who seems to have been the orator of the assemblage, addressed the men in the following terms:

Now, my brave fellows, I have come to tell you the news. The enemy is at hand, and we must up and at them. Now is the time for every man of you to do his country a priceless service—

such as shall lead your children to exult in the fact that their fathers were the conquerors of Ferguson. When the pinch comes I shall be with you. But if any of you shrink from sharing the battle and glory, you can now have the opportunity of backing out and leaving, and you shall have a few minutes for considering the matter.

Other colonels in brief, terse words seconded old Cleaveland, and then requested those who desired to retire from the proposed expedition to step three paces to the rear. No one did so, of course. Ferguson was believed to be in the vicinity of Gilbert Town. They proceeded cautiously, therefore, to that point, and the next day learned that he had retreated and that he was thought to have gone southward to Ninety Six.

In the vicinity of Beattie's Ford on the Catawba, thirty miles away, were a body of Sumter's men under Colonels Hill, who was too badly wounded to take part in the campaign, and Lacey, and a small party of South Carolinians under Williams, altogether about four hundred in number. Williams had been appointed to command the militia, and Sumter had disputed his right. Pending the settlement of the question, Sumter had withdrawn from his troops, otherwise he would have exercised chief command in the battle that was to follow. Williams, however, had remained in the neighbourhood; although Sumter's troops had refused to acknowledge him, he had gathered a small body of his own.

When this assemblage heard these mountain men had come for the purpose of taking Ferguson, Colonel Lacey made an all-night ride through the wilderness to Campbell's camp, on the Green River, which he reached an hour or so before daybreak, offering to co-operate with them and informing the mountaineers that Ferguson had not gone to Ninety Six, but was marching toward King's Mountain. They believed at first that Lacey was a Tory spy, but he finally persuaded them of his integrity, and they agreed to meet his party at the Cowpens, south of the Broad, soon to be the scene of another famous victory, the next evening, the 6th of October. Selecting some seven hundred of the best men, the mountaineers at once set out, leaving the rest to follow as fast as possible.

With scarcely an hour's sleep, Lacey mounted his horse and returned to his men, reaching them about ten o'clock in the morning, having ridden sixty miles in fourteen hours. On the appointed evening the whole party, now amounting to some eleven hundred men, rendezvoused at the Cowpens. The indomitable Lacey had succeeded in getting his men there at the hour agreed upon. Before they took up their march again they carefully selected, by a second weeding out, nine hundred and ten of the most efficient with the freshest horses, with whom they determined to push on to meet Ferguson.[3] Fifty foot soldiers resolved to keep up with the horsemen if possible.

Sure intelligence had been received that Ferguson had halted on King's Mountain. This is a low spur of the Alleghenies, sixteen miles long, running northeast and southwest. Ferguson was encamped on the southern end of it in York County, South Carolina, a mile and a half from the border. He had sent despatches to Cornwallis, whom he had been endeavouring to join, urging him to send Tarleton to escort him over the thirty miles of rough broken country between his army and Charlotte, his lordship's headquarters, for he had been apprised by two deserters of the storm that was gathering on his heels.

Not that he had any fear of being able to defend his present position, for he considered his force entirely adequate to hold it forever, although not sufficiently strong to take the offensive. The affair at Musgrove's Mills had given his troops, if not himself, a healthy respect for the mountaineers. Unfortunately for him, some of his messengers were captured, and others were forced by the dangers of the way to take such circuitous routes that they did not reach Cornwallis until the battle was over.

Ferguson had chosen the position from the point of view of the European soldier, with much skill. Professional soldiers have called it admirable for defence. He is alleged to have said, in various profane ways, that he could hold his post against any force that might be brought against him.

A great deal of unscientific criticism has been heaped upon him for this choice of position. To be sure he did not hold it against an inferior force, which seems to bear out the censures; but that force was unique in composition and its attack was an unusual one, which

3. This number was made up, according to McCrady, as follows: Campbell, 200; Sevier, 120; Shelby, 120; Cleaveland, 110; McDowell, a brother of the officer who had gone to seek Gates, 90; and Winston, a subordinate to Cleaveland, 60; making seven hundred chosen at Green River. Additional troops were selected at the Cowpens, as follows: Lacey, 100; Williams, 60, and Graham and Hambright, 50, making 210: total, 910. 200 of these were Virginians, 510 were from North and 200 from South Carolina. The foot soldiers mentioned did not arrive until the close of the action, so they are not counted. The rest were to follow as fast as they could.

no theoretical experience could have led Ferguson to expect. He could probably have held the place successfully against regular soldiers without difficulty. But the men who were after him were not regular troops. They knew nothing of the school of the soldier and cared less; their character was peculiar and their tactics in accordance.

6. King's Mountain; Launching the Thunderbolt

About nine o'clock on the night of the 6th, the army set forth from the Cowpens for King's Mountain, some thirty-three miles away. It was pitch dark and to add to their difficulties and discomforts a chill rain came driving upon them for a large part of the night. To keep their muskets dry the men were forced to take off their blankets and shirts and wrap them around the gunlocks. Chilled to the bone they urged their jaded steeds through the clogging mud and cold driving rain of the furious storm during the long night.

When day broke they reached the Catawba at Cherokee Ford, crossed it, still in the pelting rain, and plodded on. Some chroniclers aver, that, oppressed by their long, hard march, the slow progress they had made, the worn-out condition of the men, some of the officers suggested that they give over the attempt and return. Shelby, marching in the van, curtly replied,

"I will not stop until night if I follow Ferguson into Cornwallis' lines!"

So they pushed resolutely on. It continued to rain harder than ever during the morning until noon, when the storm broke and the sun came out with a fine breeze, to the great refreshment of the army. Spies and scouts sent on ahead confirmed the truth of their impression that Ferguson was on King's Mountain. At one Tory farmhouse, from which they could get no information, one of the women came out secretly and ran across the fields until she intercepted the American advance.

"How many men have you?" she cried.

"Enough to whip Ferguson if we can find him," was the reply.

"You will find him on that mountain yonder," she said, pointing to the hill three miles away.

It was two o'clock when the army reached the vicinity of the mountain after their eighteen-hour struggle in the dreadful storm. Hard on their heels followed the devoted fifty foot, who had made an unparalleled march.

The portion of King's Mountain upon which the battle occurred is an isolated hill some six hundred yards long, about one hundred feet high, and varying in width from sixty to one hundred and twenty yards across. It is a long stone-crested ridge, the sides covered with trees, the top bare and desolate. The rocks around the edge of the crest formed a natural breastwork. The narrowest part of the hill was toward the south. At this narrow end of the ridge a man standing could be seen from the foot of either slope. Ferguson's camp was pitched near the northern end, and except for the natural cover afforded by the rocks and bowlders, had no other protection. The baggage-wagons were parked along the north-eastern, the most exposed edge, near the widest part.

Ferguson had with him one hundred and twenty of the Seventy-first regulars, and some eight hundred Tory militia, about equally divided between the two Carolinas. He had had this militia under his command for some time and had drilled and exercised them with unfailing zeal and success until he rated them equal to British regular soldiery. His own troops, of course, were provided with bayonets, and he caused the hunting knives of the Tories so to be arranged that they could be fitted into the muzzles of the guns; thus the militia contingent was supplied with a formidable weapon for close quarters. His main reliance was upon the bayonet, therefore. There were no bayonets of any sort in the American army, and it was to be rifle bullet against cold steel.

The second in command on the mountain was Captain de Peyster of New York, a brave, efficient officer. It is interesting to note that, with the exception of Ferguson himself, there were probably no men of British birth in either of the two contending armies.

Riding as near the hill as they dared without being discovered, the men dismounted, with the exception of a few of the ranking officers, and were formed up in four divisions; Campbell taking the command of the right centre division; Shelby the left centre; Sevier, with Mc-Dowell's and some of Winston's men under him, led the right wing; while Cleaveland with Williams, Lacey, and the others took charge of the left wing.

A party of horse under Major Winston who knew the field of battle, were ordered to make a long detour and approach the mountain from the northern end. Campbell and Shelby were to attack the right and left sides of the mountain at the narrow lower end, Sevier and Cleaveland were to defile past them and range along the east and west sides respectively, while Winston closed the remaining gap. The attack

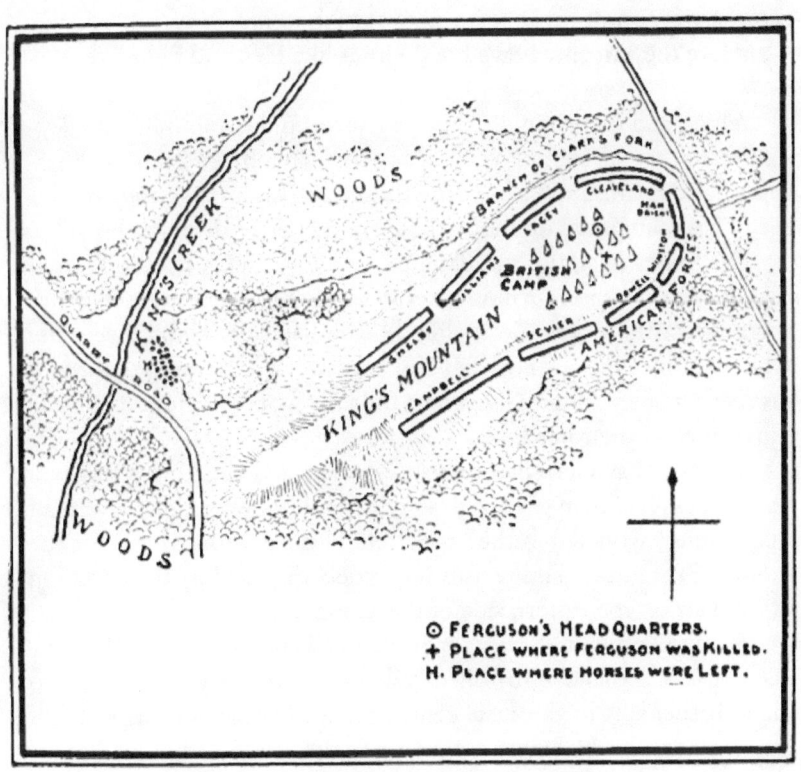

Plan of Battle of King's Mountain.

was delivered about three o'clock. The rallying word was "Buford," the name of the commander whom Tarleton had treacherously killed in the massacre at Waxhaws.

It was not until fifteen minutes before the battle began that Ferguson became aware of the threatened danger. Instantly his men were called to arms. Shelby and Campbell, having the shortest distance to go, were the first to engage the enemy. The honour of beginning the battle must be given to Campbell. The stout old Presbyterian, stripped to his shirt sleeves, led the Virginians up the hill, waving an old claymore, a weapon of his Scottish ancestors, shouting,

"Here they are, my brave boys! Shout like Hell and fight like devils!"

Yelling and firing rapidly they swarmed up the hill. When de Peyster heard these deafening yells, which he remembered from the disastrous fight at Musgrove's Mills, he turned to Ferguson saying,

"These things are ominous; these are the d———d yelling boys!"

The Englishman was not daunted by the yelling, however. Throwing his regulars upon them in a fierce bayonet charge, Ferguson drove them down the slope. Meanwhile Shelby had sustained a severe fire while getting into position and had hard work restraining the fire of his men; at last yelling, "Give them Indian play, boys!" he rode up the other slope at their head.

A similar bayonet charge by de Peyster and the Tories repulsed their attack. The men gave back so reluctantly, however, that several of them were bayoneted as they retreated. Flushed with victory for the moment, Ferguson's enthusiasm was rudely dispelled by the crackling of muskets on the eastern side of the mountain.

Yelling like fiends, Sevier's men breasted the slope of the hill. Indeed, it is said that the so-called "rebel yell," which was heard on so many battlefields in the next century, had its origin in this body of mountaineers led by Sevier. Galloping to the threatened point, Ferguson threw some of his men upon the Watauga boys. The ground here was more broken, and the same rocks which served for the British ramparts played a like purpose for the Americans. Sevier could not be driven away. He established himself on the crest of the hill behind the rocks, pouring in a deadly fire.

At the same instant Colonel Cleaveland came into action. He was a great speech-maker, this Cleaveland, and as his soldiers raced along the base of the hill to get to the position from which they were to make the ascent, he is said to have made the following speech in broken sentences:

> My brave fellows, we have beaten the Tories, and we can beat
> them again. . . . They are all cowards. If they had the spirit of
> men, they would join us in supporting the independence of the
> country. . . . When you are engaged, do not wait for the word of
> command. I will show you by my example how to fight. I can
> undertake no more. . . . Every man must act on his own judge-
> ment. Fire as fast as you can, and stand your ground as long as
> you can. . , . When you can do no better, get behind trees, or
> retreat; but I beg you not to run off.

Then pointing to the crest of the hill from which a deadly fire
was plunging, he cried, "Yonder is your enemy, and the enemy of
mankind!"

At the same instant Colonel Hambright with his brave Germans,
and Majors Winston and Chronicle of the Carolinians, closed the gap.
Williams, who had sulked because he had not been recognized or
consulted by the other officers, could stand it no longer.

"Come up, boys!" he shouted, "the old wagoner never yet backed
out!" and he rushed into action to the right of Cleaveland.

The mountain was now completely encircled. Sevier had gained
the summit and was clinging to it with grim tenacity. As Ferguson
withdrew his troops from the southern end, Campbell and Shelby
immediately turned and followed them up the hill. Both sides fought
well. Three times did the British and Tories throw themselves upon
the approaching Americans. Three times did the deadly bayonet do its
work, but they could not drive the men from the fight further than
they could continue the charge. They always came back. Campbell
had two horses shot under him. Shelby's face had been burned by
powder, so close had been the action.

The mountain was ringed with fire and covered with smoke. The
roar of the rifles and muskets could be heard for miles. Ferguson
showed himself a very paladin of courage. Mounted on a white horse
he rode frantically up and down the *plateau*, rallying his men, launching charge after charge upon whatever part of the line ventured to
expose itself on the crest. The bulk of these charges fell upon the
regiments of Shelby and Campbell, but the beleaguered force struck
out desperately on every hand. Finally a last charge furiously hurled
upon the Virginians, coupled with shouts that Tarleton was at hand,
put the regiment to flight. Imploring, protesting, swearing, the brave

"FERGUSON SHOWED HIMSELF A VERY PALADIN OF COURAGE."

commander essayed to stop the retreat of his men, but it was not until they had been driven some distance from the foot of the hill that he could get them in order again to lead them back.

Meanwhile Sevier led his men from the crest of the hill and dashed at the British in the open. At the same instant a simultaneous advance all along the lines drove the British back in every direction. The Virginians rallied and came fiercely up again. The British fell in scores.

Someone raised a white flag. Ferguson instantly ordered it down, swearing that he would "never surrender to such a d——d set of *banditti!*" Blowing the silver whistle which had rung over the field and by which he had given his commands, he rallied his forces for another final charge. De Peyster led it with the remnant of the regulars, but before they came in contact with the mountaineers, their deadly discharge reduced his line to twelve people. Another flag was raised and this time Ferguson cut it down.

But the day was lost. De Peyster realized it and advised surrender. Ferguson, however, would not see the inevitable and disdained to yield. He put himself at the head of his men for another charge and was shot by a dozen bullets and instantly killed. The British were now crowded in a huddled mass near the northeast end, surrounded on all sides by the mountaineers. To resist longer was to be slaughtered like sheep in a pen.

De Peyster raised the flag a third time. Some of the mountaineers, so ignorant of the customs of war that they did not realize the meaning of the signal, and maddened by the fighting, continued their fire, which was returned by some of the desperate British soldiers and Colonel Williams was instantly killed. The Americans yelling "Give them Buford's play," then poured a volley in on the unresisting Tories, most of whom had practically surrendered. There was a scene of wild and terrible confusion on the mountain top. De Peyster wildly protested against the butchery of surrendered men. Sevier, Shelby, and Campbell did their best to restrain their reckless, undisciplined soldiers, who continued to fire upon the huddled mass of British crying "Quarter! Quarter!" and the battle bade fair to degenerate into a massacre. Finally the mountaineers were stopped, and at Shelby's words,

"D——n you, if you want quarter, throw down your arms!" the British threw down their guns and were marched away from them.

7. AFTER THE BATTLE

The battle was over at four o'clock in the afternoon. It had lasted scarcely an hour. In the confusion some of the Tories, who wore no uniform, escaped, but the results of the battle were some three hundred killed, or so severely wounded that they had to be left on the field, and six hundred captured. On the American side the casualties were twenty-eight killed, and sixty-two wounded, the disparity being due in part to the fact that the British firing down the hill overshot their opponents, in accordance with a natural tendency under the circumstances.

They bivouacked that night upon the hill. It was a night of horror. There was but one surgeon in both armies, Ferguson's. He did what he could to alleviate the sufferings of the wounded but with little success. The Americans had gained a stupendous victory but their position was still most precarious. With a number of prisoners almost equal to their total force, they were in imminent danger of attack, for they believed Tarleton was near. Anxious hours were passed until daybreak and they took up their march in retreat.

After the first day's march information was brought them that Cruger at Ninety Six had ruthlessly hanged a number of Whigs whom he had captured. At the instance of the Carolina men, with the spirit of revenge hot in their breasts, thirty of the principal men among the Tories were tried by summary court-martial and sentenced to death. Nine of them in bunches of three were at once hanged from a huge tree near the headquarters. Among those sentenced were the two mountaineers who had deserted on the march and betrayed the advance to Ferguson. One of them was a mere boy. He was at once reprieved. The other was one of Sevier's men. The gallant soldier claimed him and begged the other officers that he might be permitted to have him. The request was granted, and the grateful man became one of the most zealous partisans of the Revolution thereafter.

One of the condemned men had a young brother among the prisoners—a mere boy. After the first group had been executed the lad begged permission to speak to his brother. Seizing his opportunity he cut the man's bonds, and he made a dash for freedom, the mountain men, cheering the daring of the boy and the desperate courage of the man, refrained from firing on him. Sevier, seconded by Shelby, thereupon interfered and the bloody reprisal ceased.

In twenty-eight days the whole army was back over the mountains, and at home again—all but those who slept on the field of their glory or who died from their wounds on the return journey and had been buried on the way. One of these was the brother of Sevier.

The heroic courage of the Scotch Presbyterian, Campbell; the resolute determination of the Welshman, Shelby; the dashing gallantry of the Frenchman, Sevier; the enthusiastic devotion of the Irishman, Lacey; the stern valour of the German, Hambright; the stubborn, dogged courage of Cleaveland, the Englishman, had won this most marvellous battle on the hills.

Success came in the very nick of time. Cornwallis in great alarm recalled his scattered forces and hastily fell back into South Carolina, thus giving the Americans time to recreate an army under General Greene, that organizer of victory. The annihilation of Ferguson greatly encouraged the South Carolina Whigs, or rebels, and coupled with the victory of the Cowpens shortly after, where Morgan with some of the King's Mountain men to assist him, crushed Cornwallis' only other successful partisan, Tarleton, paved the way to Yorktown and the end of the Revolution.

Unpublished Account of the Battle of King's Mountain

An original account, never before published, of the Battle of King's Mountain, by the Rev. Stephen Foster, a participant. The original document has been preserved by the descendants of Col. William Campbell, who commanded the American forces in the battle. Its use is allowed by Mr. T. W. Preston, now of Vicksburg, Miss., one of his descendants, and a native of South West Virginia.

★★★★★★

This battle followed the Battle of Enaree. From the latter it appears, that Col. Isaac Shelby carried off 200 prisoners beyond the pursuit of the British troops. Major Ferguson with a small party of regulars had been detached by Lord Cornwallis, to the upper section of the Carolinas, to gather troops to the royal standard and support the interest of His Majesty there. In this service he proved himself a man of energy and skill; mustered a force of a thousand men, resented the affront of Shelby, and addressed to the latter a threatening message, that if he would not cease from such depredations, he would march over the mountains and burn those villages which supplied him with men. Shelby, residing at his father's dwelling, in Sullivan county East Tenn. on receiving this message, repaired to the settlements on Watauga River, 40 miles distant. He there had ample opportunity of communicating its import to Col. John Sevier, who joined him in a sentiment of congenial heroism, for meeting so deserving and respectable an army. The message before them told them of the foe. It presented to them an enterprise of a new and daring kind. The object of this enterprise was single and distinct. This was Ferguson the whole of Ferguson and nothing but Ferguson.

The force which these gentlemen were able to muster in the two settlements, was little over 400 men, The army they were to attack was double in number; and headed by the ablest partisan leader in the land. Shelby therefore addressed a letter to Col. William Campbell of Washington Cnty. Va. to come over and join in the enterprise. Campbell at first refused, from a desire to march in a different direction, and unite his troops with those, which were then struggling in the lower sections of his own state. A second message from Shelby was successful. Campbell's division amounted to 400 men. The place of meeting was the Sycamore Flats on Watauga River, at the foot of the Yellow Mountain.

They ascended this mountain on horseback about the first of Oct. 1780. They encamped the same night in a gap of the mountain on the opposite side. The ascent of the mountain was not very difficult.

It was a road travelled before; but was impassable for waggons.

No provisions were taken but such as each man could carry in his wallet, or saddlebags. The sides and top of the mountain were covered with snow "shoe mouth deep"—On the top of the Mountain and troops paraded, here were one hundred acres of beautiful table land. A spring issuing through it ran over into the Watauga. On reaching the plain beyond the mountain, they found themselves in a country covered with verdure and breathed an atmosphere of summer mildness. The 2nd night they rested at Cathy's Plantation. The third day they fell in with Gen. McDowel, and that night held a general consultation of the officers. Gen. McDowel was without troops. Yet his rank and former services could not easily be overlooked; and at the same time these young and daring officers, impatient to inflict a decisive blow on Ferguson, were unwilling to brook the delay, that might ensue from entrusting the command to him.

It was accordingly stated in council, that they needed an experienced officer to command them; they knew Gen. Morgan was the man they wanted; they were unacquainted with Gen. Greene, and feared that their request to him for Morgan's services would be little attended to, coming as it necessarily must, from strangers. To obviate this difficulty so apparently perplexing, McDowel very generously offered to be their messenger, being personally acquainted with Greene & Morgan and his offer was gladly and promptly accepted.

It was now a matter of immediate consultation who should lead them to the intended attack. Col. Campbell having been nominated by Col. Shelby, both from a principle of courtesy and the superior number of men in his regiment, was elected accordingly.

The fourth night they rested at a rich Tory's, where they obtained abundance of every necessary refreshment.—On passing near the Cowpens, they heard of a large body of Tories about eight miles distant. And, although the main enterprise was not to be delayed a single moment, a party of 80 volunteers under ensign Robert Campbell was permitted to go in chase of them during the night. These had removed before our party came to the place, who accordingly after riding all night came up with the main body the next day.

On the next night a similar expedition was conducted by another officer without success, but without adding any delay to the march of the army. At Gilbertown, about two or three days march from the enemy, our troops fell in with Col. Williams, (who was able to select the best pilots) together with Col Cleaveland, Tracy, and Brandon, each commanding a body of men, and the whole amounting to 300. These were retreating before Ferguson, and were glad to join their forces to ours.

On the night before the day of action, a misunderstanding arose in the attempt to cross a river. Two fords were taken, and the army had separated and was crossing at both. When this was perceived by the officers, a halt was ordered, and the men rested on this side until morning. Two roads were here. And to prevent spies from passing and repassing, they were both guarded by appointed watchman. The least public of these was guarded by Lieu. John Sawyers, (since Col. Sawyers,) and 25 men were here taken in this single night. Our officers and men were so bent upon their object. So anxious to take Ferguson by surprise, and so apprehensible of his possible escape, that they could not brook the delay of footmen. 400 of them were on foot. The other 700 were mounted riflemen.

It was proposed now for the sake of despatch, that these should move in the speediest manner. And although the whole force was already too small, it was determined to risk the fate of the enterprise, in the bravery and address of 700 men. While preparations were made by the officers for this division, many of the troops in the mean time thought it a fit opportunity for refreshment. Beef was spitted at the fire, and mixed dough was in the very process of baking; when the order was given for the troops to march.—The hot meat without roasting, and the hot dough without baking, was rudely thrust by every man into his saddlebags or wallet, and the men galloped off without a murmur.

This was in the dead of night. They were 45 miles from the enemy, and nothing but the very best riding, over such roads as the country afforded, would bring them the next day to his quarters, in season to terminate the action by daylight. They were accordingly there by two o'clock, in the afternoon. Here a few intervening circumstances may be mentioned. Capt. Craig's and some other companies, on crossing a river, (probably Broad River) were made to believe by their commanding officers, for the sake of trying the courage of their men, that the enemy was upon the opposite bank. The enemy, accordingly, which was nothing else than the advanced guards of our own troops, made his appearance for their reception, retiring a little as they approached the river. They crossed the river, dismounted from their horses, and advanced to the proposed attack on the enemy. But finding no enemy there to meet them, they returned to their horses, and proceeded without further delay.

Not far onward, they were to pass a house on the right. This house formed a corner in the road. They turned it and bent their course to the right hand. Here stood a man in the decrepitude of age, leaning on a staff, and watching our men with great earnestness of visage.— He called out: "God Bless you," till his voice died in the distance of the way, and in the noise and hurry of the forward march. They now began to meet with scattered notices of the enemy's encampment in the burnt fences and trodden ground.

As the afternoon advanced, some began to talk of an encampment for our troops, and to give up the hope of meeting the enemy today.

They had now travelled about 45 miles, and during much of this time had been wet with rain. It was about 2 o'clock when coming to a place within two or three miles of the enemy, they intercepted two of his picquets, and captured the same without firing a gun.

Ferguson may have had some notice of our troops, though not immediately before their arrival. A deserter from Col. Cleaveland's division, who will be mentioned again in the sequel of the narrative, had arrived at the British quarters a day or two before and told Ferguson of the approaching attack. His appearance was said to be so shabby and unpromising as to detract much from any high regard to his statement. Yet so wary and vigilant an officer, as Ferguson was not to be taken altogether by surprise. He had chosen his position, and assumed an attitude of rigorous defence.

He was confident in his own measures, yet to secure every precaution he sent a message to Cornwallis desiring aid, at the same time stating, he had named the place of his encampment, King's Mountain, in honour of the king, and was so strongly fortified here, that if all the rebels in hell were rained downed upon him, they could not drive him from it. The message was intercepted by our men and Cornwallis knew nothing of the danger, till Ferguson was no more.

King's Mountain is a ridge running east and west, in York district, S. C. about 10 miles north of the Cherokee Ford of Broad River. A ledge of rock skirts the summit of this Mountain on the south side.

This formed a natural breastwork for the enemy, behind which they could lie with only their heads exposed, and take leisurely aim at our troops on that side. And it is a remarkable fact, which does credit to the rifles of our men, that an unusual number of the enemy, who fell, were shot through the head. Before the action, Col. Shelby remarked to the army, that he had been twice likely to be killed for an enemy by his own men. He therefore recommended, as an expedient of safety, that every man first strip off his coat and hat, and go to battle without them. This was done by himself, and his regiment, but not by others.

Col. Campbell also was induced to lay off his coat which being very peculiar in its colour and form, would have rendered him signally conspicuous from others. King's Mountain now emerged to the view of our men, and the British and Tory troops were seen through the forest rising from dinner.

The battle line was quickly formed. The main attack was to be made by Campbell's and Shelby's division up the east and steepest side of the mountain. Sevier was to ascend the left side of the mountain from these and Cleaveland on his right. Of the main body Campbell's division was on the right and Shelby's on the left. Capt. Elliot, in Shelby's division, occupied the extreme left, Lieut. Sawyers next to him, Capt. Maxwell's company next, and Capt. Webb the extreme right.

The order of march, in the companies composing Col. Campbell's division was, as nearly as the hurry of the transaction would admit, the order of the battle line from right to left, the following: Capt. Dysart; Capt. Colvil: Capt. Edmonston; Capt. Beatie; Lieut. Bowen; Captain Craig; —

But the movement forward was with so much agility, and the retreat so hurried and abrupt, that these companies not only become intermixed with one another, but also with those of Col. Shelby's. The troops were ordered to shout the Indian war-whoop, ascend the mountain and attack the enemy. This was done with great vigour, when the enemy advanced in firm platoons, fired their muskets, charged with fixed bayonets, and obliged them to give way. In the mean time Cols. Williams, Tracy, Brandon, Cleaveland and Sevier, who were to march from the left of the main body and compass the South and West side of the mountain, in the space of 15 minutes arrived there, and assailed the enemy from that direction. This gave our troops an opportunity to rally and return to the charge.

In the early part of this action, Col. Shelby was employed at some distance from his regiment to reconnoitre the enemy by a movement around the north side of the mountain, to the right of our troops. Here he discovered a spacious opening between the right of Campbell's and the left of Seviers. He viewed it to be an advantageous position for directing a constant and effectual fire upon the backs of a body of Ferguson's troops, which lay guarded in front by the ledge of rocks.

He detached Ensign Robert Campbell with about 40 men for this service, and returned to the support of his own division.

He found Col. Campbell's men in great disorder from the first shock of the British Platoons; and called Lieuts. Sawyers and some others, who assisted to rally and bring them back. In a short time after the rallying began Col. Campbells horse became exhausted; The Col. dismounted and fought through the rest of the action on foot.

This was a bay horse of thin appearance and had been nearly overcome by the fatigue of the march. The horse which Col. Campbell ordinarily rode, was a bald face black horse. After the first retreat. Col. Shelby, it is said, saw this horse and some rider on him, whom he mistook for Col. Campbell at the distance of some 200 yds from the scene.

Ensign Campbell as above directed by Col. Shelby occupied a spur of the Mountain within 40 yds of the enemy. When leading his men to this place, one of them from a view of its exposed location, exclaimed to his commander; "what! are you taking us there to be marks for the enemy?"

"No," said the other, "to make marks of the enemy." And this proved actually to be the case. For after this detachment had plied their rifles in the successive discharge of several rounds to a man, Ferguson perceived their fire to be so fatal, that he gave orders to his adjutant, McGinnis, to dislodge them. McGinnis marched his party to the charge. Campbell heard him order them to "make ready," and he commanded his own men to "stand fast," that is to stand behind the trees.

McGinnis then ordered them to fire on Campbell, who, from the narrowness of the tree that shielded him, expected to be shot through by several bullets at once. And he escaped this fate, not by the protection of the tree, but by the horizontal aim of the British muskets, which converged their bullets to a place above him, cracking the bark and splinters from the tree and shattering them down upon his head.

Campbell had now a load in his gun, which he discharged with aim at the shoulders of McGinnis, and the latter instantly fell.

The party now emerged from behind their trees, discharged their pieces with similar exactness, and the survivors of the British party retired to the main body. Campbell inspected the body of McGinnis, and saw a shot through the part of the shoulder he had aimed at.

And his party resumed their galling fire upon the backs of Fergusons men. On all sides now the fire was brisk. Our men had become cool from the first panic of the British charge; and were plying their rifles with steady effect. The matter was come to a desperate crisis.

Ferguson was still in the heat of battle with characteristic coolness and daring. He ordered Capt. Dupoister with a body of regulars to reinforce a position about 100 yds distant. But before they arrived at this short distance, they were thinned too much by the American rifles to render any effectual support. He then ordered his cavalry to mount, with a view of making a desperate onset at their head. But these only presented a better mark for the American rifles, and fell as fast, as they would mount their horses. He, then perceiving the thinnest line, which surrounded him, to be that of Ensign Campbell's Riflemen, proceeded on horseback with two militia cols, with the apparent design to force his passage through them and attempt an escape. But before reaching the line of battle he was shot and expired. He had held out with inflexible resolution beyond even the hope of resistance. His men once raised the white flag for surrender, and he pulled it down. He had a shrill sounding silver whistle, whose signal was universally known through the ranks, was of immense service on many occasions, and gave a kind of ubiquity to his movements.

Who shot Ferguson remains in uncertainty. Several have claimed it. But the honour seams distinctly accorded to none. Nor does it appear to universal satisfaction whether he was shot on horseback or sitting upon a stone.

The Americans were now in regular columns approaching the British.

A large section of Col. Campbell's troops advanced with too much rapidity, when a reserved fire from the British breastwork did more fatal execution there than in the whole action beside.

Because this forward movement brought them to a level with the British muskets, which in most instances overshot their heads.

Lieut. Sawyers to this moment kept his men at their station, from which they had been firing through most of the battle, at the distance of about twenty live steps from the enemy. Seeing the reserved fire discharged, he ordered his men to advance in order to increase the enemy's confusion. The same was done by the other companies on this side of the mountain.

And Col. Sevier, who had gallantly borne his share in the conflict, was resolutely crowding up on the other side. The British regulars and American Tories, were not only surrounded, but crowded close together, cooped up in a surprisingly narrow spaces, by the surrounding pressure of the American troops, and fatally galled by an incessant fire.

Dupoister, who succeeded in the place of Ferguson, perceived but too plainly, that any further struggle was in vain. He raised the white flag and exclaimed for quarters. Quarters were given by a general cessation of the American fire. But this cessation was not by any means complete. Some did not understand the meaning of a white flag. Others, who knew its meaning very well, knew that this flag had been raised before, but quickly pulled down again by the British Commander.

Andrew Evans was one of these. He was standing near to Col. Campbell, and in the very act of shooting, when Campbell jerked his gun upwards to prevent its effect, exclaiming; "Evans, for God's sake, don't shoot, it is murder to kill them when they raise the white flag."

Col. Campbell seems not to have been distinguished as the American commander. For, having fought as a foot soldier during most of the action, having climbed over the rocks of the enemy's breastwork with his men, who drove them away from it, he was standing in the front rank of his soldiery, his coat off and his shirt collar open like a sturdy farmer.

Dupoister came riding on a gray horse not far from the place where the Col was standing and inquired, "where is your general?" Mr. Beatie and another pointed to the place and Mr. Crow, who was not a guns length from Campbell, heard Dupoister exclaim twice, "Col. Campbell, it was damned unfair;" alluding to the above mentioned continued fire, to which Campbell made no answer but the order to dismount.—He dismounted accordingly and held his sword for deliverance to his captors, which was in the first place received by Evan Shelby and handed to Col. Campbell. The arms were now lying in front of the prisoners, without any orders how to dispose of them. Col. Shelby, from the part of the line which he commanded, rode out of the ranks with the apparent design of finding Col. Campbell. Returning without success, he exclaims, "good God, what can we do in this confusion?"

"We can order the prisoners from their arms," said Sawyers.—

"Yes," said Shelby, "that can be done." The prisoners were accordingly marched to another place, and there surrounded by a double guard. This action was on the 7th of Oct. 1780. The loss of the enemy was, 225 killed, 130 wounded, 700 prisoners, and 1500 stand of arms. The American loss was 30 killed and 60 wounded. About 700 men achieved this victory.

Sevier led about 240, Shelby 200, Campbell 400, the Carolina Cols. 300, making in all about 1140, of which, it has been stated, that about 400 were left behind for want of horses. These were met the next day and reunited with the victors in their march from the scene. So signal an exploit could not long remain a secret to Lord Cornwallis, and numerous rumours soon reached our men that he was in pursuit to recover his prisoners. Our troops, therefore, moved from the battle ground with as little delay as possible, to make sure of a victory so happily won.

And here let us pause for a moment, to answer the following question:—Why were so many killed in the American ranks, when the British platoons so generally overshot them?

1st. Because the great body of Fergusons troops were Tories, as good marksman as our own, who always sought an object for their rifles. Lieut. Edmonston was standing a moment seeking a view of an enemy to fire at among Fergusons men behind the breastworks, and was shot by a rifleman from the very place he was inspecting. This incident was an example of many. For the rocks which formed a part of this breastwork, shielded the enemy, and enabled them to fire leisurely at our men.

2ndly. The eagerness of our men for action. This was so great that it led them to exposures both dangerous and useless. Their surest and most effectual mode of fighting was to stand at the distance of a proper gun shot, and fire with deliberate aim at their enemy. But many of them were too impatient for this delay.

Moses Shelby, Fagan and some others, leaped upon the waggons of the enemy's breastwork in the useless attempt to storm his camp. But they were soon carried off wounded from the scene. Some were wounded by the charge of the British bayonets, before they would retire from the first assault. The death of Col. Williams gave a signal instance of this intemperate eagerness for action. He espied Ferguson towards the close of the action on horseback, and made for him with the full determination of a personal encounter. William Moore was close to him, and heard him exclaim "I will kill Ferguson or die in the attempt."

He spurred his horse to a speedy movement, when a rifle bullet stopped his career. He survived till the white flag told the enemy's surrender, and said, "I die contented."

3rdly. From the enemy's reserved fire at the close of the action. Lieutenant Sawyers saw the companies around him, after a general discharge from the British, go too hastily forward, and checked his own men from doing so. This movement forward near the place of the waggons brought many of our men on a level with the British.—And their reserved fire, which was then discharged in its usual horizontal direction, did fatal execution in our ranks at that place. The number killed in Col. Campbell's division during the action was 13. The action was on Saturday. On the next Saturday a Court martial was held by our Officers to try from the ranks of the Tory prisoners some offenders of a notorious kind.

Thirty two persons of this description were condemned to die, of which 23 were pardoned by the commanding officer. The remaining nine were executed the same night. This summary procedure was thought necessary; first from the unsettled condition of affairs, which precluded all hope of trial by jury; 2ndly. from the flagitious nature of the offences, one of which was the following. A man went to his neighbour's house and inquired of a little boy, "Where is your father?" to which the lad answered, "he is not at home." And the man shot him without further ceremony; though fortunately the youth recovered of his wound. 3rdly. to deter others from similar offences, and prevent these men from doing them again.

The prisoners and their captors proceeded on their march. The prisoners were every night obliged to sit upon the ground on pain of being shot by the guard, which surrounded them.

One night about two weeks after the battle, a boy was acting for one of the sentries. One of the prisoners taking notice of this contrived to move himself gradually and without rising near to the place where the boy kept guard. As soon as he was near enough to take the requisite advantage, he started with a quick jump, and was making off with speed, when the boy wheeled upon his heel, levelled his rifle and shot the fugitive through the kidneys. The man was now disabled from flight, and was drawn back again into the ranks of the prisoners.

In the morning it was ascertained by the testimony of Col. Cleaveland, that he was a deserter from the troops of the latter, and was the very man who had gone to tell Ferguson of our approach. This man, therefore, though in imminent hazard of his life through his wound, must be tried by the laws and usages of war. The court martial was equally divided, and Col. Shelby, who had been absent on a visit for the night, was called on his arrival to decide the life or death of the culprit by a single vote. The march was now delayed nearly two hours; and Shelby, though apparently of a rough and careless exterior, was so deeply concerned with his own responsibility, that while some were teasing him for an immediate decision, he would not give it in less than half an hour. He finally gave it for the man's execution: and preparations were made for it accordingly.

Two stakes were put in the ground converging towards each other at the top for him to stand upon, while his neck was fast by a rope from above, ready to hang him when the under support should be drawn away. He was permitted to stand in this attitude an hour, during which time he was constantly entreating Col. Cleaveland; "Oh, Col. Cleaveland, I pray pardon me, and I will be a good and faithful soldier ever after."

In the meantime. Col. Campbell comes up and asks; "was you the deserter, who left our troops to inform the enemy?"

"No," said the other.

"Now," added Col. Campbell, "you are quickly to stand before your Maker in judgement. Tell me in truth, if you was that deserter."

"Yes," said the other, "I was."

And his execution took place accordingly. So many of our troops, as were judged needful for safety, accompanied the prisoners a journey of three weeks from King's Mountain to the Mulberry fields, Wilkesborough in the state of North Carolina. Here they were met by a detachment of some hundreds of Carolina Militia and with these the prisoners were left in custody. Cols. Campbell; Shelby and Sevier attended the prisoners to this place; then left them and returned home.

In this expedition the exposures and privations were extreme. Four hundred or more were on foot. But these had kept up with the horse some distance beyond the Yellow Mountain. The speed of their march required bodies inured to the hardest service. The last day they rode forty five miles, and then encountered a disciplined enemy posted on a high and advantageous position. Having no baggage waggons nor public stores, every man was, from necessity, his own provider.

His fare was the plainest, the coarsest and the scarcest. His resources of provision, like the Sedonian widow's, were "a handful of meal." This placed in his saddle-bags, furnished the amount of his luxury. And when it was exhausted he was left at the mercy of fortune for the rest.

Their sick and wounded were hurried from the battle scene with all imaginable speed to avoid the assault of a pursuing enemy.

The softest accommodation that could be made ready for conveyance, was the fresh hides of the slaughtered cattle, fastened to two poles; these attached to two horses, one before and one behind, and thus the sufferer carried off in safety. To specify particulars would spin this narrative to a tedious prolixity two instances only will be here inserted:

Alexander McMillan rode all night preceding the action; of course was without sleep. The second night, that is, the night after the action, he was attending with Henry Dickenson, to the wants of James Laird and Charles Kilgore, the latter was shot with two balls through the side, and the former with one, near the middle—These were constantly in want of water. Water was of very difficult procurement. And the effort to keep them in a constant supply, employed these men with very little intermission, and without allowing them a moment of rest. The next night Mr. McMillan was on guard. Here were three nights without a wink of sleep. The fourth night he was on guard—every two hours, with intervals of rest of the same length of time.

The guard stood so thick around the prisoners, as to be able to touch each other hands by reaching. Here stood McMillan, firmly braced, with his gun in his right hand resting upon the ground. Sometime in the night, Major Evan Shelby, going the rounds of the watch to observe its order, comes to him and asks; "where is your gun?" The latter supposing it to have fallen at his feet, busily moved them without stooping down, in order to find it lying beneath him. But not finding it there, he felt constrained to reply to the unwelcome interrogatory, "really I cannot tell."

Shelby stepped aside, took it from a tree, against which it was leaning, and handed it back to the owner, with these words; "remember it is death to sleep on guard." McMillan acknowledged that this was law, but added in apology, that he had been four days deprived of sleep, from the above mentioned unavoidable causes, Shelby rejoined: "you must sleep no more upon guard;" but never divulged the secret. And for this generous forbearance on the part of the inspecting officer, McMillan has ever since, cherished for him a sense of high personal regard. Though he thinks that if measures had been taken against him, and death adjudged for neglect of duty, the circumstances of the case would have been seen to urge so strong a plea in his own justification, as to secure a reprieve from the designated punishment.

The day after Wm. Campbell was chosen to the command he proposed to Robert Campbell to lead off a detachment of men by night, and fall upon a party of Tories, eight miles distant. The offer was gladly accepted, and a body of about eighty volunteers set off for the attack. The Tories had retreated, our party had no fighting; they returned and rejoined the main body by daylight.—The next night Robert Campbell was on a similar expedition, under the command of another officer.

On the next night they began the above mentioned march of 45 miles, previous to the action. Here were three successive nights and days of the hardest service, without a moment of sleep. The next, he was requested to take charge of some part of the guard. But he stated to the officer that this was impossible, from the above mentioned incessant vigils. He then sunk down by a tree and knew nothing more till at daylight; he woke shivering in the frost. Col. Shelby that night being officer of the guard, was now seen with others, sitting at the guard fire, Campbell arose, approached the fire, and was presented by Shelby, with a bottle of rum for immediate relief. He drank of this, sat down by the fire, and undoubtedly felt the justice of the old Testament prescription; "Give strong drink to him that is ready to perish and wine to those that be of heavy hearts."

These two instances may perhaps suffice. For how can it be requisite to give publicity here, even if the writers information were adequate, to the individual suffering of the 60 wounded?—to tell of broken limbs and mangled bodies, of bullet holes through the body, probed by a sympathizing fellow-soldier, with a smoothed twig of sassafras, of mortification spreading from one limb to another, of the want of all kinds of relief from a surgeon, when none was present but a wrathful swearing British doctor?—to prove that the privations and sufferings of these men were extreme? Nor does it seem any more necessary to specify cases of individual valour. Two instances only of faltering courage have been mentioned to the writer, from Col. Shelby's division. One was of a captain lying flat upon his back in the beginning of the action. Another was of a captain who exclaimed for bullets to a comrade, who was passing him to go up the mountain.

"Bullets, bullets, my dear sir, I have not a bullet in my pouch."

"Here is enough of them," said his friend reaching out a handful to give him.

"O, they will not fit my gun," said the other, who was accordingly left to this bloodless dilemma. The rest of these men were eager for action, and determined on victory, and seemed to have answered well to the sentiment of their commander, who told them before leaving the waters of the Watauga, that he wanted no man to join the enterprise, who did not wish to fight the enemy. The troops of the other Cols. appear to have been actuated by a similar spirit.

And the whole history of the enterprise demonstrates, that our men were led to espouse it, not from a fear, that the enemy would execute his vain threats upon their villages, For to these mountaineers, nothing than such a scheme would have made prettier game for their rifles; nothing more desirable than to entice such an enemy from his pleasant roads, rich plantations, and gentle climate, with his ponderous baggage and valuable armoury, into the very centre of their own fastnesses, to hang upon his flank, to pick up his stragglers, to cut off his foragers, to make short and desperate sallies upon his camp, and finally to make him a certain prey without a struggle and without loss.

Nor was it the authority or influence of a state, which led them to engage in this hazardous service. They knew not whether to any or to what state they belonged.—From the rude circumstances of their early settlement, the difficulty of passing the wide ridges of mountains, and their constant seclusion from their eastern friends, they were living in a state of primitive independence.

And it was not till several years after this, that from the apparent and urgent necessity of the case, they created a temporary Government of their own.[1] Nor can it be expected, that that gratuitous patriotism, from which this enterprise evidently sprung, so different from that of a paper victory, a scramble for office, and for gain, can be fully comprehended by modern politicians. In those days of different principles, to know that American liberty was invaded, and that the

---

1. Note by the Rev. Mr. Foster. The Frankland Government.

only apparent alternative in the case, was American independence of subjugation, was enough to nerve their hearts to the boldest pulsation of freedom, and ripen their purposes to the fullest determination of putting down the aggressor.

The success at King's Mountain was fraught with signal advantage to America. It broke up the royal interest in the upper section of Carolina. It enabled our generals to concentrate their forces upon great objects; and was one in that series of happy incidents, which conspired in the progress of the next year, to consummate the splendid achievement at Yorktown.

Note:—The original letter is written on foolscap; the paper is yellowed with age and very much worn, but the writing is easily decipherable. It appears to have been corrected some time after it was written. There is a peculiarity in the pen work and the ink of the editor, however, which betrays him. The above follows the original in spelling, punctuation, and form in every way, as closely as I could determine it. I have not thought it necessary to correct certain obvious errors in this letter, evidently written some time after the event, into which the writer has been betrayed by his uncertain memory. But it may be well to state that the place of the battle was known as King's Mountain long before Ferguson's arrival, and its name did not refer to the English monarch, but to a settler named King who formerly lived at its foot.

C. T. B.

1

Daniel Boone, the Greatest of the Pioneers

A dirge for the brave old Pioneer!
Columbus of the land!
Who guided freedom's proud career
Beyond the conquered strand,
And gave her pilgrim sons a home
No monarch's step profanes,
Free as the chainless winds that roam
Upon its boundless plains.

1. THE LAND BEYOND THE MOUNTAINS

Beyond the Alleghenies, so long the western boundary of the new nation, lies a vast expanse of country between the Ohio and the Cumberland Rivers, cut by the thirty-seventh and thirty-eighth parallels of latitude, now known as Kentucky. No more beautiful region is to be found in the United States. Its soil is fertile and productive, its climate agreeable and invigorating. It is today one of the most delightful states in the Union, noted for the beauty of its women, the virility of its men, and the speed of its horses—to say nothing of the blueness of its green grass and the quality of its whiskey. One has to be genial and mellow even in speaking of the state and its people.

Certainly no other spot on the globe seems to be better designed for humanity, yet from the days of the mound builders to the time of the Revolution it was an uninhabited wilderness, given over to the buffalo, the elk, the deer, the bear and the wolf, who prowled through its dense forests or played in its grassy glades. From prehistoric times no race or tribe made its domicile there. Hunting parties of the Shawnees and even the distant Iroquois from the north, ranged its wildernesses and met in deadly conflict similar bodies of men from the Cherokee lands to the south, or from the Chickamauga territories on the west, so that its forests resounded often with war-cries of savage foemen.

Why it was not adopted as the settling place of one or the other of the tribes has never been ascertained. It may be that no tribe felt itself strong enough to hold the ground to the exclusion of the others. It was so desirable that its very beauty and fertility operated to make it no man's land. No tribe was strong enough to hold it alone, yet all combined to keep it free. It was not until the advent of that world-claimer, the white man, that it became a home for humanity. Danger, opposition, prior claim, never deterred the pioneers. The first settlers were usually willing to purchase the right of eminent domain if they could do so from any recognized authority or power, but if they could not—well, the earth itself belonged to the pioneer and he took any portion of it without compunctions of conscience or questions of law.

Who was the first white man to see Kentucky? Some have said that it was Moscosco, the successor of De Soto, in 1542-3, but without doubt the honour of the discovery accrues to another member of the Latin race, the great explorer La Salle, who was the first white man to put foot upon its smiling, pleasant soil in 1669-70.

Colonel Wood of Virginia and Captain Thomas Batts of the same mother state, the latter sent by Governor Berkeley, had crossed the mountain barriers in a search for a water route to China in 1664 and in 1671 respectively, but it was hardly likely that they went far into Kentucky, if they saw it at all. The first real explorer was Dr. Thomas Walker, also of Virginia, who reached the banks of the Cumberland River in 1750. It was he who first marched through that romantic pass in the mountains, which, with the mountains themselves, and the river upon which he made his camp, he called after His Royal Highness the Duke of Cumberland, the bloody butcher; and that was the first white man's name bestowed in Kentucky. It was indeed a name of ancient lineage traced down through the Cumbrians of the British Isles, the Cymry of the continent, the Cimmerians of the Black Sea, directly from Gomer, son of Japhet!

The Walker expedition amounted to little and the interior of Kentucky remained a *terra incognita* until 1767, or thereabouts, when a certain John Finley, or Findlay, explored a small section of it and returned home to North Carolina to fill the minds of the adventurous young men with whom he came in contact, with tales of its romantic possibilities. Among those to whom he told the story of his adventures was a certain Daniel Boone, a settler, farmer, hunter and pioneer, who had already some knowledge of the country.[1]

2. THE GREATEST OF THE PIONEERS

Few men have been so written about as Daniel Boone[2] and most writers have succumbed to the temptation to romance about him, too; he is quite the hardest man to tell the truth about that I have ever attempted to discuss. Let the reader who differs from what is here set down give me credit for good intention.

The investigator experiences a feeling of relief to find that Boone was born in the state of Pennsylvania. Nearly every other pioneer, explorer, discoverer or adventurer of note, in the trans-Allegheny regions, was born in the South. It is only fair to say that the West between the Alleghenies and the Mississippi was discovered, explored, settled, protected and won for the United States by the people of the Southern States—a fact not generally known, I think. Young Boone, one of a numerous family, first saw the light on the 22nd of October, 1733, at his father's farmhouse in Exeter township, Berks County, Pennsylvania, near the village of Oley, which is a few miles northeast of the present city of Reading. His father, George Boone, came from Devonshire, where he had filled the humble station of a weaver. The family originally belonged to the Church of England but had become Quakers. They removed to Pennsylvania in 1717, whither three of the older children preceded them, like Caleb and Joshua, to spy out the land.

They were plain substantial people, of limited education; sturdy, honest, independent, and capable, living simple healthy lives and usually attaining to a great age. Daniel Boone's education in arts and letters was of the most primitive character. His spelling was quite the worst I have ever come across, though, singular to state, his handwriting was rather graceful and flowing, perhaps because it partook of the physical characteristics of the man. His brother George was sufficient-

1. This inscription on an ancient beech tree still standing on Boone's Creek, a small tributary to the Watauga in Washington County, Tennessee, "D. Boon cilled a bar on tree in the year 1760," seems to indicate that Boone had hunted across the mountains long before he met Finley. But there is no evidence that the inscription is the work of Boone, and, in spite of local traditions, a probability against it.
2. Miner's excellent Boone Bibliography contains nearly one hundred and seventy-five references to lives and other sources of information concerning his career, and I have found several additional references which he does not mention.

ly well educated to teach school, and some of the family subsequently became rather noted mathematicians.

But if young Daniel Boone knew but little about books and their contents, he was one of those who found "tongues in trees, books in the running brooks, sermons in stones"—yes, we may add—"and good in everything." It was a wild primitive country in those days. The rifle of the hunter with the plough of the husbandman afforded the only means of support, and more often the hostile Indians caused the plough to be laid aside and the sole dependence put upon the weapon.

So Daniel Boone grew up to strong vigorous manhood in the forest far from urban influence, which indeed he could never tolerate. His father moved to North Carolina in May, 1750, and established himself on a frontier farm on the Yadkin, then the very outpost of civilization. Daniel, by this time, one of a very numerous family, did his share of the work necessitated by the building of a wilderness home in that day, but he was ever fonder of the chase than of the plough, and as he was the most skilful member of the family with the rifle, he speedily became the hunter for them all. This indeed was no sinecure.

In the course of time other families followed the example of the elder Boone and the country began to be thickly populated. At a very early age Daniel had married Rebecca Bryan, daughter of a neighbouring settler. One of the most heroic of that splendid breed of pioneer women, she proved herself for over half a century a worthy mate indeed for the great adventurer. Boone had prospered, he had a growing family and a good farm, yet he was not happy. Something, an instinct which he could never explain or understand, drove him forward.

He was one of those characters who are bound to be in the advance of civilization, who are made to lead it on, to "blaze" the pathway of progress. He grew restless and discontented. The advent of the settlers naturally destroyed the primeval character of the wilderness. Game became scarce and the ordinary demands of life more complex and harder to meet. Nomad that he was he felt that he must remove from his present settlement and find a new land to which to lead his family and in which to build his cabin.

Often and often he gazed at the mountains soaring into the heavens to the westward of him and wondered what lay on the farther side. When Finley came home with his marvellous tales of the beauty and loneliness of the hunter's paradise beyond the everlasting hills, he found in Boone a ready auditor to his representations.

3. The Exploration of Kentucky

A party of six men was made up in the spring of 1769 to cross the mountains under Finley's guidance and explore the country. Be it remembered that this was to be no thoughtless excursion, no adventurous foray, no mere hunter's trip to a land teeming with game; it was a movement to found a home. They went to examine a land, to discover if it were suitable for settlement or not. Boone was unanimously chosen to lead this expedition in spite of the fact that Finley had been over the mountains before. On the 7th of June, 1769, late in the afternoon, they ascended the crowning range of the Alleghenies, crossed the ridge of the divide, stood upon the western slope and gazed down upon as enchanting a panorama as was ever spread before mortal vision, their first sight of Kentucky.

In popular acceptance that name is supposed to mean "dark and bloody ground." So far as it can be determined the original meaning of the word Kentucky is "a pleasant meadow, a smiling land, whence the river flows." How it got its name of "dark and bloody ground" is perhaps not difficult to understand. Some years afterward when Colonel Henderson was negotiating with the Cherokees for the purchase of the Transylvania territory, they strove to prevent him from acquiring any land south of the Ohio. In the words of old Dragging Canoe, the war chief of the Chickamaugas, it was a bloody land, there was a gloomy shadow over it, the dark spirits dwelt there, and the white man would do well to let it alone. There was no doubt whatever that the words by which it became known, "dark and bloody ground," were apposite to its early history.

The party immediately descended the mountains and began hunting and exploring until December. Thereafter the better to cover the country they divided and Boone and a companion named Stewart plunged steadily westward through the forests and openings. Near the Kentucky River they were captured by a band of wandering Indians and spent Christmas as prisoners. Boone, already showing that marvellous sagacity he manifested in dealing with Indians, seeing that resistance would be hopeless, directed his companion to make no opposition but to affect to acquiesce cheerfully in their captivity. Their demeanour so disarmed the suspicions of their captors that after they had been in company with them for a week they found opportunity to escape in the night.

They shook off pursuit by their adroit woodmanship and finally reached the main camp. They found it plundered and destroyed and Finley and his companions gone. The four men have vanished from the pages of history. There is no record of their ever having returned to their friends across the mountains. It is believed that they were killed by the Indians and that their bones mouldered away in the country that they had helped to discover—the pioneer martyrs of a long line.

Boone and Stewart were sorely depressed by this untoward happening, but they continued their hunting and exploring, carefully avoiding hunting parties of Indians by their watchfulness. They had almost reached the end of their resources, however, and were considering a return across the mountains, when, ranging through the forest one day in the early winter, they perceived two men coming through the wood, being themselves discovered at the same moment.

The two parties took to the trees and approached each other cautiously, rifles primed and ready, each striving to "draw a bead" on the other. What was their surprise and relief, however, to find that the two men were countrymen! And their joy was the greater when Daniel Boone recognized in one of them his brother Squire—Squire being his name, not title.

The coincidence was really marvellous, that in sixty thousand square miles of territory, these two parties should find each other. Squire had come to seek for Daniel and had brought him needed supplies of powder and salt. He brought news of the family on the Yadkin, who were prosperous and well under Mrs. Boone's fostering care. The four men determined to pass the winter in Kentucky.

While hunting one day Daniel and Stewart were surprised by Indians. Stewart was shot and instantly killed, but Boone after a desperate fight managed to escape. Squire's companion also went off on a hunting expedition and never came back. It is supposed that he lost his way and died of starvation or exposure.

The brothers amassed a great store of peltries of much value. In the spring it was decided that Squire should return to North Carolina for supplies, while Daniel remained behind to protect the furs that had accumulated and to increase the stock. The redoubtable hunter was thus left entirely and absolutely alone in the midst of that vast territory; as he said, "without salt, bread, or sugar; without the society of a fellow creature; without the companionship of a horse or even a dog, often the affectionate companion of a lone hunter."

He was desperately lonely and homesick for the sight of his wife and children. Impelled by this loneliness to action he made a long detour of exploration in the southwest along the Salt and Green Rivers. He saw frequent signs of Indians and was often forced to hide himself in the cane brakes without fire to escape their observation.

On the 27th of July, 1770, his brother returned and they met at the old camp on the Red River. His brother brought with him ammunition and necessaries and two horses, perhaps the first horses ever ridden by a white man in Kentucky. The two men explored the country between the Cumberland and Green Rivers thoroughly during the year until March, 1771, when they turned northwest to the Kentucky River, where they decided to form their permanent settlement. Packing as much of their skins as their horses could carry they returned to the settlement on the Yadkin.

There is a story that the two men fell in with another body of hunters called, from the duration of their stay in Kentucky, the Long Hunters, and that the party beguiled the long hours of the evenings in the camp by reading aloud *Gulliver's Travels,* which, with the possible exception of the Bible, was the first English book read in the territory. Some of the names in the book still obtain in the state, as for instance, "Lulbegrud" Creek!

Daniel Boone had been absent over two years, during which time he had tasted neither bread nor salt nor seen any white men other than his travelling companions, who had all perished, except his brother, and the Indians. Meanwhile other parties of hunters had been exploring different portions of the country, mostly in the valley of the Cumberland, and at the same time Robertson and his North Carolinians were making the first settlement on the Watauga in the mountains of Tennessee.

4. THE SETTLEMENT OF KENTUCKY

On the 25th of September, 1773, Boone, having disposed of all his earthly goods save what could be loaded upon pack-horses, accompanied by his family and that of his brother Squire and several other families amounting in all to some fifty persons, set forth for Kentucky. It was a small humble cavalcade, a petty insignificant migration, yet it marks a momentous date in history, for it was the inauguration of "a movement for the annihilation of savagery, the extinction of the Latin and the supremacy of the Teutonic civilization in North America, parallel to that rolling westward from New England, New York, and

Pennsylvania, at the same time."

It, with the settlement of Robertson on the Watauga, was the beginning of that great drama of our history which has been described in poetic language as "the winning of the west." Many people played a prominent part in it, but certainly Daniel Boone must stand more nearly as the Columbus of the movement than any other man. But it was to be some years before he established himself and family in that promised land. As they approached the mountains a party of Indians fell upon their rear guard and killed six young men, among whom was Boone's eldest son. Alas, it was only the beginning of tragedies that dogged his family, for the Indians at one time or another made sad havoc among his kith and kin.[4]

The unfortunate incident so discouraged the pioneers that, in spite of Boone's urging, they gave over the attempt and settled on the Clinch River in Virginia. Boone's heart was in Kentucky, however, and he made several visits there, one to bring back a party of surveyors who had gone there by the order of Lord Dunmore, the royal governor of Virginia.

Boone was commissioned a captain in the royal service in Dunmore's War and had command of three frontier forts, where he did good service. He always carefully preserved his British commission thereafter, and it is alleged frequently saved his life when he was captured by the Indians, who were the allies of the British, by exhibiting it as proof of his loyalty, a perfectly justifiable stratagem, of course.

In 1775 he was sent by Colonel Richard Henderson of North Carolina, who had formed a proprietary company and purchased a vast tract of land between the Kentucky and Cumberland Rivers, which he called Transylvania, to survey a road to the Kentucky River and establish a fort there which should be the headquarters of the company. At the head of a small party of some twenty men, Boone again entered the promised land.

It speaks well for the natural skill of the man as a road builder when we learn that the path he marked out over the mountains and up through the valleys remains a great highway today, and that subsequent generations spent thousands of dollars under the direction of skilled engineers on that very "Wilderness Road," which for location they found could hardly be improved upon. Here is a letter written twenty one years after to General Shelby about that same road:

---

4. Two sons, a brother, two brothers-in-law, and other relatives were killed by Indians at different times.

Feburey the 11th, 1796.

Sir:

After my best respts to your Excelancy and famyly I wish to inform you that I have sum intention of undertaking this new rode that is to be cut through the wilderness and I think my self intitled to the ofer of the bisness as i first marked out that rode in March 1775 and never re'd anything for my trubel and sepose i am no statesman i am a woodsman and think my self as capable of marking and cutting that rode as any other man. Sir if you think with me I would thank you to write mee a line by the post the first oportuneaty and he will lodge it at Mr. John Milerson hinkston fork as I wish to know Where and When it is to be laet (let) so that I may atend at the time

    I am deer sir your very umble sarvent Daniel Boone
To his Excelancy Governor Shelby

This interesting document proves conclusively that Boone was more familiar with the rifle than the pen.

The party fought its way up through the Indians, losing several killed on the journey. They arrived at the chosen point on the 1st of April and on the 29th of the month, having been joined by Henderson and other proprietors, they began the erection of a rude fort which they called in honour of their leader Boonesborough. The fort was begun after the Battle of Lexington and completed just before the Battle of Bunker Hill, two momentous events of which the colonists were in ignorance for a long time. When they did hear the news, however, their rejoicings showed their American patriotism was above proof.

The fort, plans of which remain to us, was a very curious one, although all frontier forts, except in dimensions, exactly resembled it. It was situated on the side of a hill with one corner quite near the river. At each of the four corners there was a two story blockhouse, and along the sides of the fort a series of little cabins placed close together, their roofs slanting inward. The loop-holed cabin walls, with the palisades which filled up the spaces where there were no cabins near each of the blockhouses, enclosed a space two hundred and sixty feet long by one hundred and fifty wide. There were heavy timber gates in the front and back. The walls were about twelve feet high and there was hardly a nail or a piece of iron used in the whole enclosure.

Here, in the same year, Boone brought his wife and family; and,

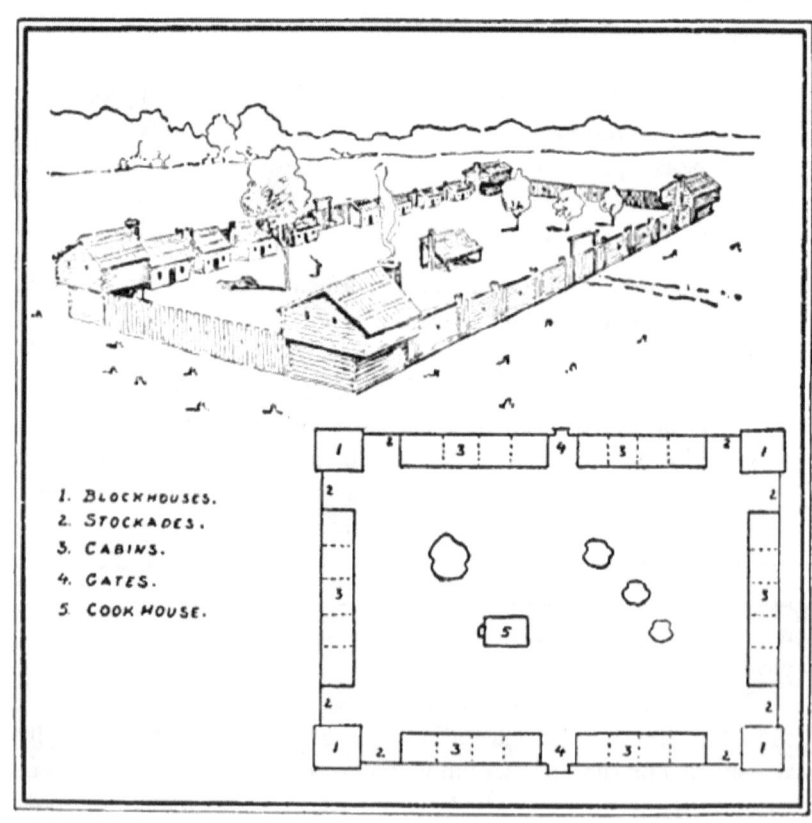

1. BLOCKHOUSES.
2. STOCKADES.
3. CABINS.
4. GATES.
5. COOK HOUSE.

PLAN AND PERSPECTIVE VIEW OF BOONESBOROUGH.

on the 8th of September, Rebecca Boone and her daughters were the first white women to stand on the banks of the Kentucky. They were followed shortly after, however, by other families who settled at Boonesborough, Harrodsburg, and elsewhere, in similar forts throughout the territory.

Thus the settlement of Kentucky was begun, but it was not maintained for many years without hardship and loss of life incredible. In thirteen years hundreds of men and women were killed by Indians. To their natural ferocity and their overwhelming desire to clear the prized hunting ground of settlers, there was added the encouragement of the British government, which was entirely willing to let loose upon its rebellious subjects the horde of savages and as a definite evidence of its desires paid liberally for the white man's—or white woman's for that matter—scalp. Hamilton, the British Governor of Detroit. "the hair-buyer general," was the prime mover in this situation.

It goes without saying that the colonists were rebels to a man, and it is interesting to know that on Tuesday, May 23rd, 1775, at the instance of Colonel Henderson, President of the Transylvania Company, a representative government was established at Boonesborough, Daniel Boone being one of the legislators.

It is characteristic of Boone that in the record of introduced bills he seems to have originated but two bills, one to preserve the game, the other to improve the breed of horses. There speaks the Kentucky hunter and sportsman! Both bills were passed, as was another to prevent "profane swearing," introduced by the Rev. John Lythe, a clergyman of the Church of England, who, on Sunday the 28th of May, under the spreading branches of a grand old elm, in the words of that most ancient liturgy, held the first religious services within the state.

5. ADVENTURES WITH THE INDIANS

Boonesborough was twice attacked by bodies of Indians, but the war parties were driven off with considerable loss to themselves and but little loss to the garrison. The prevalence of war parties often prevented the settlers from making a crop and they were forced to live mainly by the chase. Boone was easily the best shot and the keenest hunter in the settlement. This and other qualities gave him the practical leadership of all expeditions, although the proprietors were sometimes present.

On Sunday, July 14th, 1776, three young girls, the eldest Elizabeth Callaway, aged seventeen, her sister Frances, and Jemima Boone, just turned fourteen, rowed across the river in a canoe during the absence of Boone and Colonel Callaway, another of the fine spirits of the period. When they reached the other side the canoe grounded on a bar and one of a party of six Indians, who had come close to the fort unobserved, seized the bow of the boat, dragged it to land, and the girls were captured. With the spirit of the pioneer women, Elizabeth Callaway attacked the Indians with her canoe paddle and severely wounded one of them in the head. The other two girls also offered a stout resistance, which of course availed nothing.

The Indians, elated by the capture, which they rightly judged to be of importance, hurried their captives away from the fort. They strove to get the girls to put on *moccasins* in order that the betraying tracks of their shoes should not indicate their route in the pursuit which was certain to be made, but Elizabeth Callaway resisted so that they were forced to let her have her own way, and to trust to the rapidity of their movements to effect their escape.

The girls, by the intrepid Elizabeth's direction, blazed their trail by breaking twigs from the trees as they passed, and when they were discovered and prohibited, tore their dresses into bits and dropped pieces at intervals. Boone and Callaway came back to the fort that evening, when the girls were missed.

Many of the men were still away hunting and it would not have been safe to deprive the fort of all means of resistance. Two parties were organized at once, comprising some twenty men. Seven of them went with Boone, who easily caught the trail of the Indians. Among them was young Henderson, son of the proprietor, who was in love with Elizabeth Callaway, who shortly afterward married him, while strangely enough, two of the other men in the party afterward married the two other girls when they had reached what was then considered a suitable age. Women were scarce in Kentucky and the available ones never lacked for lovers and attention.

Guided by the traces left by the girls, the party pursued the Indians with furious speed, and came upon them encamped in fancied security the second day. How to effect the recapture of the girls without giving the Indians time to kill them was something of a problem. Boone and Henderson finally crawled as near the camp as they dared, and when four of the others fired on the unsuspicious Indians, they dashed upon them, placed themselves between the girls and the camp and immediately opened fire, each shooting his man as he ran. The Indians fled precipitately and the girls were saved. In the excitement of the little battle, so an ancient account says, one of the rescuers, mistaking Elizabeth Callaway, who was very dark and sat at the foot of the tree with a handkerchief bound around her head, for an Indian, lifted his gun butt to beat out her brains before he recognized her.

A few weeks after there was a wedding in the stockade between the dusky Elizabeth and young Henderson, Squire Boone, who is reputed to have been an elder in the church, performing the ceremony. This was the first marriage solemnized in Kentucky.

Boone was many times in danger from Indians. In 1777 his life was saved by the famous pioneer Simon Kenton. Several men in the fields near Boonesborough, attacked by a party of Indians, ran toward the fort, one of them being killed and scalped by the way, and their cries led Boone to sally out to their relief with thirteen men. He charged impetuously upon the Indians and was met by a lire from a concealed party. With six of his men he was wounded by a bullet, and as he lay on the ground one of the Indians attempted to scalp him. Kenton shot the Indian dead, lifted Boone in his arms and with the rest of his party succeeded in gaining the fort. Boone was very taciturn, silent and quiet, as one who had spent much time in self-communion in the wilderness. In a few brief, unemotional words, which yet meant more than a volume from another man, he thanked Kenton for his assistance.

"Well, Simon, you have behaved yourself like a man today," he said, "indeed you are a fine fellow."

On one occasion while out hunting he was captured by a party, who bound him with withes and left him on the ground in the care of some squaws, who proceeded to get very drunk on the contents of Boone's whiskey bottle. It must have been a very large bottle or contained an unusual quality of whiskey. During the night Boone rolled over to the fire, held his hands in the flames until the bonds were burned and made his escape, first blazing a tree with three deep gashes to mark the place. Years after he found the gashed tree and settled a boundary dispute by his identification of the landmark.

While hunting with his brother Edward near the Blue Licks, his brother was shot dead and again Boone fled for his life. The Indians followed his trail with a dog. The hound and the leading savage were close upon him, one of them only was at his mercy. He wisely shot the dog and escaped.

The record of his many adventures would fill a volume. His longest captivity, however, occurred in January, 1773. A great need of the colonists was salt. It was impracticable to bring it from the seaboard over the mountains, and the only way they could get it was by boiling the water from the salt springs, or "licks" as they were called, from the practice of the wild animals in licking the rocks of the ground for the salt with which they were impregnated.

With a party of thirty men Boone was engaged in this tedious but very necessary occupation. As usual he left the work to his subordinates while he hunted to provide game for the party. While hunting he was taken by a large party of Indians *en route* for Boonesborough, which they were by this time determined to capture. The garrison at Boonesborough, small at best, was greatly weakened by the absence of this party, and as they could capture Boone and his companions and then fall upon the stockade there would be no doubt but that they would take it with the women and children.

Boone affected to be delighted with his capture. He said that he and his companions had left Boonesborough for good, that they sympathized with the Indians and were quite willing to go along with them—perhaps here he exhibited his British commission. He adroitly warned them at the same time that Boonesborough was heavily re-enforced with Americans, who had in fact driven these British sympathizers away.

The Indians, who easily captured the rest of the party, were delighted with their prisoners, who had surrendered by Boone's advice; and, moved by his representations, abandoned their efforts and returned across the Ohio to their own country with their prisoners. Boone's readiness undoubtedly saved the women and children from the horrible fate of the Indian captive. His men were scattered among the tribes but were in the main well treated, and most of them finally escaped after varying periods of captivity.

There seems to have been a singular difference between the Indians of that day and place and our modern savages. Black Fish, the head chief of the Shawnees, and a warrior of no mean prowess, claimed Boone as his personal prisoner, and finally adopted him into his family, renaming him Big Turtle. Boone was separated from his men and taken to Detroit, where Hamilton, to his great credit be it said, treated him kindly and even offered to buy his freedom from the Indians for one hundred pounds. Black Fish was so charmed with his prisoner that he refused to part with him for any sum, and indeed Boone refused to be bought so far as he had anything to say about it, because he did not wish to be under any obligations of that sort to the British, especially as it might prevent his escape.

The Indians left Detroit in the spring and returned south to their own country, again taking Boone with them. He became a great favourite with all the tribe, and as usual was the hunter upon whom they depended. They used to count the charges of powder and the number of balls which he took with him on his hunting expeditions and when he returned he had to account for every charge and ball. In other words, he had to bring back game or bullets. They made no provision for a miss, which spoke eloquently of their opinion of his marksmanship. But Boone adroitly used only half charges of powder and split the bullets, trusting to his skill in stalking the game to bring him near enough to make a small charge do the work. By degrees he managed to accumulate a little ammunition this way.

The Shawnees were very busy at the time and he learned, in spite of their efforts at secrecy, that they were mustering in great force for an attack on Boonesborough, which they hoped to capture in his absence. Fearfully anxious for his family and others he sought desperately for means of escape, and finally succeeded in getting away on the 16th of June, and in four days he traversed the distance between the Indian village and Boonesborough, over one hundred and fifty miles, during which time he only had a single meal. Part of the time he was on horseback, it is alleged. He was not a good swimmer. When he came to the Ohio he found a deserted canoe on the banks which enabled him to cross the wide swift river. When the starved exhausted woodsman reached Boonesborough he was received with rejoicings as one risen from the dead. His wife, deeming that he had been killed, had gone back to North Carolina with her children.

6. The Defence of Boonesborough

The fort, which had fallen out of repair, was at once put in shape for defence when the news that he had brought became known. Boone naturally took charge of everything. Hoping that he might deter the Indians from coming, or stop their advance, while the rest were busily engaged in working on the stockade he led a party of twenty men to the Scioto River, where he encountered a larger force of Indians, defeated them and drove them back. But learning that the main body was already *en route* for the fort Boone and his companions retraced their steps, succeeded in passing the Indians and reached Boonesborough in safety, after a terrific march, just before the savages appeared.

The party entered the fort shortly before sunset, Sunday, September 6th, and that night the Indians appeared on the other side of the river and the next morning they crossed without opposition and invested the fort. The Indians were not alone, however, for they were accompanied by eleven French Canadians under a young captain, whose name was Dagniaux de Ouindre, although he is usually referred to in the histories as Du Quesne, and one extravagant romancer actually identifies him with the family of the great marquis for whom the celebrated fort was named! The party advanced under the French and English flags, strange to say. The real commander of the expedition, which numbered four hundred and forty-four Indians beside the Canadians, was Boone's adopted father Black Fish, very much cut up at his quondam son's desertion and defection.

Contrary to their usual practice, instead of at once beginning an attack, the Indians through de Quindre proposed a parley, in which the surrender of the fort was demanded under promises of kind treatment and so forth. Boone's conduct in his late captivity inspired them with the hope that they could effect their end without resistance. The wily hunter asked for two days to consider, which was at once granted by the unsuspecting allies, who carried their complaisance so far that when the cattle of the settlers, returning in the evening as was their wont, presented themselves before the gate the Indians made no objection to their entrance.

Meanwhile the people in the fort, amounting to thirty men, twenty boys, and the women and children, worked like beavers, strengthening the palisades and getting a supply of water from a spring outside. It is a strange thing that almost every fort that was erected in Kentucky was forced to get its water from some external source. At the end of two days, their preparations having been completed, Boone calmly informed the Frenchman that under no circumstances would he surrender and at the same time thanked the besiegers for allowing him time to complete his preparations for defence.

Discomfited by this unlooked-for check to their hopes, they did not yet abandon their endeavours for a further treaty. Boone was very anxious to gain time. Expresses had been sent to Virginia and North Carolina asking that troops be despatched to aid them and raise the siege. The longer he waited the more was the likelihood of their arrival. He therefore consented to a further discussion of the question of surrender.

The next day was appointed for a council. Nine Americans were to meet a party of Indians and Canadians, all unarmed, outside the walls of the fort. Boone stationed a number of his best riflemen in the blockhouse nearest the meeting-place with instructions to fire upon the Indians should any treachery be manifested.

The nine Americans, among whom were Boone and his brother, secure in this protection, held a grand *powwow* with the Canadian and Indian delegates, who were present in considerably greater numbers at the treaty place between the fort and the Indian encampment. A singular treaty of peace, hard to understand from the meagre accounts which have come down to us, was proposed, to which the Americans agreed. After the matter had been apparently amicably settled de Quindre and his allies thought that nothing remained to them but to take possession of the post; but before they parted they proposed that the treaty should be ratified by a general handshaking. This request was acceded to by Boone, who, to tell the truth, does not seem to have shone as a diplomatist. Instead of shaking hands singly two Indians at once endeavoured to grasp the hands of each American, and as soon as the savages seized the pioneers they started to drag them toward the Indian camp.

But they reckoned without their hosts. If Boone was little of a negotiator he was much of a fighter. Shouting to his men he jerked himself free from the two who held him and struck out right and left with his fists, in the good old Anglo-Saxon style, a way the Indians knew nothing of. His example was followed by his companions and the whole party ran for the fort pursued by the Indians. At the same time the rest of the savages who had not attended the council ran from their camp by the river bank and opened fire; but a steady and well-directed fire from the blockhouse killed a number of the pursuers and enabled Boone and his men to reach the gate in safety with no one killed, though Squire Boone was severely wounded.

Concealment and pretence were now at an end. The Indians poured a furious fire upon the fort, which was returned with deadly effect by the Kentuckians. A renegade negro slave who had stolen an extra long-range rifle amused himself by ascending a tall tree and from there picking off the exposed garrison. Boone by an extraordinary shot brought him down.

The Indians besieged the fort for nine days, using every stratagem and artifice of which they were capable to effect the capture, and finally resorted to the unheard-of expedient of attempting to undermine the stockade. Their endeavour was detected by the great quantities of mud which they threw in the river and Boone at once began a countermine.

Tradition has it that much rude banter was exchanged between the combatants. "'What are you red rascals doing there?' an old hunter would yell in Shawnese from the battery to the unseen Indians on the river bank below. 'Digging,' would be the return yell. 'Blow you all to deveil soon; what you do?' 'Oh!' would be the cheerful reply, 'we're digging to meet you and intend to bury five hundred of you.'"

The little garrison was constantly on the walls, its efforts being seconded by those of the women, who moulded bullets, loaded rifles, and in many instances even joined in the actual fighting, when one face or the other was assaulted. On one occasion the Indians set fire to the roofs of the cabins with blazing arrows and torches, but a fortunate rain which had saturated the logs prevented the spread of the fires and saved the fort.

The rain flooded the badly constructed mine the besiegers had made, the bank caved in, and their whole work was ruined just as they had carried it within striking distance of the gate. In utter discouragement they raised the siege on the 16th of September and retired, having sustained a very heavy loss. Exactly what, however, is not known, although the Kentuckians counted at least thirty-seven killed outright beside many wounded. Two of the defenders had been killed and four were wounded.

So furious had been the fire that after the battle they picked up one hundred and twenty-seven pounds of lead bullets from the ground around the fort, and this takes no account of the vast number which had buried themselves harmlessly in the trunks of the trees. The gallant defence undoubtedly saved the fort from being overwhelmed and the settlement wiped out at this juncture. Indeed it may be said to have saved Kentucky, and the sturdy little band of backwoodsmen desperately defending the fort in the wilderness deserve as well of their country as the men of Bunker Hill and Valley Forge.

7. THE LAST BATTLE OF THE REVOLUTION

After the repulse of the Indians from Boonesborough Boone, who was a major in the county militia, was promptly brought to trial before a court-martial, first for surrendering at the Salt Licks, and second for the parleying and treatying at the fort. He was immediately acquitted, being able to show that the motive for his actions had been the protection of the settlement and had resulted for the best in both cases, and he was at once promoted in rank to a lieutenant-colonel. Hereafter he is invariably styled Colonel Boone.

The disastrous repulse of the Indians and the springing up of other stations nearer the Ohio combined to render Boonesborongh secure from any further attacks. The fort was still maintained, but the constantly increasing number of settlers flowed out of its constricted area and built their cabins in its vicinity. Soon a thriving town grew up around the battle-scarred enclosure and then Boone, who had gone to North Carolina and brought his family back to Kentucky, felt it necessary to move on.

Abandoning his land claim, to which, indeed, he found through some carelessness he had no complete title, and having lost nearly all his movable property by robbery, he moved across the Kentucky River and settled in the wilderness again at a place which he called Boone's Station, another small frontier fort where he resumed his occupation of hunting and trading.

On the 16th of August, 1782, a mounted messenger came dashing up to the station, his horse in a lather of foam, carrying the news that Bryan's Station, a very important point further westward and five miles from the present city of Lexington, had been attacked by an overwhelming force of Indians and white men, and that the place was in desperate straits. Boone himself happened to be at Boonesborough at the time, but the men at the station immediately mounted their horses and galloped to the succour of their brethren.

Meanwhile the messenger was despatched to Boone and the next day found the old pioneer on the march with all the men of the vicinity to the relief of Bryan's Station.[5] The siege there had been raised by as desperate a defence as was ever exhibited in a frontier fort, when the rescuing parties arrived. Messengers had been sent in all directions and on the evening of Saturday, August 17th, pioneers to the number of one hundred and eighty-two had assembled at Bryan's Station, and several hundred men under the command of Colonel Benjamin Logan were hourly expected.

There was a great preponderance of officers among the men already at the station, and long and anxious were the councils which were held to determine their course. It was a principle of border warfare that no savage foray should be allowed to go unpunished, although it was known that the allies, who were commanded by Campbell and McKee, renegades from the American cause with the infamous Simon

5. *Siege of Bryan's Station and The Battle of Blue Licks* by Reuben T. Durrett, Bennett H. Young, Henry T. Stanton and George W. Ranck also published by Leonaur.

Girty and a large party of Wyandottes, among the fiercest warriors on the continent, greatly outnumbered the Kentuckians, and it was finally determined to pursue them at once, without waiting for the advent of Logan.

Early on the next morning the party, consisting of horse and foot under the command of Colonels John Todd, Stephen Trigg, and Daniel Boone, set forth. The Indians and Canadians had marched very deliberately and had taken particular care that their trail should be easily followed, even to the extent of blazing it, by gashing the trees as they passed. This itself was a very serious indication, but the backwoodsmen were indifferent to odds and the Kentuckians dashed on rapidly, so rapidly that they marched thirty-three miles the first day. In the two days that had elapsed the allies had marched thirty-eight miles, so that the two forces encamped for the night but five miles from one another.

The next morning they took up the march again and in a short time came to the Licking River, a stream easily fordable, at a place called Blue Licks, one of the salt springs which from time immemorial had been the haunt of the buffalo and deer. The river here makes a loop enclosing a piece of land shaped like a sugar-bowl. The trail, a buffalo "trace," led straight across the river and up an open ridge, the sides of which were heavily timbered, and cut by ravines running at right angles to the ridge. It was the place where Boone had been captured when with the salt party years before. With that wonderful topographical instinct which had enabled him to find his way in the densest wilderness, every detail of the position was fresh in his memory.

A few Indians were seen on the other side of the river upon the ridge. As the Kentuckians approached them they leisurely disappeared. A party of scouts was sent forward but found nothing. Their inspection must have been perfunctory, for the woods and ravines were filled with Canadians and Indians in ambush, waiting just such an opportunity as this. There was something very suspicious about the whole situation, however, and the place was so dangerous that the assemblage was halted while a council of war was held.

Boone, as the most experienced Indian fighter and as the man of the highest importance among them, was asked for his opinion. He pointed out that the situation was grave indeed. He felt certain that the Indians were ambushed on the other side of the river, and that the Kentuckians should at once select a defensive position on their own side and hold it until the arrival of Colonel Logan and his men. Only a man of Boone's courage could have offered such counsel and their only salvation, as it happened, would have been in its acceptance. But with all his reputation and powers Boone does not seem to have been a leader of men. His prowess was individual and his reputation likewise, so his counsel was disregarded by the majority and it was determined to attack.

Boone then proposed that a party should be detached to march secretly up the river and fall upon the rear of the Indians and Canadians, at a prearranged signal, while the main attack was delivered in front. While this dangerous proposition was being discussed,—for there was enough military talent among the allies to have enabled them to overwhelm one detachment before the other arrived, if the manoeuvre were detected, which would almost certainly happen,—a Major McGary, a man of headlong and impetuous valour, but without discretion, disgusted with the apparent hesitation of the Kentuckians, and, as he states, chafing under the taunt of cowardice which had been flung at him the day before when he had suggested waiting for Logan, suddenly broke up the council, after much bickering, by turning his horse to the ford of the river and dashing across it shouting, "Let all who are not cowards follow me! "

It was one of those foolish appeals which always produce disaster and the consequences of which are usually terrible. Large parties of the men immediately broke after McGary and the wiser and older officers found themselves committed to a course of action entirely at variance with their knowledge and experience. McGary ought to have been shot by someone before he entered the river, but the authority of the officers was of a very indefinite character. The men were all equals and they obeyed just about as it pleased them, or nearly so. There was nothing for Boone, the Todd brothers, Trigg, Harlan, and the rest, to do but follow and endeavour to restore such order as they could in the mob into which their men had degenerated.

The force passed the river unmolested, and advanced up the broad buffalo trail toward the top of the ridge. Some semblance of order was restored as they progressed. McGary led the advance party of twenty-five men, Trigg took command of the right, Boone of the left, and Todd of the centre. Preferring to fight on foot a majority of the troops dismounted and left their horses on the bank. The bare ridge was about three hundred and fifty feet long and the thin attenuated line barely covered it. As they approached the top a rifle shot rang out,

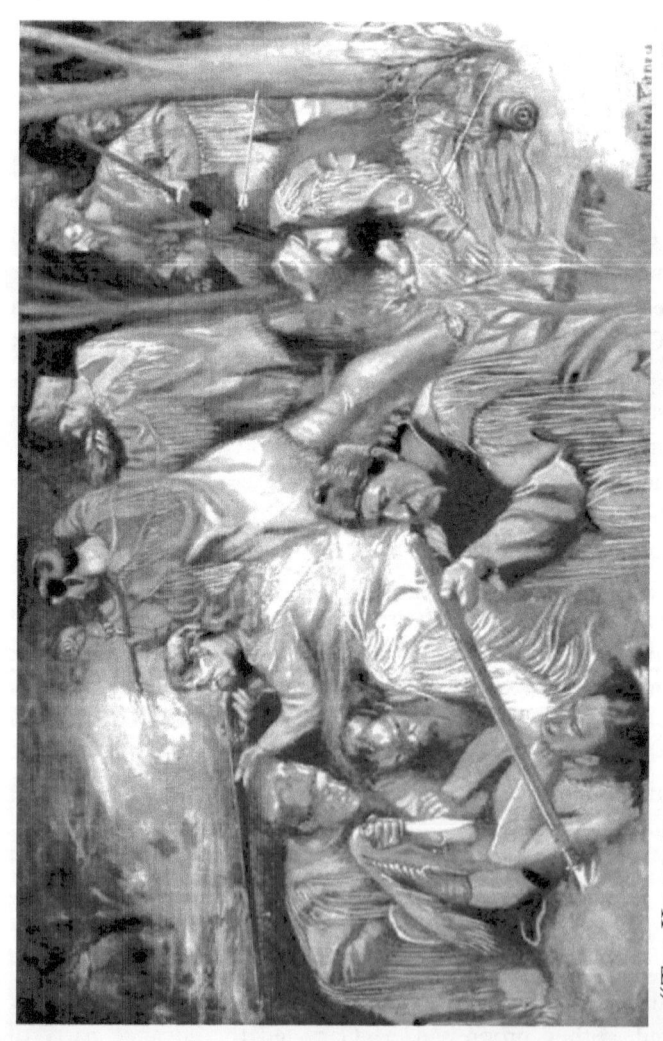

"The Kentuckians stood to their ground manfully, and returned the fire."

followed by a stunning volley. Of the twenty-five men in the advance twenty-three were instantly shot down, McGary being one of the two who escaped. Fate must have been asleep at that moment, for if ever a man deserved death it was he.

Following the first volley the Canadians appeared in force on the ridge, while on either flank the Indians opened a deadly fire from the ravines. The Kentuckians stood to their ground manfully and returned the fire, inflicting quite a heavy loss, but in an instant the open was black with men. Boone and his men, however, advanced gallantly and drove the Indians back on the left, but only temporarily. The Indians, especially the Wyandottes, were as fearless and as reckless as the Iroquois, and after the first volleys they came bursting through the smoke tomahawk in hand.

The Kentuckians with unloaded rifles and knives were no match for the Indians with tomahawks, especially when outnumbered three to one. Nearly every officer of rank was instantly killed. The Indians overwhelmed the right wing and extended their lines around that flank, the centre then gave back before the tremendous pressure and the advancing left became isolated. In another moment the Kentuckians would have been entirely surrounded and a massacre would have ensued. *Sauve que peut* became the order of the day at once.

The Kentuckians fled pell-mell in wild confusion to the river, those mounted galloping madly down the buffalo trail, others seeking to gain their frightened horses and escape. Boone, fighting desperately with knife and clubbed rifle in defence of his life, his horse having been killed, found himself far in advance of his line, cut off by the Indians who had gathered between him and the river. His son Isaac, a private in his company, lay dying at his feet.

Seizing the boy in his arms with superhuman strength he burst through the encircling foemen and by his knowledge of the place gained shelter in a ravine through which, still carrying the wounded lad, he made for the river. Although he had escaped observation for the moment his discovery was certain. The Indians and Canadians were ranging the woods and butchering everybody they came across. The helpless wounded upon the field were immediately killed. As it chanced, the poor boy died in his father's arms and Boone put his body in a sheltered recess in the rocks and finally succeeded in escaping across the river.

Major Netherland, who was better mounted than the others, gained the opposite bank of the river. With cool hardihood he stopped every man who came across until he had gathered quite a party about him. Charging their rifles they waited until the main battle came rolling toward the stream. The Kentuckians in advance plunged into the water, the Indians close after them. Netherland's force by steady firing checked the pursuit at the bank of the river until their exhausted comrades got over, when they immediately scattered in the woods. The Indians attempted little or no pursuit on the other side of the river.

Sixty-seven Kentuckians were killed outright or were murdered on the field after the battle. Seven were captured, of whom four died by torture, and many of those who escaped were wounded in some way or other.

Half way to Bryan's Station the fugitives met Colonel Logan with four hundred men coming to their support. In the face of this disastrous defeat, in which over forty *per cent*, had been lost, and ignorant of the number of the allies, which rumour had magnified to an extraordinary degree, Logan deemed it prudent to retire to Bryan's Station.

The return of the defeated brought desolation and sorrow to the whole territory. A few days after the battle the army, greatly re-enforced, marched out to the battlefield, which was, it may be imagined, a scene of horror. The Indians had carried away their dead, the Canadians had buried theirs, and their loss was never certain. Compared to that of the Kentuckians, however, it was inconsiderable. Logan and Boone buried the dead on the field, covering their remains with a huge mound of stones.

What must have been the thoughts of the old pioneer whose advice, if they had taken it, might have prevented this fearful slaughter! He had lost his brother, two of his brothers-in-law, and two of his sons in battles with the Indians. Certainly he had paid a heavy price for his part in the settlement of Kentucky!

He accompanied George Rogers Clark in the expedition which was organized after the Battle of the Blue Licks, which devastated the Indian country, and did good service there. But the Indians came no more to Kentucky. The treaty of peace which closed the Revolution deprived them of their British backing, and left the United States free to deal with them, and it is a notable fact that this sanguinary and disastrous engagement was the last battle of the Revolution. The contest which began at Lexington, Massachusetts, ended at the Blue Licks, Kentucky, a place that had never been dreamed of when Pitcairn shot down the minute men, so rapid even under adverse circumstances had been the growth and expansion of our country.

8. THE END OF THE OLD PIONEER

After the war Boone's carelessness in complying with the legal requirements caused him to be dispossessed of his second attempt at land claim, and in 1795 he removed to Missouri, then a part of the Spanish territory of Louisiana. Here, with his children and grandchildren around him, he passed the remainder of his days, his passion for hunting existing to the very last. Long past the age of threescore and ten the old hunter and pioneer made excursion after excursion through that yet unexplored west which still rose before him with all the allurements that it held in the days of his youth. There, in 1813, his faithful wife died. She had been a helpmeet to him indeed.

A dirge for the brave old pioneer!
A dirge for his old spouse!
For her who blest his forest cheer
And kept his birchen house.
Now soundly by her chieftain may
The brave old dame sleep on.
The red man's step is far away.
The wolf's dread howl is gone.

When Louisiana passed to the United States Boone again found that he had neglected to secure his land title from the Spanish government and was again dispossessed of his claim, so that he who had spent his lifetime in discovering, acquiring, protecting, the vast territory of the United States west of the Alleghenies, found himself at last without a rood of ground to call his own. In his extremity he appealed to the legislature of Kentucky, and at their urgency the government of the United States through Congress granted him a tract of land in Missouri, where he died on the 23rd of September, 1820, in the eighty-sixth year of his age.

As was fitting and proper, his remains with those of his wife were brought back in 1845 to rest in the soil of Kentucky, which justly cherishes his memory as one of the fathers of the commonwealth. Not often has there been in our history so admired and beloved a pioneer. He stands for a class which has vanished, and which circumstances will never permit to reappear, but a class which performed great services in the development of this country, and which will always be held in grateful remembrance. The hunting shirt and the axe, the long rifle and the powder horn, the handful of parched corn, and the coon-skin cap, these should be incorporated in our escutcheon, for these were the means by which was won to us that great country between the Alleghenies and the Mississippi.

2

The Women and Children of Bryan's Station

1. THE WIVES OF THE PIONEERS

In discussing *Border Fights and Fighters*, the battles, sieges, and adventures whereby was brought about that great winning of the west justly so celebrated in song and story, the attention of the historian is usually given particularly to the men, and well it may be. But in many instances the women played as brave a part as their husbands or fathers, and the chronicles and traditions of the rude times teem with thrilling instances of sturdy courage and heroic daring on the part of the feminine pioneers. Generally speaking, the wives of the frontiersmen indeed showed themselves worthy helpmates to their cool and adventurous husbands. If some of the things that these women did were set down for modern delectation they would be regarded as utterly incredible, and the most exuberant imagination of the most daring dime novelist of other days could scarcely match the truth.

For instance, in 1787, there was Mrs. John Merrill of Nelson County, Kentucky, who, when her husband desperately wounded staggered into his cabin and fell on the floor at her feet, succeeded in shutting and barring the door upon the assaulting Indians, and when they broke into the house through a shivered plank of the door, killed four of them in succession with an axe—the axe, strange to say, being the favourite weapon of the women, as the rifle was that of the men! And when the savages gave over that attempt and tried to enter by the chimney, with ready wit she emptied her feather bed on the flames and smoked them away, keeping them at bay till help came and her loved ones were saved.

Then there was Elizabeth Zane, a young miss just come from

boarding school in Philadelphia to her father's house on the frontier in 1777. The people of the settlement being besieged by Indians and rangers under Girty, in Fort Henry, where Wheeling now stands in West Virginia, suddenly found themselves without powder and facing certain capture. Not a man could be spared from the weakened garrison which had already lost over half its members, but the brave girl volunteered to run to an outlying cabin, her father's, and bring back thence a keg of powder which had been left there. She succeeded in her desperate undertaking in spite of a heavy fire poured upon her by the Indians, delivered the powder to the garrison, and saved the fort![1]

I recall the story of two other women who held their cabin against an overwhelming force, the husbands of the two weltering in gore upon the floor—one dead, the other dying, in fact. The Indians repeatedly tried to set the cabin on fire and the women put out the flames again and again, first with their scanty supply of water, and when that was exhausted, by the use of raw eggs, and when the store of these in turn was gone, with the bloodstained garments of their husbands, saving their children and themselves from a fate too horrible to dwell upon. And there are hundreds of similar instances that might be mentioned.

But the women of Bryan's Station exhibited a greater degree of heroism than perhaps any other body of women in the new settlement of Kentucky. Bryan's Station was situated about five miles north of the present city of Lexington. It was originally founded by the Bryan brothers, their families and friends. One of these brothers had married a sister of the famous Daniel Boone, as had another of the settlers, and both men lost their lives in Indian conflicts. Boone's wife, by the way, was a sister of these Bryans.

2. An Old-Time Frontier Fort

The station was a rude log fort enclosing about forty cabins. It was about six hundred feet long, two hundred feet wide and twelve feet high. The cabins were placed at intervals around this parallelogram, and the spaces between filled with a heavy palisade, the outer walls of the cabins, with the palisades, composing the walls of the fort. There were two entrances closed with two heavy wooden gates. In each corner a two-story block-house was built which projected four feet beyond the walls, giving the defenders an enfilading fire. The roofs of the cabins sloped inward from the edge of the palisades, or outer

---

1. See my book *Woven with the Ship*: Saved by Her Slipper.

walls, so that a small person crouching upon the inner edge of the roof would not be visible from outside of the stockade.

Like almost every other frontier fort in Kentucky there was no water in the enclosure, a terrible mistake, but accounted for by the fact that the springs were generally on low ground not suitable for defensive works—still they might have dug wells in the forts, but the fact remains they rarely did. A short distance from the northeast corner of the fort there was a bountiful spring from which the garrison could get water when there was nobody there to prevent.

There had been terrible doings on the frontier during the spring and summer of 1782. The British and Indians had made raid after raid through the land. Two years before a certain Colonel William Byrd of Westover, Virginia, a Tory, who seems to have been a gentleman and a soldier, led some eight hundred Indians with a detachment of soldiers and some artillery into Kentucky. None of the forts was proof against artillery, nor was there any in the territory except that in the possession of George Rogers Clark, which was not available. Two stations, Martin's and Ruddle's, were attacked in succession and easily captured. Their garrisons and inhabitants were murdered and tortured with shocking barbarity. It is to the eternal credit of Colonel Byrd, that, finding himself unable to control the Indians, he abandoned his expedition and withdrew, otherwise the whole land would have been desolated.

The bulk of the invading Indians were Wyandottes, who were easily first among the savages of the northwest for ferocious valour and military skill. The opposing forces being exactly equal, a detachment of them defeated a certain Captain Estill by a series of brilliant military manoeuvres which would have done credit to a great captain, being indeed upon a small scale Napoleonic in their conception and execution.

Two years after Byrd had withdrawn, William Campbell and Alexander McKee, notorious renegades, with the infamous Simon Girty, whose name has been a hissing and byword ever since he lived, led a formidable war party consisting of a few Canadians and four hundred Indians into Kentucky. The first place they attacked was Bryan's Station. Another place called Hoy's Station was menaced by a different party of Indians and express messengers had ridden to Bryan's Station to seek aid, which the settlers were ready to grant.

The American party was being made up to go to Hoy's Station early in the morning of the 16th of August, 1782, when as they approached the gate to ride out of it, a party of Indians was discovered on the edge of the woods in full view. The party was small in number, comparatively speaking, yet its members exposed themselves, out of rifle range, of course, with such careless indifference to consequences, or to a possible attack, as inevitably to suggest to the mind of Captain John Craig, who commanded the fort at the time, that they were desirous of attracting the attention of the garrison in the hope that their small numbers might induce the men of the station to leave the fort and pursue them.

Craig was an old Indian fighter who had been trained in Daniel Boone's own school. He was suspicious of any manoeuvre of that kind. Checking the departure of the relief party, he called his brother and the principal men of the station into a council and they concluded at once that the demonstration in the front of the fort was a mere feint, that the Indians were anxious to be pursued and that the main attack would come from the other direction.

3. RUSE AGAINST RUSE

The surmise was correct. With cunning adroitness Campbell had massed the main body of his forces in the woods back of the fort with strict instructions for them to remain concealed and not show themselves on any account until they heard the fire coming from the front of the station, which would convince them that their ruse had succeeded. Then they were to break from cover and rush for the back wall of the fort, which they supposed would be undefended, scale it, and have the little garrison at their mercy. It so happened that the spring, referred to above, from which the fort got its water supply, lay within a short distance of the main body concealed in the thick woods which surrounded the clearing with the fort in the centre. The situation was perfectly plain to Craig and his men. They determined to meet ruse with ruse and if possible defeat the Indians at their own game.

Before they could do anything, however, they must have a supply of water. On that hot August day life in that stockade, especially when engaged in furious battle would become unsupportable without water. Only the ordinary amount sufficient for the night had been brought in the day before. The receptacles were now empty. After swift deliberations the commandant turned to the women and children crowded around the officers, and explained the situation plainly to them. He proposed that the women, and children who were large enough to carry water, should go down to the spring with every vessel they could carry and bring back the water upon which their lives depended. He also explained to them that the spring was probably covered by concealed masses of the enemy who were waiting for the success of the demonstration in front of the fort to begin the attack.

He said further, that it was the opinion of those in command, that if the women would go to the spring as they did under ordinary circumstances, as was their custom every morning that is, the Indians would not molest them, not being desirous of breaking up the plan by which they hoped to take the fort and have everything at their mercy. The men in the fort would cover the women with their rifles so far as they could. It would be impossible for them to go and get water; as it was not the habit of the men to do that, the unusual proceeding would awaken the suspicions of the Indians and the men would be shot down and the fort and all its inmates would be at the mercy of the savages.

Every woman there was able to see the situation. The theory upon which they were proceeding might be all wrong. The Indians might be satisfied with the certainty of capturing the women thus presented, and the women and children might be taken away under the very eyes of the helpless men. On the other hand, it was probable, though by no means certain, that Craig's reasoning was correct and that the Indians would not discover themselves and the women and children would be allowed to return unmolested. Still nobody could tell what the Indians would do and the situation was a terrible one. Capture at the very best meant death by torture. The women in the fort had not lived on the frontier in vain. They realized the dilemma instantly. A shudder of terror and apprehension went through the crowd. What would they do? They must have the water; the men could not get it, the women did!

Mrs. Jemima Suggett Johnson, the wife of an intrepid pioneer and the daughter and sister of others, instantly volunteered for the task. She was the mother of five little children and her husband happened to be away in Virginia at the time. Leaving her two little boys and her daughter Sally to look after the baby in his dugout cradle, she offered to go for the water. This baby was that Richard Mentor Johnson, who afterward became so celebrated at the Battle of the Thames where Tecumseh was killed, and who was subsequently Vice-President of the United States.

Taking her little daughter Betsy, aged ten, her eldest child, by the hand, the fearless woman headed a little band of twelve women and sixteen children, who had agreed to follow where she led; among them were the wives and children of the Craig brothers. The little ones carried wooden piggins, and the women noggins and buckets. The piggin was a small bucket with one upright stave for a handle—a large wooden dipper as it were—while the larger noggin had two upright staves for handles.

Carefully avoiding any suspicious demonstration of force on the part of his men, Captain Craig opened the gate and the women marched out. Chatting and laughing in spite of the fact that they were nearly perishing from apprehension and terror, they tramped down the hill to the spring near the creek some sixty yards away, with as much coolness and indifference as they could muster. It was indeed a fearful moment for the women, and no wonder that some of the younger ones and the older children found it difficult to control their agitation; but the composed manner of those valiant and heroic matrons like Mrs. Johnson somewhat reassured the others and completely deluded the Indians. Probably the younger children did not realize their frightful danger and their unconsciousness helped to deceive the foes in ambush.

It took some time to fill the various receptacles from the small spring, but, by the direction of Mrs. Johnson, no one left the vicinity until all were ready to return. This little party then marched deliberately back to the fort as they had come. Not a shot was fired. The Indians concealed within a stone's throw in the underbrush had looked at them with covetous eyes, but such was the unwonted discipline in which they were held that they refrained from betraying themselves, in the hope of afterward carrying out their stratagem. As they neared the gate some of the younger ones broke into a run crowding into the door of the stockade which never looked so hospitable as on that sunny summer morning, and some of the precious water was spilled, but most of it was carried safe into the enclosure.

With what feelings of relief the fifty-odd men in the station saw their wives and children come back again can scarcely be imagined. Despatching two daring men on horseback to break through the besiegers and rouse the country, Craig immediately laid a trap for the Indians. Selecting a small body he sent them out to the front of the fort to engage the Indians there, instructing them to make as much noise and confusion as possible. Then he posted the main body of his men at the loop-holes back of the fort, instructing them not to make a move, nor fire a gun, until he gave the order.

"It was indeed a frightful moment for the women."

The ruse was completely successful. Deceived by the hullabaloo in front the Indians in the rear, imagining that their plan had succeeded, broke from cover and instantly dashed up to the stockade, shouting their war cries, and expecting an easy victory. What was their surprise to find it suddenly bristling with rifles as Craig and his men poured a steady withering fire into the mass crowded before them, fairly decimating them. They ran back instantly, and concealment being at an end, returned the fire ineffectually. Immediately thereafter from every side a furious fire from four hundred rifles burst upon the defenders. All day long the siege was maintained. Once in awhile a bullet ploughing through a crevice in the stockade struck down one of the brave garrison, but the casualties in the station were very few.

On the other hand, when an Indian exposed himself he was sure to be killed by a shot from some unerring rifle. One or two Indians climbed a tree seeking to command the fort therefrom, but they were quickly detected and shot before they had time to descend. At last they attempted to burn the fort by shooting flaming arrows up in the air to fall perpendicularly upon the buildings. The children, the little boys, that is, and some of the older girls, were lifted up on the inclined roofs, where they were safe from direct rifle fire, though in imminent danger of being pierced by the dropping arrows, with instructions to put out the fires as fast as the arrows kindled them, which they succeeded in doing. Meanwhile, the women were busy moulding bullets and loading rifles for the men, and many of them took their places on the walls and aided in the defence.

The mothers of our forest land,
Their bosoms pillowed men;
And proud were they by such to stand
In hammock, fort, or glen;
To load the sure old rifle,
To run the leaden ball.
To watch a battling husband's place,
And fill it should he fall.

Finding their efforts unavailing the Indians ravaged the surrounding country. They killed all the cattle belonging to the pioneers, burned and destroyed the fields of grain, and turned the environment into a bloody desert. In the afternoon a succouring party from Boone's Station appeared, but without Boone, for he was absent at the time, and succeeded in entering the fort. The newcomers included some sixteen horsemen with thirty footmen from the Lexington Station.

The horsemen approached unobserved and deliberately dashed through the Indian lines. The suddenness of their onset and the great cloud of dust raised by their horses disconcerted the Indians and they succeeded in breaking through without the loss of a single man, although they were shot at by numbers of savages.

The footmen, however, who were some distance away, hearing the noise of the horsemen's battle, disobeyed orders through friendly gallantry, and instead of endeavouring to gain the fort turned aside with the intention of succouring the horsemen who had already rushed through. They found themselves in a cornfield, confronted by an overwhelming body of Indians, and incontinently ran.

Fortunately for the hunters these Indians had just discharged their pieces at the horsemen and there had not been time to reload. The rifles of the Kentuckians were still charged, and even the most implacable savage hesitated to attack a loaded rifle with a tomahawk.

Keeping the Indians back by threatening them, the footmen gave over the attempt to reach the fort and succeeded, with the exception of six killed, in escaping. These Kentuckians did not fire until they had to, and every time they did they brought down a man. The Indians pursued them for some distance, but as Bryan's Station was their object the pursuit was soon abandoned. The fugitives scattered in every direction rousing the country.

Meanwhile the battle around the station still kept up. Toward evening, however, the Indians having sustained severe loss, and seeing no prospect of capturing the place, which was as stoutly defended as ever, reluctantly determined to raise the siege and withdraw. Before they did so Simon Girty resolved to try what he could effect with persuasion. Cautiously advancing toward the fort and taking cover behind a huge sycamore tree, he held a parley. Declaiming his name and position, he advised the garrison to surrender at once, promising immunity and kind treatment on the part of Hamilton, the British commander at Detroit. His faith was better than Girty's, but that of both of them amounted to nothing.

Girty told the garrison that the beleaguering force would be supplemented on the following day by artillery, and if the station did not immediately surrender it would receive the fate which had been meted out to Martin's and Ruddle's Stations. The address was listened to in gloomy silence. Everybody knew what had happened at those two stations, and small wonder that many a heart sank at the prospect.

There happened to be in the fort, however, a young man named Reynolds, a reckless dare-devil sort of a fellow, who took upon himself without authority the answering of Girty. He told him that he knew perfectly well who he was, that he knew his character, also; that he had a little dog that was so utterly worthless that he had named him Simon Girty, because he could think of no other name so beautifully appropriate; that he didn't believe they had any cannon, and that if they would just wait outside the fort until the next day they would have the whole of Kentucky upon them, and if they knew what they were about they would get away in short order!

Girty retired in great discomfiture, followed by the laughter of the Kentuckians, and greeted by the sneers of the Indians. It was a long and anxious night they spent in the fort thereafter, the defenders keeping on the alert for any demonstration, but in the morning the Indians were gone. They had decamped as silently as they had approached, the siege was raised, the battle was over. They had taken Reynolds' advice.

All day eager settlers from every direction poured into the settlement, and in their hot desire to punish these Indians they sallied out soon after with an inadequate force and, as we have seen, were badly defeated by Campbell and his allies at the disastrous battle of Blue Licks.

4. The Story of the Morgans

One further romantic incident of the siege is worthy of mention. A man named Morgan had settled with his wife and child in a cabin outside the fort. When the Indians appeared, he concealed his wife in a recess beneath the slab floor of his cabin, I surmise perhaps because she was ill and it was impossible for her to escape. At any rate, thinking he had left her in a place of safety he took his baby in one hand, grasped his rifle in the other, and broke through the Indians and gained the forest.

Unfortunately the Indians burned the house, while he looked helplessly on from his place of concealment with his anguish intensified by his utter inability to do anything at all. The Indians discovered him after a time, and he had a desperate struggle to get away. He reached Lexington at last, left the baby there, and at once joined the relief party which fought the Indians in the cornfield.

When the siege was raised the frantic man searching among the embers found the charred remains of a human body. Crazed by his loss he was among the first to cross the river and engage the Indians at the battle of Blue Licks. Recognizing a portion of his wife's clothing worn by an Indian, he killed him in a hand-to-hand struggle, but he was shot and frightfully wounded. Retaining strength enough to crawl away from the battlefield he concealed himself in the wood, lying down to die. There he was found by his wife, who had been taken prisoner and had escaped in the confusion of the battle. She dragged him into a further place of concealment, cared for him as best she could, and when the Indians departed after the battle she contrived to get him back to the fort in safety.

The bones he had found in the ashes of the cabin were those of a wounded Indian, who had crawled in there and died. The Indians had set fire to the house and the woman had been forced to discover herself. The savages had not had time to torture her, and so the family was united once more.

The men, of course, conducted themselves heroically in the siege, but the honour of the defence which they were enabled to make certainly rests with those pioneer mothers and daughters of Kentucky. A monument around the spring, the tribute of the Daughters of the American Revolution, one of the few that have been erected to women, serves to commemorate their heroic self-sacrifice and valour, for it takes more courage to go to a spring and get water in the face of four hundred Indian rifles pointing at you from out of a dark wood, than it does to stand behind a wall and fight all day long.

1

The Massacre at Fort Mims

1. THE BEGINNING OF THE CREEK WAR

On the evening of Tuesday, the 31st of August, 1813, a little canoe floated ashore near Fort Stoddardt, Alabama, a rude frontier stockade on the west bank of the Mobile River, some twenty-five miles above the city of that name. In the bottom of the canoe lay an exhausted, half-delirious negro woman, a slave, whose only name was Hester. She was suffering from a huge, ghastly bullet wound in her breast. Lifted by tender hands from the bloody canoe, in which she was prostrated, she was carried into the fort and questioned by the commander.

She told a tale of massacre and destruction which froze the blood of the listeners. She believed herself to be the sole survivor of the garrison, and the people who had collected at Fort Mims, on Lake Tensaw, some twenty miles further up the river, just below the "cut-off," or the confluence of the Alabama and the Tombigbee, which thereafter make the Mobile River. The story they heard from the lips of the wretched woman, who had managed, she knew not how, to conceal herself till nightfall in the cane brake and then escape in the boat in which they found her, was one of the most appalling recitals of savage fury that has ever been told in any of our Indian wars.

The great Tecumseh, in the previous year, had succeeded in engaging the major portion of the powerful Creek nation in behalf of his Confederacy. The Creeks were the most notable of the southern Indians. For enterprise and valour, for progress in a rude sort of civilization, for the development of an organization which possessed some of the properties of government, they were only to be compared with the Iroquois, or Six Nations, in the north.

Those who know the red man only through touch with the modern Indian of the plains are accustomed to sneer at the conception of him which is exploited, let us say, in Cooper's novels; but the Creeks and the Iroquois were very different from the modern Indian, and Cooper's pictures, so far as these two peoples are concerned, do no violence to the facts. The Creeks were, however, as ruthlessly cruel and bloodthirsty in warfare as, for instance, Geronimo[1] and his Mescalero Apaches. The men were tall, magnificent specimens, and some of the women are said to have been beautiful; I think, however, that could only be by comparison with other Indian squaws. The Creek Nation numbered some thirty thousand, of whom at least seven thousand were approved warriors. Among them were many half-breeds, who inclined either to civilization or savagery, as the case might be, and exhibited the traits of the white man or those of the Indian, according to their rearing and environment.

There was a division in the tribe as to joining the conspiracy of Tecumseh, and the smouldering embers of a civil war were beginning to glow among them, when the War of 1812 broke out. Such an auxiliary for the British to work with, in conjunction with the Spanish authorities in Florida, was not to be despised. Supplied with English guns and incited by British rewards offered for scalps, even of women and children, the great body of Creeks declared for war, although some remained friendly to the Americans. The half-breeds, or men of mixed blood, were divided between the two sides. The principal war chief of the Indians was a half-breed named Weatherford, who was called in the Creek language, "The Red Warrior."

After a skirmish at a place called Burnt Corn, which resulted in the defeat of the settlers, the alarm spread all over Alabama and the frightened inhabitants, including those half-breeds who were, to all intents and purposes, Americans, gathered for protection in the little forts and stockades which dotted the country on every hand.

There had lived for many years in Alabama, near Lake Tensaw, a wealthy half-breed named Samuel Mims. His house was a large and substantial wooden structure of one storey, with several outbuildings. It was situated some little distance from the water, on low, sandy ground surrounded by woods, marshes and swamps, which on the east were traversed by several ravines overgrown with cane brakes. The house was surrounded by a low stockade, made by driving parallel rows of open stakes at suitable intervals, the spaces between being filled with loosely piled fence-rails. At three and a half feet from the ground five hundred loop-holes were pierced. The stockade was seventy yards

1. *Geronimo* by Geronimo published by Leonaur.

square and enclosed an acre of ground. On the southwest corner on a slight rise a blockhouse was begun but never completed. There were two large gates in the centre of the east and west faces. From the north and south faces projected small square enclosures called bastions, made of the same pickets.

Thither at once resorted all the inhabitants of the vicinage, and many small houses were built in the enclosure to shelter them. To them in the latter part of July, General Claiborne, the United States military commander of the territory, sent one hundred and seventy-five volunteers, commanded by Major Daniel Beasley, with Captains Jack, Middleton, and Batcheldor. Major Beasley found a lieutenant and sixteen soldiers in the fort and some seventy other men who were organized into a battalion, and one Dixon Bailey was elected their captain.

Most of the soldiers were full-blooded whites, although some of the settlers were of mixed blood. Bailey himself was a half-breed. There were nearly six hundred people in the enclosure now, which was too small to contain so great a number with comfort or safety, and Beasley erected a second stockade some sixty feet beyond the east wall with which it was connected on either side, forming an outer enclosure, in which he stationed the bulk of his troops.

2. Careless Defenders

General Claiborne visited the place soon after and charged the defenders straitly to complete the blockhouse and strengthen the palisades. At first they worked heartily enough, and kept a fairly vigilant watch, but so many false alarms were brought to them that they grew careless and indifferent at last. Beasley was a poor commander, though a brave man. He presently allowed the work to languish. The blockhouse was never completed, and latterly, except at night, they kept no watch. He also imprudently weakened his command by sending away small detachments to garrison other points.

The summer was very hot. Many of the people crowded together in that low, marshy ground became ill. On the 29th of August two negroes who had been herding cattle came rushing back to the fort in terror, exclaiming that they had seen a large body of Indians. The foolish Beasley, declined to credit their tale, and, angry at the commotion and alarm their news had created, actually ordered them to be flogged!

The owner of one of the negroes, a certain Fletcher, refused to

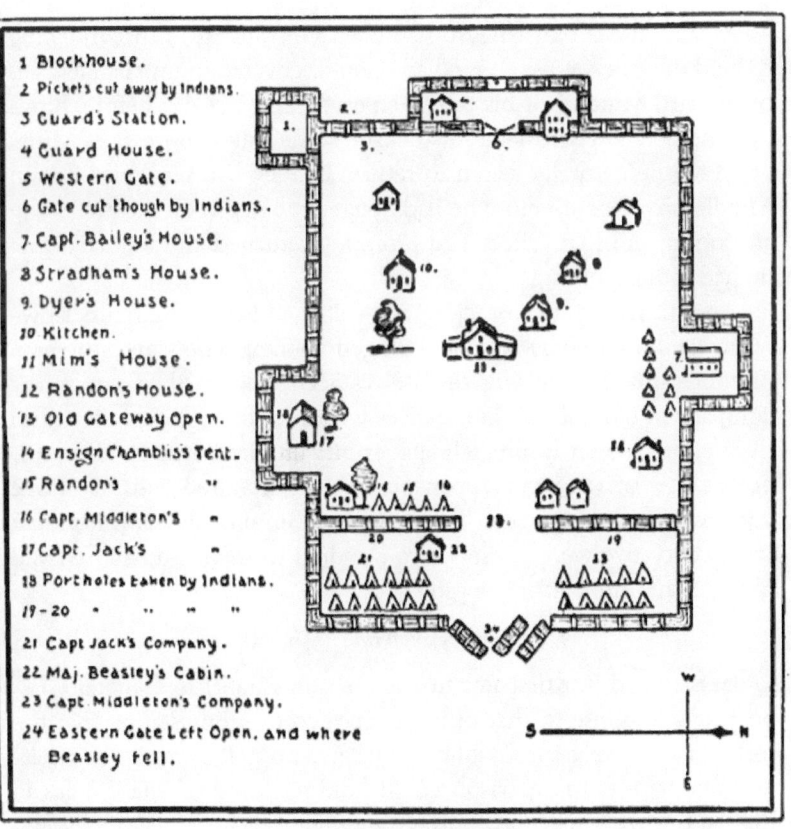

1 Blockhouse.
2 Pickets cut away by Indians.
3 Guard's Station.
4 Guard House.
5 Western Gate.
6 Gate cut though by Indians.
7 Capt. Bailey's House.
8 Stradham's House.
9 Dyer's House.
10 Kitchen.
11 Mim's House.
12 Randon's House.
13 Old Gateway Open.
14 Ensign Chambliss Tent.
15 Randon's   "
16 Capt. Middleton's "
17 Capt. Jack's   "
18 Portholes taken by Indians.
19 - 20   "   "   "   "
21 Capt Jack's Company.
22 Maj. Beasley's Cabin.
23 Capt. Middleton's Company.
24 Eastern Gate Left Open, and where
   Beasley fell.

PLAN OF FORT MIMS.

allow his man to be whipped, but the owner of the other, making no objection, the unfortunate negro was tied to a stake and soundly lashed. Beasley shortly informed Fletcher that he must either allow his slave to be flogged, or leave the fort with his large family the next morning. The alternative was not to be thought of. After considering it all night Fletcher reluctantly gave his consent just before noon on Monday, August 30th, 1813, and the negro was accordingly triced up to a post preparatory to receiving a lashing.

Meanwhile the first negro had been sent out again that morning to herd the stock as usual, and had again discovered unmistakable signs of Indians. Mindful of his bitter experience of the day before, however, he fled to Fort Pierce, a stockade some miles above Fort Mims, to which he naturally feared to return. Beasley had sent out Captain Middleton to scout before he had flogged the negro on the preceding afternoon, and that officer had promptly returned and reported that he had found nothing.

The morning was hot, close and sultry, and the long hours slowly dragged along. The soldiers lounged in their tents, some of them playing cards, or amusing themselves according to their fancy; the company cooks and the housewives were preparing the midday meal throughout the enclosure, while over one hundred little children disported themselves in the open places. Five hundred and fifty-three persons were in the fort at the time, of whom probably two hundred and twenty-five were soldiers, two hundred women and children and old men and the balance negro slaves.

3. Paying the Awful Penalty

Beasley had just despatched a letter (still extant) to General Claiborne, in response to that officer's repeated cautions, stating that the fort was absolutely safe, and he was to give himself no concern whatever about it, as the garrison could hold it against all the Creeks in the nation. By some miracle the messenger reached the general and delivered the letter after all was over. At the time he was writing a great body of a thousand Indians, a small portion of whom the two negroes had seen and reported, had actually surrounded the fort unperceived. They lay hid in the forests, or concealed in the canebrakes, although the most of them were crouching beneath the brush in the nearest ravine in front of the east gate, to reach which they would be compelled to pass over an open field.

Beasley was standing in the door of his own house in the outer enclosure when the drums beat the noonday mess call. That was the prearranged signal for attack. Instantly the open field was covered with a mass of "Red Sticks," the name given to the Creek warriors from the red clubs they always carried in battle. These, however, were armed with the best modern muskets as well. Silent as death, they dashed rapidly toward the open gate. They had actually come within thirty yards of it before anyone saw them, which tells a tale of the negligence of the guards.

Beasley saw them first. Shouting "Indians! Indians!" he ran through the little enclosure toward the great, ponderous east gate, frantically striving to close it in the face of the charging enemy, now yelling madly and coming on gallantly. The soil was sandy and the wind had drifted it against the gate. With the strength of despair, Beasley threw himself against the timbers. The sand held for a fatal moment. But the major bent his back and pushed like mad and the gate began slowly to swing toward the post. Before he could close it the foremost Indians threw themselves upon it, thrust it back, fell upon Beasley with tomahawks, cut him down, and rushed over his body toward the troops in the outer enclosure.

The men had scarcely time to seize their arms before the Indians burst upon them in a perfect torrent through the open gate. Beasley had crawled aside and they heard his voice from the midst of trampling feet, shouting to the men just before he died, "For God's sake, fight on!" The major portion of the soldiers fled through the second gate into the vacant part of the fort and manned the wall. This inner gate was left open for a time, but was finally closed. Those who could not get away were slaughtered to a man in the outer enclosure, which was now full of Indians. At the same time the palisades were attacked on all other sides. The soldiers and settlers fought desperately. Many of the women took part in the defence. One, Mrs. Daniel Bailey, actually thrust a bayonet into one man who played the craven and forced him to get up and fight!

Dixon Bailey, the brave half-breed, upon whom the command, after Beasley's death, had devolved, showed himself a hero. The Indians under Weatherford were no less courageous. The fighting was so close that sometimes a soldier and an Indian would discharge their guns through the same port-hole at the same moment and both would be killed. The carnage on both sides was fearful, and after some three long hours of the hottest kind of fighting, the defenders being encouraged thereto by the heroic efforts of Bailey, who was everywhere animating

"THE MAJOR BENT HIS BACK AND PUSHED LIKE MAD."

his men, the savages began to draw off with the plunder of the houses outside the stockade.

Weatherford, riding a magnificent black horse that day, the very incarnation of a savage war chieftain, bitterly protested at the retreat, and finally led his men forward for a final attack on the post. This time there was no withstanding them.

Some of the houses in the enclosure were set on fire by burning arrows. The east gate was entered by an irresistible charge. The west gate was cut through with axes, after all the defenders had been slain, and another storm of Indians poured into the enclosure that way. The south wall was next gained. The defenders fought desperately from house to house, while the roofs were burning over their heads. Mims' house, from which, through apertures in the roof, a deadly fire had been kept up, was set on fire. In it were many of the women and children, who perished miserably, either by flame if they stayed, or by tomahawk or scalping-knife if they came out. The Indians did not waste blows or weapons on the small children, either. They killed them with their naked hands!

Soon the whole enclosure, save the north bastion, which was Bailey's particular command, was filled with frantic savages. Into the last refuge of the frail little enclosure of the bastion poured a perfect stream of frenzied humanity, trampling each other to death in their mad terror. The place was packed so full that there was scarcely room to move in it, much less to defend it. Bailey appealed for someone to attempt to get away and bring succour. He was already severely wounded. When no one else volunteered he tried to go himself but was prevented by his friends. The place was entirely surrounded now at any rate.

Those in the bastion were forced to see those outside killed in the most shocking manner. It is not possible to write of the barbarous deaths that these people died. Weatherford commanded, protested, implored, but he could not restrain his followers, now roused to a pitch of savage madness. They even threatened his own life, and he was at last forced to let them alone. He had loosed the storm; he could not control it. He regretted the slaughter to the last day of his life.

Presently the Indians broke into the bastion. All was soon over. Some dozen soldiers tore openings in the palisade and managed to escape from the place of death. The rest were slaughtered where they were; most of them, even the women and children left, fighting heroically to the last. Bailey was among those who got away, but only for a short distance in his case. He reached the swamp, but was so badly wounded, and in five places, that he lay down and died, bidding the men to leave him and to try to make their escape without him.

The number of the slain was never accurately known, but not a white, or half-breed, man, woman, or child, survived, except those twelve soldiers; the killed certainly numbered over four hundred and fifty. The poor negro who had been left tied to the post to be whipped was killed in the first onset. The only persons whose lives were spared were some of the negroes who were reserved as slaves by the warriors. It may be, or may not be, an evidence of their civilization, but it is a fact that many of the Creeks owned numbers of negro slaves.

The fort was burned to the ground. The Creeks had lost terribly in the assault, for over four hundred warriors out of the thousand who had made up the party had been killed and many wounded, such had been the desperate character of the defence. They made some effort to bury their own dead, but soon gave over the attempt, and taking what plunder they had gained, they moved away to attack other posts.

The bodies of the men, women and children, negroes, half-breeds, whites and Indians, were left lying on the field. They were found there some days afterward by Major Kennedy with a relief expedition, and they buried what had been left of them after the ravages of bird and beast in one common awful grave. For desperation in defence, persistency in attack, and absolute courage on the part of both parties, the affair was, and remains, almost without a parallel.

A wave of indignation and horror swept over the southwest, penetrating even to the sick chamber of Andrew Jackson, lying almost helpless from a ghastly wound in his shoulder, the result of a duel. Rising from his bed, suffering agonies, but sustained only by his indomitable will, he called to his aid the militiamen of Tennessee, and began that campaign which after many hard-fought battles of varying fortune, ended in the annihilation of the Creek warriors on the bloody field of Tohopeka at the Horse-Shoe Bend of the Alabama River.

No Indians on the continent, except the Iroquois, ever fought in hand-to-hand conflict with the whites with such courage and success as these Mobilians. They manifested not a little of the spirit of those Indians, their ancestors, who, two hundred and seventy-three years before, had brought De Soto's expedition to the verge of annihilation, under that redoubtable warrior Tuscaloosa. [2] While we abhor their cruelties we may at least admire their courage.

---

2. See my book, *Colonial Fights and Fighters*: De Soto, (published by Leonaur)..

2

Jackson's Victory at Tohopeka

1. The Last Stand of the Creeks

On the morning of the 27th of March, 1814, that most redoubtable and successful of Indian fighters, General Andrew Jackson, at the head of an army of two thousand regulars and volunteers, arrived before the most formidable fortification which had ever been erected by savage warriors on the American continent. One hundred and sixty miles from even the ragged edges of civilization, in the heart of the Alabama wilderness, the Creek Indians, one of the most powerful and intelligent of the southern savage tribes upon the continent, had chosen to make a final stand in that war which they had entered upon at the instigation of that most capable and ferocious savage Tecumseh, and under the influence of the fanatical ravings of his brother, the prophet, a man less known as well as less able, but possibly more dangerous than the famous warrior.

After their overwhelming success at the bloody massacre at Fort Mims on August 30th, 1813, they had been defeated by Coffee at Talluschatches on the 3rd of November, and most disastrously by Jackson at Talladega on the 9th of November. Their spirit, however, had remained unbroken by these reverses and after the withdrawal and dispersion of the American levies, in a series of predatory forays they had continued ravaging the border. A determined effort was needed to crush them and bring them finally into subjugation.

To Jackson was entrusted this duty. The Creeks were immediately aware of the projected movement and with spirit undaunted they concentrated their forces and resolved to stake their cause on one last desperate effort. The spot in which they had elected to make their stand was singularly well adapted for defensive purposes by the arrangement of nature.

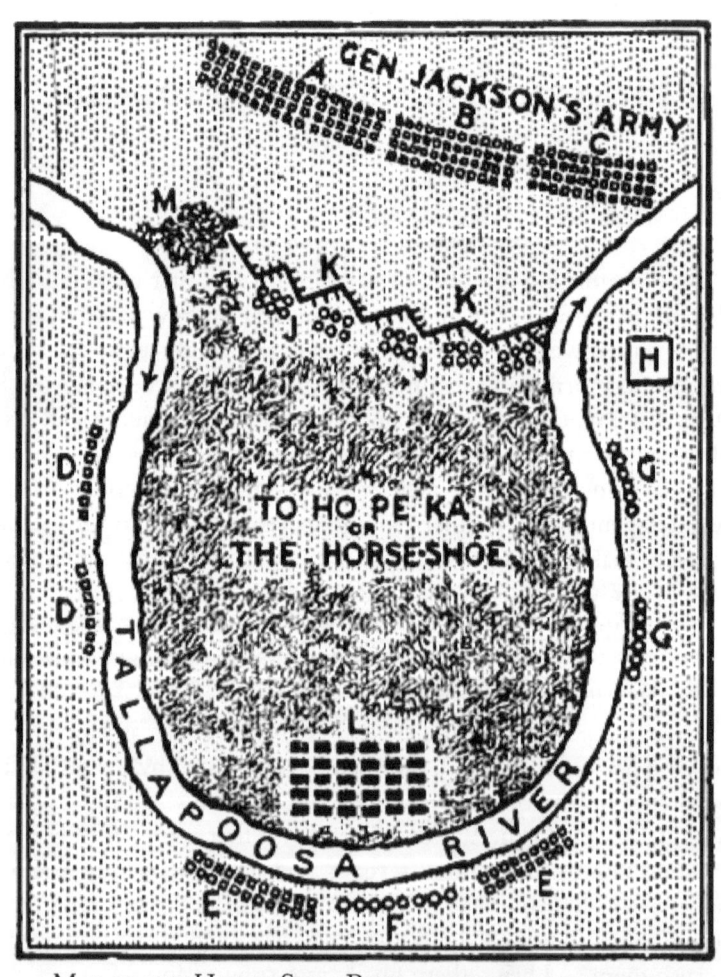

MAP OF THE HORSE-SHOE BEND AND PLAN OF THE BATTLE.

The Tallapoosa River, an affluent of the Alabama, is one of those tortuous southern streams which, in their many windings, drain a vast extent of territory. About the middle of the eastern side of the present state the river bends sharply upon its course enclosing a piece of ground about one hundred acres in extent in the shape of a horseshoe—called from that fact, *To-ho-pe-ka*, by the Indians. At the neck of the peninsula, three hundred and fifty yards across, the Indians had erected a breastwork of logs about six feet high and piled in zigzag fashion somewhat like an old-fashioned snake fence, the interspaces being filled with smaller timber and brushwood.

By the construction of this breastwork, which indicated a higher degree of skill than usually possessed by savages, who are supposed to know nothing about fortification, an enfilading fire was secured which would sweep the lines. It has been surmised by many writers that the character of the breastwork implies the work of a white man's brain, but this is not a necessary conclusion. The breastwork had been pierced with two rows of loop-holes.

In that season the Tallapoosa was unfordable. The Indians had taken care to secure all the canoes on their side of the river under the bluffs around the bend, and the height of the shores presented a further obstacle to any attack from the rear.

Within the enclosure were gathered some nine hundred warriors, the flower of the nation, indeed practically the last of it, with three hundred women and children. Three prophets—we would call them medicine men now—were a not unimportant factor in the defence. These, like other charlatans in other wars all over the world, had promised immunity from the white man's bullet to the savage braves. The promise may have added a certain degree of intensity to their determination, but as events showed, it was not necessary to enable them to put up one of the best defences that the Indians ever exhibited. The savages were well provided with rifles and muskets, in the use of which they were expert, and with ample food and unlimited water supply, they confidently awaited the American attack.

The whole outlook, when Jackson arrived at the fort, was sufficiently forbidding, yet he was quick to see that once he could effect a lodgement in the bend, or get across the breastworks, the Indians would be at his mercy! They would be trapped! The Creeks reasoned, it is supposed, that if Jackson succeeded in rushing the entrenchment they could retreat by the river. Jackson took care of that. He despatched the redoubtable General Coffee with seven hundred horsemen by a circuitous route to a ford of the river which had been discovered by one of the friendly Cherokees, the implacable enemies of the haughty, overbearing Creeks. The cavalry succeeded in gaining the rear of the Indian position unobserved, although, of course, separated from it by the river. Coffee dismounted and disposed his troops so they could cover every egress from the bend. Having done this some of the Cherokees, bolder than the others, swam the river, cut the fastenings of the canoes and towed them to the other bank.

Meanwhile Jackson had opened fire upon the breastworks from an eminence about eighty yards distant, with the two cannon of his army, a three and a six pounder. The Indians laughed in derision as the little cannon-balls buried themselves harmlessly in the huge logs of the barricade. It was half after ten in the morning when the engagement began, and for several hours, while Coffee was making his detour and dispositions, it continued with but little effect on either side.

Jackson could not make up his mind, from consideration for his troops, to storm those formidable breastworks. Death would meet a great many of them in the attempt. His men, less thoughtful than he, clamoured to be allowed to go forward, but the general with his usual hard-headed commonsense, refused to be influenced by the popular opinion of his army.

This hesitation arose from no excess of caution or lack of courage on the part of Jackson. He was without doubt one of the bravest and most intrepid men, and one of the hardest fighters, that ever lived, and he proved his courage, moral and physical, in hundreds of ways. [1] He was even then suffering from a terrible wound, which he had received in a duel and which would have incapacitated any ordinary man from duty for years to come. His shoulder had been dreadfully shattered, so much so, that during this campaign he could scarcely bear even the weight of a coat-sleeve on it, and in all his military experiences he was never able to wear the heavy bullion epaulets of his high rank.

It must have been a source of grief and humiliation to him that in a private quarrel he had expended his blood and strength, now so sorely needed in the service of his country. He kept up in this instance by the exercise of that indomitable will which he possessed in such large measure. It was with no thought of himself, therefore, that he restrained his men through the long hours of that battle.

About noon, however, the main army heard from Coffee. After

1. See my book, *American Fights and Fighters*; The Battle of New Orleans, (also published by Leonaur).

his success in obtaining possession of the canoes he determined to send over a party to beat up the quarters of the Indians behind the breastworks. Colonel Morgan was detailed for this duty. Accompanied by a small body of men he passed the river, set fire to the Indian huts and made a brilliant diversion in the rear. His band was too small for a sustained engagement and the attempt was only partially successful, for while the Indians detached parties from their front line to meet the new danger, and succeeded in driving off Morgan, they still held to their breastwork in force. However, the whole force had been disorganized by the occurrence and now, if ever, was the time for an advance. Jackson gave the signal which had been waited for.

2. The Heroism of Young Sam Houston

It was about half after twelve when the drummers beat the long roll. The eager men took up the advance and scrambled through the broken and heavily timbered ground on the run. The Thirty-ninth United States under Colonel Williams took one side, and the East Tennessee brigade of volunteers under General Bunch, the other. Jackson on horseback led them. They succeeded in reaching the rampart which towered above their heads, though not without severe loss on the way, When they reached the breastwork there was some hesitation. The men poked their guns through the portholes and fired point blank at the Indians, who returned the fire.

This interchange of shots was productive of some loss, but nothing whatever could be determined by it. Something had to be done and done quickly. Two officers, realizing the necessity, leaped for the top of the breast- works, calling upon the others to follow them. The first one was Major L. P. Montgomery of the Thirty-ninth Infantry. He had scarcely reached the top when he pitched forward, dead, a bullet in his forehead—the first man over! The second man was Ensign Sam Houston of Tennessee,

As Houston gained the top he stood for a moment in full view. Rifles cracked, bullets sang about him, but left him untouched. An arrow, however, made a deep wound in his thigh. Sword in hand Houston, then but twenty years old, leaped down amid the Indians. He was at once followed by a portion of his men. On the other flank the volunteers emulated the example of the regulars and the breastwork was finally gained. The Indians were swept from the line of defence to which they had clung so stubbornly.

But the savages were by no means defeated. The bend was heavily wooded and filled with brush-heaps and log-huts, and every house, every brush-heap, every tree clump, every copse, became a rallying point for defence. The woods were filled with flame and smoke into which the American soldiers plunged to get at their red foemen.

Conscious of his wound at last Houston leaned against the breast-work and begged the lieutenant of his company to pull out the arrow, which was, of course, barbed and firmly imbedded in the flesh. The lieutenant made two ineffectual efforts to pull out the arrow, but failed on account of the barbs. Maddened by the pain Houston raised his sword at the officer and vowed he would cut him down if he failed a third time. Under this stimulus the lieutenant jerked the arrow from the wound. It was, of course, followed by a gush of blood which nearly left the boy helpless.

He scrambled over the breastworks again and went back to the surgeons in the rear. Jackson saw him while his wound was being dressed and ordered him to retire from the action. The boy begged and implored permission of the general to return when the flow of blood was stanched, but Jackson curtly refused his plea. The battle was still raging all over the bend. It was too much for Houston to stand. As soon as he was released by the surgeon he deliberately disobeyed his orders, scrambled over the breastworks, found his company, and continued the fight.

It was nearly all over but the killing. Surrounded by overwhelming numbers of soldiers there was nothing left for the Creeks to do but to die, and they died game. No one asked for quarter, no one appears to have thought of surrender. As they were forced from line to line, from place to place, those alive at last reached the river bank. They were appalled to find their canoes gone, but plunged dauntlessly into the ford, only to be met by the cool, steady, withering fire from Coffee's riflemen, lining the banks on the farther side.

Jackson was not a merciless man, as he was popularly supposed to have been, and he did his utmost to stop the carnage, but on that smoke-covered, blood-saturated peninsula, in that almost impenetrable tangle of primeval forest, it was impossible to get hold of his men; and the Indians themselves, in their proud disdain to ask for quarter, in their determination to continue the fight, rendered his efforts abortive. The battle stopped about three o'clock in the afternoon. It stopped because one side had been wiped out. There were no more Indians to be conquered, but in its ending was seen its most dramatic feature.

A party of desperate Indians took position in a deep ravine near

"THEY PLUNGED DAUNTLESSLY INTO THE FORD, ONLY TO BE MET BY THE
FIRE FROM COFFEE'S RIFLEMEN ON THE FARTHER SIDE."

the river bank which had been covered by heavy logs. There appeared to be only one way to get at them and that was by a rush at the entrance, which was fully covered by the savage rifles. Jackson called for volunteers to storm the place. No one responded to his appeal until, with his usual impetuous headlong valour, young Sam Houston, in spite of his wound, sprang to the front.

Seizing a musket and calling upon the men to follow him he made a rush at the entrenchment. The men made a forward movement but stopped after going a few feet, and Houston, not noticing that he was unsupported, ran forward alone, raising his piece to fire as he approached. He received the entire discharge of that last desperate band of Indians. As he neared the entrance to the ravine two bullets struck him, one in the arm, the other in the shoulder. His musket fell from his hand and he stood helpless in this dangerous position.

Seeing at last that he was unsupported he deliberately turned around, still under fire, walked back out of range to his soldiers, and fell helpless. No one else tried to rush that position. The Americans found means to set fire to the covering logs, thus forcing the Indians out into the open, where they were killed as fast as they appeared.

The battle was over. Of the nine hundred warriors who had manned the place five hundred and fifty-seven were killed outright and their bodies were found where they had fallen. There do not seem to have been any wounded to speak of, at least the writers make no mention of them. It is estimated that over two hundred were shot or drowned in attempting to cross the river and probably nearly all of the few who succeeded in getting over perished in the surrounding woods, through which the American soldiers ranged for some time, taking pot shots at every Indian they saw. The fighting force of the tribe was blotted out then and forever. There was no more Creek war, for there were no more Creeks.

The Americans had paid a high price for their victory, however, for the killed and wounded numbered over two hundred. Among the most seriously wounded was young Sam Houston, who had so distinguished himself on that day. When he was brought back to camp the surgeons, deeming his wounds mortal, paid little attention to him, devoting themselves to those whom they thought they had a chance of saving. He lay all night on the ground with little or no care. They did extract one bullet, but made no attempt to probe for the other.

In the morning, finding him still alive to their great surprise, they put him on a rude litter, improvised out of trees and branches, and carried him seventy miles to Fort Williams. He survived this journey, and the fact that he had done so gave the surgeons an idea that probably he might be worth looking after. He was attended at Fort Williams with such rude surgery as the frontier afforded and after some time removed to another post.

Two months after the battle he reached his home in west Tennessee, after a journey of several hundred miles in a horse litter! He was so emaciated by his terrible hardships, his face was so changed from the effects of his unhealed wounds—and they remained unhealed to the end of his life, by the way—that his own mother did not recognize him. But, as we shall see, he lived to take part in another more important and more famous battle, two decades later, in which he was the commander instead of a subaltern.

3

When the Seminoles Fought for Freedom

1. THE INJUSTICE OF THE UNITED STATES

To put all the Indian wars in which the United States has engaged
under one censure, or to include them in one category, is unscientific,
because it takes no account of the facts. Some of the wars were as
justifiable as any which have ever been waged by our people. Some
of them were brought upon the Indians by their own deliberate actions. For the war of the Apaches under Geronimo upon the United
States no defence of the Indians whatever can be urged. Nor is there
much to be said, to use an older instance, in behalf of the Creeks, who
commenced their famous war by the Battle of Burnt Corn and the
Massacre at Fort Mims.

On the other hand, there is no justification for the United States
for—to cite a modern illustration—the Nez Perces war, and there is
but little for that in which the following incidents occurred.

The Seminoles of Florida and southern Georgia were among the
ablest and bravest Indians on the continent. The name means "runaway," and they were mainly of the famous Creek stock which had furnished many instances of capacity and courage. They were leavened by
the remnant of the ancient aborigines of Florida who had escaped the
inevitable extermination attendant upon Spanish occupation. They
were a small tribe, probably never able to put more than two or three
thousand warriors in the field.

Their country was to the southern states after the war of 1812 just
what Oklahoma and the Indian Territory were to the western states
a few years since. Nominally under the government of Spain, which

146

pretended to do little and could do less in keeping order, their country was the refuge of every outlaw and vagabond who wanted to escape from the law and justice; and especially was it a convenient asylum for the fugitive slave.

The negroes by no means gained their freedom among the Seminoles, but they enjoyed a quasi-liberty which made their condition much more tolerable than that of complete servitude. And when to this state of affairs were added facilities for wild and savage life, to which their natural inclination directed them, it is not strange that many of them embraced the opportunity for change, and crossed the line as they had or could make a chance.

There was constant friction back and forth between parties of slave-catchers, officers of the law, and the Indians. When the territory was ceded to the United States in 1821, after Jackson's vigorous foray, conditions became even more intolerable. Whatever may be said of the rights and wrongs of the situation, never in the history of the world has it been, and I presume never will it be, that a vast body of fertile and arable land suitable for settlement could be withheld from a people who were willing to go in and cultivate it, in the interests of those who simply wished to retain it as a game preserve, and who were unable or unwilling to use it themselves. A rude tribal government will not be permitted to exist in contravention to a civilized administration. The weak have always had to go to the wall; whether they always will is a question. But there are ways and ways, and the United States chose a bad way and paid for it.

It was proposed to remove the Seminoles beyond the Mississippi, the government paying them a small sum for the lands thus opened for white settlement, promising them an annuity for a short time, and further agreeing to assume the expenses of transportation. After much persuasion the Seminoles, who had already been crowded down into what is now Florida, at last agreed to go, at least a portion of them did; but to make a long story short, when the time came for signing the treaty and starting the exodus, only a few of them were willing to leave.

Now the land by ancient usage and long occupation, belonged to the Seminoles. The United States had no vested right to take it from them or to force them to leave against their will, yet that is what the United States proceeded to do. Matters came to a crisis in November, 1836, when Charlie Amathla, a chief who had sold his lands and received his stipend, agreeing to go, was shot by a party under the leadership of Micanopy and Osceola.

Micanopy was the head chief of the Seminoles. Osceola was a half-breed, the son of an Englishman named Powell. He had been reared with the tribe, however, and was to all intents and purposes an Indian. He was the most implacable and persistent, as well as the ablest, antagonist of the United States among the Seminoles, and his talents for war, his administrative and executive ability, speedily raised him to a position of the first importance. He had many noble qualities and for an Indian he stands upon a very high plane, although he was not altogether the magnanimous hero which popular imagination depicts him.

For instance, when they found the American gold which Amathla had received for his lands upon his person after they had murdered him, Osceola would not permit his band to appropriate any portion of it, but threw it away, saying that it was blood-money and that its possession would invite disaster!

One dramatic incident in his career has often been repeated. When he was asked with other chiefs to sign a treaty agreeing to the translation of the tribe beyond the Mississippi, he walked to the table, drew a knife and drove it through the parchment by a blow of his powerful arm, remarking grimly that thus and thus only would he sign the treaty.

The United States, being fully determined to remove the Seminoles willy-nilly, Osceola promptly began hostilities. Before they got through with him and his the country paid a price for Florida which staggered humanity—humanity being more easily staggered in those days than now. The war was protracted by these two or three thousand Seminole warriors through seven years. It cost the United States twenty million dollars and the lives of fifteen hundred regular soldiers and certainly more than as many of the settlers and volunteers.

Reputations were made and lost—the latter, mainly—by successive commanders, and Osceola was finally captured by an act of the blackest treachery. This was nothing less than a flagrant violation of a safe conduct and a flag of truce, by General Jessup, of the U. S. Army, who had invited a conference with the chiefs, promising them absolute liberty to go as they had come, and who seized Osceola forcibly, when he trusted his person to American honour. The dauntless chief was thrown into prison and died at Fort Moultrie of grief and despair, after a short captivity.

In the end, of course, the Seminoles were defeated. The bulk of those who were left were sent beyond the Mississippi and a few who were harmless were allowed to remain in Florida. The country was at last open to settlement.

The Indians were able to protract the contest for seven years, first, on account of their splendid qualities as irregular fighters, and second, by the almost inaccessible character of the Everglades to which they repaired. They were not beaten until the warriors were practically exterminated. In many respects their superb fighting reminds us of that of the Boers in South Africa. Their magnificent valour and their desperate determination, the capacity of their chiefs, and the consecration of their warriors, sustained them to the end. Right was made only by might, in this instance.

2. THE MASSACRE OF DADE AND HIS MEN

The most terrible happening during the war was the occurrence which practically began it, and which is known as "The Dade Massacre." The word "massacre "is a very easy one to bruit about, but how a body of troops who are surprised by an enemy in war time and who fight without asking quarter, until they are all killed, can be said to be massacred, in an invidious sense, is an open question. However, to the story.

In the fall of 1836, there were some five hundred United States regular troops in Florida, ten companies in all; one company at St. Augustine, six at Fort King in the centre of the state, nearest the scene of hostilities, and three at Fort Brooke on Hillsboro Bay, near what is now known as Tampa. Two companies were ordered from Fort Brooke on the 16th of December, to meet a force from Fort King near the forks of the Withlacoochee River, or Ouithlacoochee, as it used to be spelled, in order to undertake a punitive expedition.

To have taken one hundred men away from Fort Brooke would have left it practically defenceless. The commander, therefore, did not obey the order of General Clinch, the commander-in-chief in Florida, until a re-enforcement of forty men under the command of Major Francis L. Dade reached him from Key West. Dade was a captain and brevet major in the Fourth Infantry, the same regiment which had, under Boyd, fought so gallantly at Tippecanoe twenty-five years before.

Immediately on his arrival the expeditionary force was made up. Drafts from Dade's Fourth Infantry men were made to complete two full companies of fifty men each of the Second Artillery and the Third

Infantry, commanded by Captains Gardiner and Frazer respectively, with Lieutenants Bassinger, Henderson, Mudge and Keais, and Assistant Surgeon Gatlin. as their subordinates. Captain Gardiner was to command the expedition, but on the morning of the start Major Dade discovered that Captain Gardiner's wife was seriously ill and he therefore volunteered to lead the party so that Captain Gardiner could remain at the post to care for his wife.

The offer was accepted by the grateful captain and the party, comprising one hundred and nine effectives and a Spanish negro guide, set out, carrying ten days' provisions and accompanied by one six-pounder drawn by four oxen and one light horse wagon. The departure was taken at 6 a.m. on the 24th inst.

A short time after they left the post Captain Gardiner learned that a comfortable transport was to sail immediately for Key West, and as members of his wife's family and other friends were stationed there at the time, it was decided that it would be advisable to send Mrs. Gardiner thither on the transport. Accordingly they placed her aboard the ship, and her husband bade her farewell, galloped after the detachment, which had been delayed by the breaking down of the ox train, and succeeded in reaching it that evening, raising the muster to one hundred and ten officers and men. It was a pity Gardiner had not gone with his poor wife.

Dade had halted his advance, sent back for horses to draw the cannon, and when they were provided marched on. The troops progressed slowly toward the designated rendezvous. It took them four days to make sixty-five miles. They were under Indian surveillance from the start. It was afterward learned that their guide was a traitor who had betrayed the route, and the Seminoles had resolved to intercept them. The usual precautions were observed, however, on the march and the camps were made carefully and thoroughly protected by sentries.

They were not molested, though conscious of observation, until the 28th of December. They had crossed the fork of the Withlacoochee and were marching along the trail which served as a road. The ground was an open barren. On one side, however, there was a small pond surrounded by a stretch of swamp overgrown with grass five feet high and interspersed with scrubby *palmettos*. On the left side of the road the ground, save for the pine trees, was open and unencumbered.

Here the Indians had chosen to attack. They wished and expected to annihilate the detachment, and they selected a place which offered the Americans no concealment, so that none of them could get away.

At eight o'clock in the morning the advance came slowly trailing up the road.

Osceola had intended to direct the attack in person, but he was busy the day before, killing General Thompson, the Indian agent, his aides and the other settlers, and did not reach the scene of the battle until long after it was over. The Indians, however, were ably led by Micanopy. Some two hundred of them lay hidden in the tall grass overlooking the road which passed close to them. They had received strict orders from their chief not to fire on any account until he gave the signal, which would be the discharge of his own piece.

There do not seem to have been any flankers thrown out on this occasion. The place was the most unlikely one for an ambuscade that could have been conceived. There were numberless spots on the march where they might have been assaulted, narrow defiles, thick woods enclosed by impassable morasses, but here the country on one side was open and on the other the grass would have afforded cover to no force but an Indian one.

In high spirits the troops marched along. Captain Frazer and Lieutenant Mudge led the advance, which seems to have been strung out in a long line. After them came Major Dade with the main body with the six-pounder and the wagons in the midst. With cool and terrible patience Micanopy waited until the whole line was under the guns of his troops. Taking careful and deliberate aim at Dade he shot him dead.

Instantly the grass was alive with smoke and fire. Over half of the American force was shot down at the first volley. Captain Frazer was instantly killed and Lieutenant Mudge was mortally wounded. Lieutenant Henderson had his left arm broken, and Lieutenant Keais both arms broken. Captain Gardiner, Lieutenant Bassinger and Dr. Gatlin were the only officers unhurt.

The suddenness of this appalling attack with the terrible losses consequent upon it, to the credit of the soldiers, be it said, in no wise disorganized them. There was no panic, the men abandoned the road instantly and took to the trees which abounded, in true Indian fashion, and poured a heavy fire upon the Seminoles. For some forty minutes the battle raged furiously, the Americans husbanding their fire and not delivering it until they caught sight of an enemy, when the Indians actually withdrew.

Hastily collecting the wounded who could be moved Captain Gardiner, who seems to have acted with great courage, moved back

151

a short distance, bringing with him the six-pounder, which had been rapidly served by Lieutenant Bassinger. He had between forty or fifty men able to continue the battle. Instantly they set to work to fell trees to make a breastwork which he drew out in the form of a triangle.

They all worked with fervent desperation but did not succeed in raising the breastwork more than three small tree trunks high when the Indians appeared once more. They had been re-enforced and returned to the attack. The battle recommenced with fury. The other side of the road where the grass was thickest was a little higher than the place where the troops had attempted to make the breastwork in their haste, which, unfortunately, was in a slight depression. The Indians who surrounded the little fort on all sides easily commanded it with their fire.

Lieutenant Henderson, in spite of his broken arm, continued to load and fire his musket until he was shot down. Lieutenant Keais lay in the breastwork, leaning his head against a log, helpless with his broken arms slung by a handkerchief, until he was shot again and killed. Dr. Gatlin, who had two double-barrelled shotguns which he used effectively, was finally killed by a bullet in the head. Captain Gardiner was mortally wounded and fell, crying, "I can give you no more orders, lads. Do your best!"

Lieutenant Bassinger, who had fought his piece of artillery which was exposed on the outside of the fort until every man detailed to it had been killed, and himself seriously wounded, crawled into the fort thereafter and continued the battle until every man had been killed or wounded. When the Indians perceived that the fort was silent, about two o'clock in the afternoon they ceased firing and swarmed into it.

They took many scalps but did not mutilate the bodies nor even rob them, except to take the officers' coats. Almost immediately they left the scene of action. The reason for their sudden departure was that they expected General Clinch's men, the troops from Fort King, which they must prepare to meet at once.

3. AFTER THE BATTLE

After they left the battlefield, however, a party of some fifty negroes appeared who began to kill and plunder the bodies. Lieutenant Bassinger, the only officer left alive, had, with some of the others, lain perfectly quiet while the Indians were in the fort, feigning death. When he perceived the intent of the negroes he struggled to his knees and begged for his life and the lives of his men. With brutal wicked-

"I CAN GIVE YOU NO MORE ORDERS, LADS. DO YOUR BEST!"

ness they cut him down with hatchets and mutilated his body in a fearful manner. They, too, were in a hurry, and three living private soldiers escaped their attention. Two others had managed to get away during the confusion of the fight, both severely wounded.

Ransom Clark, one of the living, had been wounded five times. His head had been struck by a bullet and he was covered with blood. One of the negroes had seized him to kill him, but another crying that the man was already dead as his head was blown open, the negro dropped him to the ground. He and the others had to lie perfectly still, not daring to give vent even to their anguish. Finally at evening one of the men left alive struggled to his feet and darted across the little breastwork. He was instantly shot dead by a lurking Indian.

Ransom Clark and a man named Cony, the remaining two, waited until dark and then started to return to Fort Brooke; Fort King was much nearer, but they did not know the way, and the Indians were between them and the troops. The progress of the two wounded men was attended by the most excruciating agony and was frightfully slow. They were so badly injured that they were compelled to crawl the greater portion of the way on their hands and knees.

The next morning a mounted Indian observed the two fugitives. As the only chance for life they divided. The Indian pursued Cony and shot him, but Ransom Clark, urged to impossible exertions by the desperation of his case escaped from him. After three days he had dragged himself, or crawled, over the sixty-five miles that intervened between the place of the fight and Fort Brooke. He and the other two men referred to were the only persons who escaped, and the other two died of their wounds shortly after reaching the fort, leaving Clark as the sole survivor.

Clark was in a pitiable condition when he reached Fort Brooke, but he survived his awful sufferings for several years, dying as the result of them in 1840. He had led an adventurous life indeed, and had more than once escaped from sudden death, the last occasion being a few years before when he was the only man saved from a boating party which had gone out from Fort Morgan for a sail and had been overtaken by a storm.

The story of that battle sent a thrill of horror throughout the country, and sealed the fate of the Seminoles. Those who had been inclined to show them pity, or to temporize, were now equally resolved with the others to wage war relentlessly until the end.

It was not until the following February—in the interval several battles having taken place—that an expedition reached the place where Dade and his command had been exterminated. The Inspector General thus reports what he found :

Western Department,
Fort King, Florida, Feb. 22, 1836.

General—Agreeably to your directions, I observed the battle ground six or seven miles north of the Withlacoochee River, where Major Dade and his command were destroyed by the Seminole Indians on the 28th of December, last, and have the honour to submit the following Report:

The force under your command, which arrived at this post today from Tampa Bay, encamped on the 19th instant, on the ground occupied by Major Dade on the night of the 27th of December. He and his party were destroyed on the morning of the 28th, about four miles in advance of that position. He was advancing towards this post, and was attacked from the north, so that on the 20th instant we came upon the rear of his battle ground, about nine o'clock in the morning. Our advance guard had passed the ground without halting, when the general and his staff came upon one of the most appalling scenes that can be imagined.

We first saw some broken and scattered bones; then a cart, the two oxen of which were lying dead, as if they had fallen asleep, their yokes still upon them; a little to the right, one or two horses were seen. We then came to a small enclosure, made by felling trees in such a manner as to form a triangular breastwork for defence. Within the triangle, along the north and west faces of it, were about thirty bodies, mostly mere skeletons, although much of the clothing was left upon them.

These were lying, every one of them, in precisely the same position they must have occupied during the fight; their heads next to the logs over which they had delivered their fire, and their bodies stretched with striking regularity parallel to each other. They had evidently been shot dead at their posts, and the Indians had not disturbed them, except by taking the scalps of most of them. Passing this little breastwork, we found other bodies along the road, and by the side of the road, generally behind trees, which had been resorted to for covers from the enemies' fire.

Advancing about two hundred yards farther, we found a cluster of bodies in the middle of the road. They were evidently the advanced guard, in the rear of which was the body of Major Dade, and to the right that of Captain Fraser.

These were doubtless all shot down by the first fire of the Indians, except, perhaps, Captain Fraser, who must however have fallen very early in the fight. Those in the road, and by the trees, fell during the first attack. It was during a cessation of the fire, that the little band still remaining, about thirty in number, threw up the triangular breast-work, which, from the haste with which it was constructed, was necessarily defective, and could not protect the men in the second attack.

We had with us many of the personal friends of the officers of Major Dade's command, and it is gratifying to be able to state, that every officer was identified by undoubted evidence. They were buried, and the cannon, a six-pounder, that the Indians had thrown into a swamp, was recovered and placed vertically at the head of the grave, where it is to be hoped it will long remain. The bodies of the non-commissioned officers and privates were buried in two graves and it was found that every man was accounted for. The command was composed of eight officers and one hundred and two non-commissioned officers and privates. The bodies of eight officers and ninety-eight men were interred, four men having escaped; three of whom reached Tampa Bay; the fourth was killed the day after the battle.

It may be proper to remark, that the attack was not made from a hummock, but in a thinly wooded country; the Indians being concealed by *palmetto* and grass, which has since been burned.

The two companies were Captain Fraser's of the 3rd Artillery, and Captain Gardiner's of the 2nd Artillery. The officers were Major Dade of the 4th Infantry, Captains Fraser and Gardiner, Second Lieut. Bassinger, Brevet Second Lieutenants R. Henderson, Mudge and Keais, of the Artillery, and Dr. J. S. Gatlin.

I have the honour to be, with the highest respect, your obedient servant,

E. A. Hitchcock,
Captain 1st Infantry, Act, In. General.

Major General E. P. Gaines,
Commanding Western Department, Fort King, Florida.

The bones of the officers and soldiers were afterward exhumed and reinterred at St. Augustine with appropriate ceremonies and a monument erected over them. There is also another monument to Dade at West Point, of which, by the way, he was not a graduate. It bears this significant inscription :

TO COMMEMORATE THE BATTLE
OF THE 28TH OF DECEMBER,
BETWEEN A DETACHMENT OF 108 U. S. TROOPS
AND THE SEMINOLE INDIANS, OF FLORIDA,
IN WHICH ALL THE DETACHMENT
SAVE THREE
FELL WITHOUT AN
ATTEMPT TO RETREAT.

In this connection, one phrase of Captain Hitchcock's report is worthy of note. The men had been shot at their posts! The bodies were found drawn up in the lines as they had fought. In the face of that appalling disaster, bereft of their officers, confronted by a sure and awful death, they had gallantly maintained the heroic traditions of the American Army, dying on the battle ground in their appointed stations. Honour to them!

1

George Rogers Clark and the Great North West

1. THE ORIGIN OF A GREAT IDEA

The first white man who penetrated the heart of the territory bounded by the Ohio, the great Lakes and the Mississippi, was that redoubtable explorer and heroic soul, Robert Cavelier, Sieur de la Salle. In 1669-70 he traversed what is now Indiana and explored the country along the beautiful Ohio as far as the Mississippi, claiming the whole vast region for France. For nearly one hundred years thereafter the white flag of that sunny land fluttered from the stales of small forts, which were erected from time to time at strategic points commanding the river highways, in accordance with the military genius of the French soldiery. These strategic points became centres of trade, agriculture, and commerce in the succeeding centuries.

In 1727 the Sieur de Vincennes established a military post on the Ouabache (Wabash), where the town of the same name now stands in southern Indiana. In 1735 a few families settled there, and their number was slowly augmented during the century. The fort, although nearer the province of Quebec, was in the territory of the district of Illinois, of the province of Louisiana. The headquarters of the district were at Kaskaskia, situated where the river of the same name empties into the Mississippi, and the capital of the province was New Orleans.

In 1736 the gallant commander and founder of Vincennes was killed, bravely fighting, by the English and Indians in a war against the Natchez, and the Chickasaws, when d'Artaguiette met with overwhelming defeat. Says Charlevoix, "Vincennes ceased not until his last breath to exhort the men to behave worthy of their religion and their country." D'Artaguiette and fifteen of his companions were captured and burned at the stake. Louis St. Ange de Bellerive was appointed to the governorship of the little Indiana town in 1736, and remained in charge until 1764; in this long tour of duty proving indeed a father to his people.

Perhaps nowhere on the continent has humanity dwelt in such peaceful simplicity as in the little settlement at Vincennes. Even the Indians lived in amicable relations with the colonists in the main. Cut off from intercourse with the rest of the world, it passed them by unheeding and unheeded, the fleeting years leaving the people unchanged. In hunting and fishing, in agriculture of the most primitive kind, with implements which might have been used two thousand years before; in trading down the river to New Orleans; in feasting, in frolic, with all the gayety of their French nationality, the uneventful days glided by.

Except at Kaskaskia there was not a school in the whole vast territory, although incredible as it may seem, there was a billiard table in the settlement on the Wabash! The little education the inhabitants received was imparted by the faithful and devoted missionaries who dwelt among them.

In 1763, on the completion of the Seven Years' War, the whole country from the Great Lakes to the Gulf of Mexico on the hither side of the Mississippi fell into the hands of England by treaty, although, owing to the fearful outbreak of savage passion, engendered and stimulated by Pontiac, except Tecumseh the ablest Indian who ever lived, the English were not able to take immediate possession of it. Kaskaskia and Fort Chartres, the principal military post, were turned over to them in 1765, and the post at Vincennes sometime later. On the western side of the river France ceded her claims to the territory to Spain.

The conquest made little difference to the inhabitants. They had not been greatly concerned in the war which had resulted in the transfer of their allegiance and they were not greatly concerned with another more important event which happened later on. They lived on just as they had done before—perhaps a little less cheerfully, a little less happily, under the Union Jack than under the *Fleur-de-lis*, but there was not much difference.

Meanwhile all of the vast territory west of the Allegheny Mountains which had hitherto proved a barrier to the settlements having their origin on the seaboard, was attracting the attention of such bold, adventurous spirits as Boone, Robertson, and Sevier. Among other empire builders who surveyed it with eager, if not prophetic vision, was George Rogers Clark.

Like many of the pioneers he was a native of the great state of Virginia, where he was born on the 19th of November, 1752. The west was settled by men from the south of Mason and Dixon's line, except in the case of Pennsylvania. Without belonging to the landed gentry, the Clark family was respectable, and he himself received such education as the western part of the Old Dominion afforded. Like George Washington and many young men of the day, he became a surveyor, in which vocation he displayed great proficiency. But at best his acquirements were limited. His spelling was simply awful, although his diction and his chirography were somewhat better. However, spelling was thought somewhat lightly of by many gentlemen who had enjoyed more advantages than this young Virginian.

He was a strongly built, heavy set man, with broad brow and keen blue eyes, with a dash of red in his hair from a Scottish ancestress, which corresponded with the fighting qualities of the man. He was a young man of sufficient consideration in the community to receive a commission as captain in Lord Dunmore's war, a school which graduated many officers into the more serious conflict which followed hard upon it. Clark was one of Dunmore's staff, apparently, and therefore did not participate in the famous battle of Point Pleasant on the Kanawha. After the war he went to Kentucky, which he had before visited on a surveying expedition. Subsequently he became one of the most prominent of the pioneers in that famous territory.

The Revolution found the Clark family intense and zealous patriots. The two oldest brothers immediately enlisted in the Continental line and served with credit—the elder one with distinction—during the whole of the war. George Rogers, the third, was not less ardent in his patriotism than the other two, and he displayed his qualities on a more splendid field. The remaining brother, too young for the Revolution, showed his qualities in the famous Lewis and Clark expedition across the continent in 1804-6.

When the war began, the Indians, stimulated thereto by the British, inaugurated a series of ruthless forays, not only into the "dark and bloody ground" of Kentucky, but everywhere on the borders. The few frontier settlements in Kentucky, with which we are at present concerned, were at once put on the defensive and forced to fight for their lives. With the forethought of state builders, desirous of organizing a civil government of some sort in the trans-Allegheny region, and of representing their defenceless condition to Virginia, which they rightly considered their mother territory, they called a convention at Clark's instance, at Harrodsburg in 1775. He was delayed in reaching the convention when it opened, and found, when he did arrive, that he and one other had been elected to the Virginia legislature from Kentucky, which at that time had no legal existence and therefore no right to send delegates to the assembly. However, he made the long arduous journey across the mountains to Williamsburg only to learn that the legislature had adjourned before his arrival.

He and his companion at once made representations to the Governor, the redoubtable Patrick Henry, concerning the situation beyond the Mississippi, asking for five hundred pounds of powder to defend themselves against the savages, and suggesting also that some steps be taken for the establishment of civil government in this wild and lawless expanse of territory. There was in existence at the time a Transylvania Company, so called, of which Colonels Henderson and Campbell were chief promoters, which claimed the right of eminent domain over Kentucky, and the Virginia government felt some hesitation about assuming any rights over this country.

The authorities were perfectly willing to lend five hundred pounds of powder to their neighbours in Kentucky on the guarantee of Clark himself, but Clark was shrewd enough not to fall into a trap of this kind. He rejected their proffer and wrote them a brilliant letter in which he said that a country that was not worth defending was not worth claiming. This sharp intimation that he would endeavour to get help elsewhere brought the commissioners to terms. Clark got the powder. It was his first success. Not only did he get it after the order had been given—and the two things were not synonymous, then; it was hard to get powder in those revolutionary days, since it was in so great demand—but he actually succeeded in getting it safely into the hands of the people. This in spite of savage attacks and perils of a journey well-nigh unsurmountable. He also succeeded, through his representations, in having Kentucky formed into a county of Virginia, and brought under the operation of the civil law of that state, a service of inestimable value.

Meanwhile the British, in pursuance of their well-devised plan, continued to launch the savages on the backs of the Americans in the fond hope that they would thus be enabled to work their will with the harassed revolutionists on the seaboard. Major Stuart and chiefs

McGillivray and Oconostota raised the Creeks and Cherokees on one hand, while Lieutenant-Governor William Hamilton, of Detroit, who seems to have been one of the chief villains in the plot, incited the Indians in the northwest to the war-path with great success. Campbell, Shelby, Sevier and Robertson held them in check to the southwest; God raised up another leader to cover the frontier to the northward.

It was hard living in Kentucky in those days, and the one man there who saw something else to do than fight recklessly and desperately when the savages came, the one man who divined how these forays might be stopped and who realized that in the stopping of them great benefits would accrue not merely to Kentucky, but to the United Colonies as well, was George Rogers Clark.

He realized that the old French posts of Detroit, Kaskaskia, and Vincennes were the points from which the Indians secured the necessary supplies to carry on the war, as well as the stimulation which enabled them to sweep the borders. Securing information concerning their strength and weakness from two spies whom he sent out, he conceived the magnificent design of capturing these points, holding them, and thus establishing for the United States a claim to the great territory of the northwest.

Neither he nor anyone else dreamed for a moment of the great, populous and wealthy states which were enshrined potentially within that wilderness. No one could imagine that upon the barren shore of one of the lonely lakes tossing its fresh waters in the sunlight should presently rise the second city of the Union and one of the great cities of the world. How could he, or any one, anticipate the future growth of the struggling colonies? The boldest imagination could not comprehend the possibility, much less the realization, of that great deluge of men, which, starting from the shores lapped by the ocean-tide, should break over the mountain-crest hitherto considered a natural boundary, and flood the wilderness until it reached the banks of the faraway Mississippi. And as for the empire beyond it over which the same tide rolls and still sweeps on, that was beyond the most extravagant dream, even. Yet with instinctive prophetic vision something of this Titanic conception of national destiny seems to have come to this young man.

2. The First Success

In 1777 he went back to Virginia and laid his daring project before Patrick Henry. The stupendousness of the idea impressed the sagacious old governor; he caused a council to be called to consider the suggestion of the borderer, a council composed of himself, Thomas Jefferson, George Mason, and George Wythe. To these men, Clark, not much more than a boy, just twenty-five years old in fact, expounded his plan. They realized at once what there was in it. Not merely the protection of the settlements south of the Ohio in Kentucky, not merely a check to Indian aggression, but the extension of the borders of the United States to the Mississippi, the control of that vast territory between the mountains and the river. Room to grow, room to grow for thousands of years, they may have thought, instead of barely for a century. At any rate they approved the plan.

Few more momentous councils have ever been held, although even now it is scarcely noticed in history. Clark was naturally selected to lead the expedition. He was given twelve hundred pounds in depreciated Virginia currency, a commission as a colonel, an order for ammunition at Fort Pitt, and authority to raise seven hundred and fifty men for three months' service where he could. Then they sent him out with their blessing and their goodwill. Such were the inadequate means provided for this gigantic achievement.

The plan was kept strictly secret by Clark and the four men who had determined upon it. His public instructions from Patrick Henry ordered him to proceed to Kentucky and take measures for the defence of the colonists with such troops as he could enlist. A private letter, however, authorized him to take and hold Kaskaskia, Vincennes, and the whole northwest territory.

Many difficulties beset the enlistment of his soldiers, but he finally succeeded in assembling several hundred men on Corn Island, at the Falls of the Ohio, opposite where is now the great city of Louisville. The thickly wooded island has since been stripped of its trees, and washed away by the rapid current. Many of his troops deserted from time to time, especially when they learned the real purpose for which they had been embodied, and he found himself left at last with about one hundred and fifty men; and the time was approaching for them to start upon their projected expedition.

He had chosen to camp upon this island because, on account of its isolation by the rapid falls, he could prevent further desertion. It was a good place, too, in which to drill and train the men in accordance with his limited experience. What he lacked in military training and technical knowledge he made up in zeal and innate capacity to command, and he soon got his little army under excellent control.

163

A number of families which had followed him down the river settled on the island around a blockhouse which he built for their protection. Then he set forth to accomplish his comprehensive purpose. He left his camp on the island on the 24th of June, 1778, and embarked his men, divided into four companies, in *bateaux*, rowing back up the river until he could gain the channel through the rapids, much more dangerous then than now, through which they made an exciting passage.

The departure of the expedition was dramatic in the extreme. As the boats were whirled down the mighty river by the swift current, though it was early in the morning, the land was enshrouded in almost total darkness from an eclipse of the sun; a bad omen thought some of the party, but Clark was no believer in omens. For four days they swung down the river, reaching at last an abandoned French post called Fort Massac. It had been built by the garrison of Fort Du-Quesne fleeing from the advance of Forbes in 1759.[1]

There they were met by a party of hunters who had recently come from Kaskaskia, the capital and principal town of the province. They reported it to be lightly garrisoned and negligently guarded. Learning of the destination of the expedition, they asked Clark's permission to join his party, for which one of them offered to act as guide. The offer was gladly accepted, and although the guide temporarily lost his way and was in imminent danger of death at the hands of the indignant and suspicious Americans, he proved his loyalty and gave them good service in the end. For six days the party marched westward over the prairie. They had no wagons or pack-horses, and no baggage except what each man carried himself, consequently their progress was unusually rapid.

On the evening of the 4th of July they reached the east bank of the Kaskaskia River, opposite the town, undiscovered. Marching up the bank in the night they found a farmhouse. They put the inmates under guard, seized the boats belonging to them, crossed the river, and marched down toward the town. The commander of the place was M. de Rocheblave, a Frenchman. The garrison was made up of Creole militia. De Rocheblave had implored to have British regular troops sent him, but none had appeared. It was not thought possible that the post would be attacked by the Americans, and the King had use for his soldiers elsewhere. On that evening no one dreamed that

---

1. See my book *Colonial Fights and Fighters*. The Struggle for the Valley of the Ohiom, (also published by Leonaur.).

"CLARK, WITH TRAGIC INTENSITY, BADE THEM GO ON WITH THE DANCE."

the Kentucky pioneers were at hand.

One dramatic account of the capture of the place says that Clark surrounded the town, disposing the greater portion of his troops so that none could escape from it, and with the rest marched silently toward the fort. The story goes that the officers were enjoying a dance at the time in one of the large rooms, and that Clark, admitted to the fort through the postern by one of his prisoners, left his men outside the barracks and then walked boldly into the room. No one happening to notice his entrance he stood quietly by the door, with an inborn love of the dramatic, folding his arms and looking grimly upon the scene of gayety.

Presently an Indian caught sight of him and recognized an enemy, perhaps because of the buff and blue he wore, and rent the air with a terrific war-whoop. The women shrieked, the music stopped, and Clark, with tragic intensity, bade them go on with the dance, but to remember that now they were to dance in honour of Virginia and of the United States, instead of Great Britain! I take it that they were in no humour for further merriment. Whether the story be true or no, and some good authorities give it credence, the fact remains that the fort was surprised and captured without the loss of a man on either side.

Clark was most anxious to get hold of the papers of the commander. One naive historian says that Madame de Rocheblave succeeded in concealing them in her bedchamber, and that rather than violate the sanctity of her apartment and thus affront her modesty, the American officers suffered her to do what she would with them.

"Better," writes the gallant old chronicler, "better, yes, a thousand times better, were it so than that the ancient fame of the sons of Virginia should have been tarnished by insult to a female."

It is a pity to spoil a pretty story, but the papers, at least an important portion of them, were forthcoming, however they were secured. The British relations with the savages were revealed in them; the English guilt was clear.

By this time the inhabitants of the town were in a great state of terror, and Clark purposely fostered it. He ordered them to repair to their houses and stay there under pain of death, and they passed a night of anguished foreboding. In the morning, permission being given, they came to him begging him to spare the lives of their wives and children, offering themselves as slaves in that contingency, to the American chief of the "Big Knives," as they called the Kentuckians.

What was their joy and relief when Clark proclaimed that their lives would be spared, their property respected, and that all should en- joy freedom. While they were enthusiastic with this news, he invited their allegiance to the American cause, which it was not difficult to secure, in view of the great tidings which he brought them of the capture of Burgoyne and the American alliance with France.

Thereafter the French and Americans were indeed brethren. Their mourning was turned into joy and they made haste to hoist the stars and stripes which, for the first time, July 5th, 1778, floated near the waters of the Mississippi. Cahokia received the Americans in the same ardent way, and the conquest of the northwest, so far as they were concerned, was complete. In October, 1778, Virginia inaugurated the first civil government in the northwest by establishing the County of Illinois, comprehending all the new territory beyond the Ohio, with Colonel John Todd as Governor, and Clark as supreme and independent military commander.

There yet remained of the British posts to be dealt with, Vincennes and Detroit, before the conquest of the country could be called complete, the former being of more present importance because nearer. Among the inhabitants of Kaskaskia was a certain Roman priest named Father Gibault, whom Clark, with finer regard for euphony than spelling, referred to in his letters as "Mr. Jeboth." This devoted French missionary agreed to go to Vincennes, which was at that time without a garrison, to secure the allegiance of the populace to the new government and new flag. He faithfully fulfilled his commission, and the French residents willingly assented to the change of government, and hoisted the American flag over the fort, which they subsequently delivered to Captain Leonard Helm, who was appointed commandant and Indian agent at the post by Clark.

Meanwhile Clark administered the military affairs of the province of Illinois with great vigour, by his resolution and tact compelling the Indians to bury the hatchet and make peace, which obtained for a considerable period. For the first time in years Kentucky and the borders of Virginia were comparatively free from war-parties. The settlers could lay aside the rifle and ply the axe and speed the plough in safety.

Clark's methods of dealing with the Indians were always fine. He knew that kindness and gentleness would be taken by them as indications of weakness. Therefore he was boldness itself toward them. Years afterward, while making a treaty with several hostile tribes, he over-

awed them and compelled them to make peace in the following way:
Some three hundred hostile Indians in full war-paint met him in council at Fort Washington. Clark had seventy men in the stockade. The Shawnees were arrogant, boastful and full of fight. They came into the council-house with a war-belt and a peace-belt. Throwing them both on the table they told Clark to take his choice. He swept them both to the floor with his cane, rose to his feet, stamped contemptuously upon them, and sternly telling the Indians to make peace instantly or he would wipe them off the face of the earth, ordered them to leave the hall. They fled his presence, debated all night, swallowed the insult, and buried the hatchet.

3. "THE HAIR-BUYER GENERAL"

There lived at Detroit at this time a certain British officer named William Hamilton, who occupied the important position of Lieutenant-Governor of the province. History has written severe indictments against this man. There are still in existence letters in which his employment of Indians to carry on "civilized" warfare is proved beyond doubt. He is accused of having offered rewards for American scalps and of having paid them, and the facts are indisputable. Early in 1778, he wrote to Carleton, governor of Quebec, that a party of Indians had just come into Detroit with seventy-three prisoners and one hundred and twenty-nine scalps! On the 16th of September in the same year, he wrote to Haldimand, who had superseded Carleton, that another party had arrived bringing twenty-nine prisoners and eighty-nine scalps. Among these scalps were many that had been wrenched from the heads of women and children!

This subornation of savagery is the most dastardly action by which a brave soldier can ruin his reputation. To employ ruthless Indians to prey upon women and children and defenceless non-combatants is the act of a villain and a coward. There is this to be said in explanation, though not in justification, of Hamilton's action, that he acted under orders of his government, upon which the odium primarily rests; but orders or not, no man should ever commit such a crime. Rather should he surrender his commission. No, Hamilton's course is indefensible. The blood of innocent women and children is upon him.

When Hamilton heard, as he did presently, of Clark at Kaskaskia, and that he had raised the American flag at Vincennes, he determined to march down the Wabash from Detroit, retake Vincennes and then proceed westward and capture Clark. With a motley force of Indians together with thirty British regulars, and fifty Canadian volunteers from Detroit, he appeared before Fort Sackville, Vincennes, on December 17th, 1778. The French militia of the garrison at once fled to their homes and left the defence of the fort to the redoubtable Helm and one valiant soldier named Moses Henry.

Helm, of course, could make no defence of the dilapidated stockade, but he had partaken in large measure of the spirit of Clark He resolved to bluff. Clark was the greatest bluffer in the history of the northwest. He was always willing to make good so far as he could, but generally he had so little force that he accomplished his ends by his assurance. Helm was like him. He charged the one serviceable cannon he possessed to the muzzle, ran it out at the gate of the post, placed his solitary soldier by it with a blazing match, and swore to Hamilton, who had demanded his surrender, that no man should enter the fort until he knew what terms would be granted him.

Inspired by his dauntless bearing, and ignorant of the force with which he might have to contend, and with the added argument of a loaded cannon trained upon his troops, Hamilton agreed that the garrison should march out with the honours of war, if they would surrender. Withdrawing the match. Helm and Moses marched out solemnly between the disgusted British and Indians, and Hamilton got the fort. He retained Helm as prisoner, but the genial qualities of the jovial American won the affections of his captors, and his imprisonment was a light one.

A more vigorous commander than Hamilton would have immediately pushed on to Kaskaskia and completed the conquest of the country by capturing Clark, but Hamilton, satisfied with his expedition so far, and deterred by the wretched weather, the lateness of the season, the difficulties of the way, concluded to wait until the springtime.

He did detach a party of Indians and rangers to attempt to abduct the American commander, if they could find him, but beyond alarming the inhabitants of Kaskaskia they effected nothing. Clark was soon apprised by his scouts of the capture of Vincennes. This was a serious blow to the project he had formed. How to meet it was a question. He was not yet informed of Hamilton's further intentions, nor was he in possession of accurate information as to the force of the garrison which the British held at the post.

To him, in his uncertainty, in the latter part of January, 1779, came one Francis Vigo. Vigo was a Sardinian, born at Mondovi, before the middle of the seventeenth century. He had been an officer in the Spanish army, and in that capacity had come to America. He had resigned his command and entered upon the business of a trader, hunter, etc., with headquarters at St. Louis, where he had amassed a large fortune. He was a man of liberal and enlightened views, and had extended a hearty hospitality to Clark when he arrived in that country. He had done more than that. He had accepted the depreciated Virginia currency at par, and by giving it his countenance, had made it pass current among the natives. He had cashed Clark's drafts for large sums, and in fact it is difficult to see how the expedition could have succeeded without him.

He had gone on a trading expedition to Vincennes, where he had been captured and brought before Hamilton. Hamilton had no authority to hold a Spanish subject, and he had released him on parole, requiring him to report daily at the fort. The inhabitants of Vincennes, with whom Vigo was a great favourite, protested so vigorously against his detention, going to the length of refusing to supply the fort with provisions unless he were immediately released, that at last their efforts prevailed to secure his freedom. He had refused to be enlarged on condition of his doing nothing to prejudice British interests during the war, and Hamilton was forced to let him go on his promising to do nothing to hinder the cause of British arms on his way to St. Louis.

Vigo strictly kept his agreement. He passed the mouth of the Kaskaskia without stopping, and repaired to his home in St, Louis. Having now kept his promise to the letter, he took horse and made his way with all speed to Kaskaskia, where he arrived on the 29th of January, 1779. There he acquainted Clark with the state of affairs in Vincennes. Hamilton had dismissed all his Indian allies for the winter, and held the fort with eighty white troops. It was his purpose, however, so Vigo in- formed Clark, to assemble them all in the spring-time, and with heavy re-enforcements from Detroit, march to the Illinois country. In that case there would be little hope of a successful resistance.

What was to be done? It was midwinter. Could the Americans march to capture Vincennes then? To wait for spring and the British to come was to give up all. Clark at once determined upon an immediate attack. He "flung his gauntlet in the face of Fate and assumed the offensive." He would not wait for pleasant weather to bring Hamilton and his horde upon him, he would carry the war into Indiana at once. I do not suppose he had ever heard of Scipio Africanus, but his methods were those advocated by the famous Roman.

Fort Sackville had been thoroughly repaired and put into a complete state of defence by Hamilton, It was provided with artillery and manned by a garrison sufficient to hold it against any force which Clark could possibly assemble. Nevertheless the American determined upon its capture. The day that he received the news from Vigo was the real crucial moment of the expedition, and it is not too much to say that the history of the northwest territory turned upon his decision.

To anticipate the course of events a little, France and Spain in the negotiations for peace at the close of the war were only too anxious to limit the western boundary of the United States to the Alleghenies, a desire which England naturally shared. Spain bent all the resources of a diplomacy by no means insignificant to bring about this result. The one argument by which Franklin and his fellow-counsellors were able to insist that the western boundary should be the Mississippi and not the Alleghenies, was the fact that the country had been conquered by Clark, retained by him, and was now actually in the power of the United States. That conquest would not have been complete, however, and the retention impossible, if Hamilton had been left in possession of Vincennes. Therefore it was not only for his own safety, not only to hold Kaskaskia, but in order that he might establish a valid claim to the whole great territory that Clark determined upon action.

4. The Terrible March

He made his preparations with the same promptitude as he made his decision. A large *bateaux* which he called the *Willing* was hastily improvised, loaded with provisions and supplies, and provided with two pieces of artillery and four swivels. Captain Rogers, a kinsman of the general, was placed in command with forty men and ordered to make all haste *via* the Mississippi, the Ohio and the Wabash, to an appointed rendezvous near Vincennes.

Clark, with the balance of his officers and men and two companies of French Creoles, who volunteered to accompany him, commanded respectively by Captains McCarty and Charleville, made ready to march overland. Clark's original force had been reduced to one hundred men. By pleadings and promises he had induced that number to remain with him after their three months' term of enlistment had expired. These he took with him. The Creole additions raised the total force to one hundred and seventy, with a few pack-horses to carry the scanty supplies they could procure.

They set forth on the 4th of February, 1779, so rapid had been their preparations, upon one of the most memorable marches ever undertaken under the American flag. One hundred and forty miles as the crow flies, and some two hundred over the usual trail lay between him and his destination. The only undertaking in our history that can be compared to it is Arnold's march up the Kennebec to attack Quebec. The weather was cold, damp and rainy. The season had been a very wet one, and the prairies were turned into lakes and quagmires. They marched as rapidly as possible over the desolate, damp, wind-swept plains.

Every river and creek they passed was in full flood and presented serious obstacles, until, on the 15th of February, they came to the two forks of the little Wabash. Ordinarily there is a distance of three miles between the two channels. Now the whole country lay under water, icy cold at that, for five miles to the opposite hills. There were no roads, no boats. The provisions they had carried were nearly exhausted. The game had been driven away by the floods, and they were without food or fire.

Plunging into the icy water Clark led his men, carrying their rifles and powder-horns above their heads, over the bottoms until they reached the channel of the river. They had built a rude canoe and a small raft on the bank, and now standing up to their waists in water—in some places it was up to their necks—they removed the baggage from the pack-horses, ferried it across one channel, built a rude scaffold of drift-wood and logs upon which they stowed it; swam the horses over the second channel, loaded them again, drove them through the flood until they reached the other fork of the river, where they repeated the process, and at last got on emergent though water-soaked ground. The passage took two days, during which they had no opportunity to rest. No one had a dry thread upon him. Orders were given to fire no guns except in case of dire necessity, for fear of giving alarm to the enemy they hoped to surprise. Provisions were lower than ever.

The next day they marched along through the water, resting for the night upon a damp hill, and on the 17th they reached a river, well called the Embarrass, which flows into the Wabash a short distance below Vincennes. Here they found a more serious condition prevailing. Both rivers had overflowed, and as far as they could see was a waste of water. They sent out parties to look for the *Willing*, to find fords, to secure boats, anything. No success attended their efforts.

Meanwhile they set to work to make canoes. They were literally starving, having had no provisions of any sort for two days! That day they captured a canoe with some Frenchmen in it, who had been sent out of the fort to scout. These they detained as prisoners. The Frenchmen added to their discouragement by informing them that the whole country around Vincennes was overflowed, and it would be impossible for the Americans to reach the fort. Clark, however, pushed on down the bank of the Embarrass until he reached the Wabash.

At this juncture one of the men shot a deer, which was divided among the one hundred and seventy and furnished them with the first food they had had for over two days! It was a scanty allotment for so many starved, half-drowned men, but it put new heart into them, and they determined to press on. Indeed, that determination was never out of Clark's mind.

In the canoes they had made as best they could they crossed the Wabash on the 21st.

At this juncture the spirit of some of the Creoles gave out, and they wanted to return. The desire to retreat was communicated even to the Kentuckians, and the whole enterprise trembled in the balance. Clark, however, was equal to the occasion. The story goes that in one of the companies there was a big six-foot two-inch sergeant, from Virginia. A little drummer-boy, whose antics and frolics had greatly amused the men, was mounted on the shoulders of the tall sergeant. By Clark's command, the drummer beat the charge, while the sergeant marched into the water.

"Forward!" thundered the commander, plunging into the icy flood. The men laughed, hesitated, and followed to the last man. That night they rested on a hill, lying in their soaked clothes without provisions or fire.

For two more days they struggled on through the waters until on the 23rd they were fortunate enough to capture a canoe with some Indian squaws in it, in which they found a quarter of buffalo and some other provisions. Broth was soon made and given to the most exhausted of the little band. Some of the hardier men refused their portions and generously gave them to their weaker brethren.

At this time they had drawn near enough to Vincennes to hear Fort Sackville's morning and evening guns. They were so near, in fact, that they expected to attack that night.

When they began the final march in water varying in depth from breast to neck, Clark took another method for putting heart into any recalcitrants. He detached Captain Bowman, his best officer, with

173

twenty men, and told them to bring up the rear and to shoot the first man who faltered. No one did so. They struggled on throughout the morning in the most desperate of straits. The water was covered with a thin coating of ice, which they broke as they plunged in. They had managed to get together a number of canoes by this time, and into these they put the weaker men. They suffered horribly. Clark himself, in spite of his resolute will and magnificent strength, almost gave way. Finally about one o'clock they reached an elevation about two miles from the town. It was covered with trees, and from their shelter, themselves unseen, they could examine at their leisure the goal of their endeavours.

The terrific march of these iron men was over. For the last ten days they had been struggling through water and ice. They had enjoyed neither fire nor rest. Three or four scanty meals had served them during that awful period. They dried themselves as best they could in the cold sunshine, revelling in anticipations of the meal which they hoped they could get if they ever succeeded in capturing the place. Clark now hesitated; should he fall on the town at once, or should he first attempt to secure the neutrality of the people, which he believed he could do without difficulty? He wisely decided for the latter plan. By one of his French prisoners he despatched the following crafty letter:

To the Inhabitants of Post St. Vincents:

Gentlemen:—Being now within two miles of your village with my army, determined to take your fort this night, and not being willing to surprise you, I take this method to request such of you as are true citizens, and willing to enjoy the liberty I bring you, to remain still in your houses. And those, if any there be, that are friends to the King, will instantly repair to the fort and join the Hair-Buyer General [2] and fight like men. And if any such, as do not go to the fort shall be discovered afterwards, they may depend on severe punishment. On the contrary, those that are true friends to liberty, may depend on being well treated. And I once more request them to keep out of the streets; for everyone I find in arms on my arrival, I shall treat as an enemy.

G. R. Clark.

Hamilton and his officers had carried things with a high hand, and the inhabitants were rejoiced at the approach of the Americans. No-

---

2. Alluding to the fact that Gov. Hamilton had offered rewards for the scalps of Americans.

body appears to have betrayed them to the British commander, who was yet in total ignorance of their proximity. He had sent out Captain La Mothe to scout, and the party, surrounded by the floods, had not come back. Clark waited until nightfall, divided his army into three companies, in order to surround the post, and then marched forward to the attack.

5. The Capture of Vincennes

Fort Sackville was an irregular enclosure, the sides varying in length from sixty to two hundred feet, and enclosing some three acres of ground. The stockade was stoutly built of logs about eleven feet high. The garrison was ample, and there were several pieces of artillery and swivels mounted on the walls. It was strong enough to have bidden defiance to one hundred and seventy starved and half-drowned troops without artillery of any kind, but it did not.

It is to Clark's credit that he refused to allow the Piankeshaw Indians, who were there in large numbers, and who volunteered their services, to take part in the attack. Marching silently through the town Clark surrounded the fort, which stood on the bank of the river, the men taking cover behind houses and trees. He quickly threw up a slight breastwork in front of the gate of the stockade, and announced his presence by opening a smart rifle fire.

It is related that Captain Helm and Colonel Hamilton sat in the latter's headquarters playing cards while a bowl of apple toddy was brewing before the fire. Having learned from the French inhabitants which were Hamilton's headquarters, some of the Kentuckians, in sport, opened fire upon the chimney, surmising that that bowl of apple toddy would be brewing beneath it. As the rifles cracked, some of the plaster fell into the apple toddy as they had intended.

"That's Clark," said Helm, "but d—n him, he needn't have spoiled my toddy!"

The garrison were even yet so unsuspecting that they imagined that the firing was caused by some drunken Indians, and it was not until a sergeant was struck in the breast by a bullet and seriously wounded that they awakened to the situation. There was a beating of drums and a hurrying to arms, and through the night a smart fire was kept up between the contending parties, the British blazing away fruitlessly in every direction, the Americans, who were scantily provided with powder, husbanding their fire and endeavouring to make every shot tell. Nothing had yet been seen of the *Willing*, and the supply of powder on the American side was perilously low. Fortunately they procured enough from one of the friendly inhabitants to keep up the engagement. From the same friendly source they also got a good breakfast, which was as useful almost as the powder.

Learning from the inhabitants that Captain La Mothe's party was still at large, and being desirous of capturing the British force intact, Clark withdrew some of his men during the night, and left the way open for La Mothe to enter the fort, which he did, the Americans by their commander's orders withholding their fire. Clark was sure that he had them all then. When the morning came the surprised Hamilton found himself completely surrounded by the besiegers, of whose numbers he was entirely ignorant, although the fact that they were there at all was evidence of their quality. The firing was kept up with such effect by the rifles of the Kentuckians that it became impossible for the British to serve the guns. As soon as a port-hole was opened a stream of bullets was poured into it. The condition of the British was serious, so they thought at any rate.

Early in the morning Clark sent the following peremptory letter to Hamilton :

Sir.—In order to save yourself from the impending storm that now threatens you, I order you immediately to surrender yourself, with all your garrison, stores, etc., etc., etc. For if I am obliged to storm, you may depend on such treatment as is justly due to a murderer. Beware of destroying stores of any kind, or any papers, or letters, that are in your possession; for, by Heavens, if you do, there shall be no mercy shown you.

G. R. Clark.

To this he received the following reply :

Governor Hamilton begs leave to acquaint Colonel Clark that he and his garrison are not disposed to be awed into an action unworthy of British subjects.

Nevertheless by this time the British were badly scared, and after another interchange of shots Hamilton asked first for a truce of three days and then for a parley. Finally a meeting was appointed. Hamilton, attended by Major Hay, his second, and Captain Helm, his prisoner, met Clark. The American general was furious. He refused to listen to any proposed arrangements. It was surrender at discretion, or nothing at all. It was many long years after that day that a certain little man from Illinois made the world ring with the phrase "Unconditional Surrender," yet that was the purport and nearly the wording of Clark's terms.

He vowed he would put to death any Indian partisans in Hamilton's command, and when asked whom he meant, replied that Major Hay had been one of those who had led war-parties against the settlements. When Helm attempted to interfere and say a word in favour of the British, Clark sternly silenced him, telling him as a prisoner he had no right to discuss the matter. Hamilton promptly offered to release Helm, and Clark with equal promptness refused to accept him then. Hamilton begged hard for other conditions, but the inflexible American, regarding him also as a murderer as well as a coward, would grant no terms. Therefore Hamilton returned to the fort, having been given an hour to make up his mind.

A party of Indians friendly to the English, who had been on a scalp hunt, came back during the morning with the ghastly trophies of their prowess hanging at their belts; one scalp was that of a woman. Ignorant of the presence of the Americans, they ran right into their arms, and two were killed, two were wounded, and six captured. While the conference between Clark and Hamilton was going on, the six captured Indians were taken out before the fort, where the garrison could see them, summarily tomahawked, and their bodies cast into the river. Clark was not actually present when the savage and bloody reparation was taken, but it was by his orders, and he was responsible. Hamilton was unable to resist the clamour of the garrison after this sight and, upon Clark's final agreement to treat them as prisoners of war, he surrendered the fort at discretion.

The next morning the British marched out and delivered their arms to the Americans, who marched in and hoisted the stars and stripes for the second time in Indiana. The Americans fired a salute of thirteen guns from the British cannon. During the progress of the salute twenty cartridges for the six-pound guns blew up and wounded some of the Kentuckians. Among them was the brave Captain Bowman, who died several months after, it is believed, from injuries received in this disaster.

Save one wounded soldier these were the only casualties on the American side in the expedition. The loss in killed and wounded on the part of the British was also small. The *Willing* came up soon after, and Captain Bowman was sent forward with a party of soldiers to intercept a convoy of provisions and supplies from Detroit, which he did in a handsome manner, capturing everybody in the escort.

The campaign was ended. The English plans to repossess Indiana and Illinois failed in every direction; indeed, save for one abortive attempt, nothing further was done to dislodge the Americans. On the other hand, Clark could never assemble sufficient force to enable him to take Detroit, which was the sole position held by the British at the end of the war; with that exception the country remained in his possession.

6. FORGOTTEN!

Clark performed other services during the war; finding himself on one occasion in Virginia when Arnold invaded it, he joined Von Steuben as a volunteer, and fought gallantly under him. Virginia promoted him to be a brigadier-general, and presented him with a sword, which, by the way, owing to the straitened finances caused by the war, was a second-hand one, although the best that could be procured at the time. Clark continued in the service of the state, headed several expeditions against the Indians, got himself mixed up with the Spanish authorities and had his actions disavowed by the United States, and was finally dismissed the Virginia service, on the plea of poverty, which was true enough.

He had never enjoyed a commission in the Continental service, and the dismissal left him without employment. The remainder of his long life is a sad story of disappointment and neglect. He was still a young man, and his years might have been filled with valuable service to his country. His marvellous campaign had evidenced his qualities, but he became so embittered by the ungrateful treatment he had received that he fell into bad habits. He drank to excess. He had no wife or children, and lived alone for many years, hunting, fishing, and indulging his appetite with such of his old friends or comrades as chanced to visit his cabin, which was erected on a six-thousand-acre grant of land Virginia made to him when she ceded the northwest territory to the United States. He was land-poor and lonely.

Four years before he died he was stricken with paralysis. He was alone in his cabin at the time and fell into the fire, which so severely burned one leg that it had to be amputated. It is related that he desired a fife and a drum to be played outside the house while the operation was being performed. It was before the days of anaesthetics, and the grim old soldier sat in his chair and had his leg taken off without an expression of emotion, while martial music was being dinned in his ears. He found a home in his last helpless years in the house of his sister, Mrs. Croghan, opposite Louisville, and there quietly slept away his life on February 13, 1818. He did much and suffered much—we may forgive him the rest.

There is a story that when his means were at last exhausted, and he could not obtain any settlement of his just claim against the state, he thrust the sword which Virginia had presented to him in the ground, broke it off at the hilt, and threw the pieces away with the bitter remark, "When Virginia wanted a sword, I gave her mine. Now she sends me a toy. I want bread!" In his paralysis, the state, leaving his claims still unsettled, seems to have sent him another sword!

Years after his death the tardy government of the United States settled his claim against it for the expenses incurred in his heroic campaigning, in which he had exhausted all his private fortune. It was not until 1877 that the claim of the heirs of Francis Vigo for a portion of the money which he had given to assist the northwest territory was allowed! As Vigo left no wife or children the money was paid to collateral heirs. Even poor old Father Gibault, who had done such good service in securing Vincennes and had given his own little property to Clark, in the endeavour to circulate the depreciated paper of the government, died in abject poverty, unrequited.

I do not know a more heroic achievement in our history than Clark's capture of Vincennes. I do not know in our history of greater results from slenderer means than Clark's subjugation of the northwest. I do not know in our history a sadder picture than the broken, paralyzed old man, alone in his cabin; and lastly, I do not recall in any history a more moving example of national ingratitude than that experienced by the priest, the Spaniard, and the soldier.

2

Tecumseh and William Henry Harrison

1. The Greatest of the Indians

To decide who is the greatest man of a race, a nation, or a period, is by no means easy; and any determination that may be arrived at, is likely to find as many opponents as advocates. Yet I am of the opinion that mature reflection will concede the fullest measure of greatness among the red men to Tecumseh. In four centuries of American history, at least three, and possibly four, Indians may be called great, even when measured by civilized standards. Joseph Brandt, or Thayendenegea, the Iroquois, who is the possible fourth, but who would popularly be considered first, may not be taken as a fair representative of his race, for he was educated and his character formed by civilised influence, though the results of this influence—from the stand-point of civilization—were not always apparent.

To be sure he was no worse than, in fact not half so bad as, many of his British contemporaries. But the three pure-blooded Indians who became what they were in the natural savage environment of their race and time, stand far above this veneered Iroquois in character, purpose, or achievement. The third in degree was the first in point of time. Metacomet, the Wampanoag, known as King Philip, was the engineer of that formidable conspiracy which had as its object the sweeping of the English into the sea. and as its hope the clearing of the new land of those European invaders with whom the savage chief found himself engaged in a struggle of life or death to his race.

King Philip belonged to the Algonquin family. Nearly a hundred years after his death in 1676, Pontiac, the great war-chief of the Ottawas, born a Catawba, and therefore of the Mobilian family, launched his formidable conspiracy upon the English posts from Fort Pitt to Michilimackinac in 1763. Although he captured eight forts out of the twelve attacked, and inaugurated a campaign of devastation and horror upon the borders of the northwest, he failed at Detroit, and in the end was assassinated by a hired traitor belonging to a petty Illinois tribe.

Tecumseh, the greatest of the trio and the man who stands higher than any Indian who ever lived, had a deeper view of the situation. While perhaps not so romantic as King Philip, nor so bold and fierce as Pontiac, he was the one solitary Indian who had, in addition to the traditional characteristics of a warrior, the qualities of a statesman. Philip fought to drive the English into the sea. Pontiac to restore the supremacy of the French in the land. With these two, war was the end and aim of their conspiracies. In the case of Tecumseh, it was the inevitable result of his endeavour, but it was not its primary object.

With a discernment and prescience which would not have been out of place in a modern philosopher, Tecumseh realized that the object of the struggle, as well as the advantage of the situation, lay in the possession of the land.

He declared that the land occupied by the different tribes of Indians belonged to them all in common; that they could only hold it in severalty as tenants; that each tribe had title to the land it actually occupied, only while it occupied it; and that no cession of territory of whatsoever degree could be made to the white man by any tribe for any purpose, without the general consent of all the tribes! To enforce this profound and catholic principle, and to make it operative, he formed a league of the Trans-Allegheny tribes, extending from the Great Lakes to the Gulf of Mexico.

He, and he alone, seems to have discerned the folly, from the Indian point of view, of the alienation by particular tribes of vast bodies of land to the Americans. He saw that in a very short time there would be no foot of land owned by the Indian on the hither side of the Mississippi, hence the league. This evidences his capacity, his genius, and his title to pre-eminence. Alone of all the Indians he entertained this idea and he came perilously near putting it into operation. Had he been a Greek, a Roman, a Frenchman, a German, or an Englishman he would have been called a patriot and a hero. James Parton says of him:

Every race produces superior individuals, whose lives constitute its heroic ages. Investigation establishes that Tecumseh, though not the faultless ideal of a patriot prince that romantic story represents him, was all of a patriot, a hero, a *man*, that an Indian can be. If to conceive a grand, difficult, and unselfish project; to labour for many years with enthusiasm and prudence in attempting its execution; to enlist in it by the magnetism of personal influence great multitudes of various tribes; to contend for it with unfaltering valour longer than there was hope of success; and to die fighting for it to the last, falling forward toward the enemy covered with wounds, is to give proof of an heroic cast of character, then is the Shawnee chief, Tecumseh, in whose veins flowed no blood that was not Indian, entitled to rank among Heroes.

General William Henry Harrison adds this testimony to his character and abilities :

He was one of those uncommon geniuses which spring up occasionally to produce revolutions, and overturn the established order of things. If it were not for the vicinity of the United States, he would, perhaps, be the founder of an empire that would rival in glory Mexico or Peru. No difficulties deter him. For four years he has been in constant motion. You see him today on the Wabash, and in a short time hear of him on the shores of Lake Erie or Michigan, or on the banks of the Mississippi; and wherever he goes he makes an impression favourable to his purposes.

Three boys were born at a single birth in the latter part of the eighteenth century, date uncertain, near where is now Springfield, Ohio. Their father was a Shawnee (Algonquin) and their mother a captive Creek (Mobilian). Thus they represented in their own persons the great ethnic divisions of the Indian race, a fact of no little importance in their subsequent career.

One of the trio may be dismissed from consideration, since nothing is known of him but his name. The eldest of the triplets was called Tecumthe, at least this appears to be the approved orthography, but he has gone into history under the name of Tecumseh, and it is not now worthwhile to change it. His name means "the wild cat that leaps upon his prey." He is described as a tall, athletic, handsome man, of noble and commanding presence. To his well-earned reputation as a warrior was added a fluent and persuasive oratory. Although he was not born a chief he easily raised himself to a position of general leadership by his talents. He was a formidable foeman indeed.

The second child was known as "the Prophet;" his Indian name being Elkswatawa, the word signifying "the man with the loud voice." It is probable that neither of these names was bestowed upon the boys until advancing years had given their elders some inkling of their characters. Indeed, it is asserted that Elkswatawa was a drunken, dissolute vagabond in his early years, and for his capacity for imbibing liquors was formerly known as "The Open Door." He had lost an eye in some drunken brawl which did not improve his sly and sinister cast of countenance. His brother, it is supposed, finally reformed him. That is, he outwardly reformed him. Elkswatawa quit drinking and abandoned his wicked courses, but the fund of lies with which he had been charged was got rid of so slowly that he never exhausted his stock. He had nothing whatever of the nobility of soul, the breadth of thought, or the depth of intellect of Tecumseh, yet he was shrewd, cunning, and in his way, capable.

He lent to the league the element of the supernatural. He gave to the plan of Tecumseh the sanction of religion. He posed as the prophet of the new undertaking of which Tecumseh was the leader. And because he was small in character and did not measure up to the greatness of his brother, by his folly he gave the opportunity by which the blow was dealt that broke up what was undoubtedly the most formidable savage confederacy with which the American border was ever menaced. It is probable, indeed, that he finally imposed upon himself, and believing in his own prophecies, was thereby "*hoist by his own petard!*"

Exhibiting a remarkable degree of patience and self-restraint, for several years Tecumseh worked at his plans with indefatigable energy, travelling from one end of the country to the other and gradually organizing the tribes into his confederacy, and impressing upon them his great idea. The Indian character is not favourable to such confederacies or combinations, but had it not been for the precipitate action of the prophet it is possible that Tecumseh might have met with so large a measure of success in his attempts as to have changed the history of the border to a great degree.

2. The Protagonist of the League

It is a singular fact that the whole scheme tumbled to pieces like a house of cards, at a single bloody touch in the northwest, although in the south there was a long and hard-fought war, especially with the Creeks, which was entirely due to the efforts of the great Shawnee. The man who shrewdly took advantage of Tecumseh's absence and the folly of Elkswatawa, to break up the league, and finally to cause the death of the great chieftain, was William Henry Harrison. The history of three years was a sort of duel between the two, with the northwest territory, as the reward of success; and, as is always the case, the white man won.

It is only of late that the reason for the importance in which the battles of Tippecanoe and the Thames have been held instinctively by the people of the central west has come to light. They were small affairs, as battles go, though gallantly fought on both sides, but their consequences were far-reaching; the one broke up the scheme, the other removed the schemer!

If Tecumseh could have matured his plans without molestation, if he had had time to have brought all the Indians on this side of the Mississippi into subserviency to his will, and had thrown them upon the American border, in let us say, the war of 1812, as he did those whom he could influence, the situation would have been grave indeed. The border would have been devastated, the frontier settlements wiped out, the war of 1812 would have been indefinitely prolonged with horrors indescribable. As it was, had it not been for him and his Indians, a large part of western Canada would have belonged to the United States by conquest.

Harrison was a Virginian. The west was explored, conquered, and protected, generally speaking, by men from the south of Mason's and Dixon's line—a fact usually lost sight of in our histories. His ancestry, which included a signer of the Declaration of Independence from Virginia, could be traced back to one of Cromwell's indomitable Ironsides, and far beyond. After graduating from Hampden-Sydney College he secured a commission in the regular army, against the advice of Robert Morris, his guardian. His first military experience was enjoyed under the personal instruction of that splendid revolutionary and border campaigner, Anthony Wayne.

He was one of Wayne's *aides* in the war in the northwest which culminated in the victory of Fallen Timbers; where, by the way, Tecumseh is alleged to have distinguished himself on the Indian side. He was a close student of military matters, and his native talents as a soldier enabled him, a boy of nineteen, to prepare an order of march for the army as it advanced through the country of the hostile Indians, which was adopted unanimously by Wayne and the veteran officers to whom it was submitted.

Harrison was the incarnation of personal daring and romantic gallantry. He married his wife in opposition to the wishes of her father, a certain Judge Symmes, uncle of the man who originated the absurd "Symmes Hole" theory of the North Pole.

"Well, sir," sternly said the old judge to the young captain when he learned of the wedding, "I understand that you have married Anna."

"Yes, sir."

"How do you expect to support her?"

"By my sword and by my right arm," was the doughty reply. And it may be said that no woman ever depended upon two more reliable things than those.

At the age of twenty-four he resigned the army, was made secretary of, then delegate to Congress from, the northwest territory; and was subsequently (1801) appointed the governor of the newly erected Indiana Territory, which owes much to his fostering care and judicious administration.

By the summer of 1811 Tecumseh's league had become so formidable that he ventured formally to protest against a treaty which had been signed at Fort Wayne in 1809, by some of the tribes, ceding some three million acres of Indiana land to the United States for some eight thousand dollars and annuities aggregating less than twenty-four hundred dollars!

This tribal action was in opposition to his communal principle, and a council was appointed to discuss the matter. In violation of agreement Tecumseh came to Vincennes with four hundred armed Indians. The proceedings of the council were interrupted by the threatening attitude of the Indians. Harrison at one time drew his sword and rallied his small company of guards about him, fearing he would have to fight the angry Indians at once. Only his courage and coolness prevented a serious and bloody rupture then and there.[1]

Matters were patched up, however; time was not ripe for Tecum-

1. Tecumseh refused to go under a roof to hold this council.

"Houses," he said haughtily, "were built for you to hold councils in; Indians hold theirs in the open air."

After he had finished his speech one of Harrison's *aides* pointed to a chair, saying, "Your father requests you to take a seat by his side."

"My father!" replied the chief scornfully, as he stood erect before them; "the sun is my father, and the earth is my mother. On her bosom I will recline," he added, as he sat down upon the ground.

"MESSENGERS BROUGHT LETTERS ... APPEALING FOR
VENGEANCE OR PROTECTION."

seh's revolt yet, and it was finally agreed that the matter should be referred to the President of the United States. As it would take some time to hear from this referee, whose decision might easily be imagined, Tecumseh, who had been merely playing for time, left the northwest and hastened south for a final appeal to the Indians of that section, leaving the charge of affairs of the northwest to the Prophet, with strict instructions to permit no rupture during his absence. His departure was fatal to his hopes, a mistake which caused the downfall of the confederacy. The Prophet's control of the Indians was not nearly so complete as that of his brother, and a series of petty forays, farm-burnings, murderings, and so forth, exasperated and irritated the settlers almost beyond endurance. Messengers brought letters to the Governor from all parts of the territory appealing for vengeance or protection. They had been hot for a punitive expedition from the first; indeed it is likely that one would have been undertaken if the Indians had remained quiet, so splendid a chance being afforded the Americans by Tecumseh's absence in the south. It was therefore soon determined that Harrison should march into the disputed territory and make a demonstration in force which should at least compel the Prophet and his followers to observe the *status quo* until the President had been heard from, and which, if opportunity served, might do more serious work. As usual in our Indian difficulties, there was black treachery on both sides.

Troops had already been assembled at Vincennes, the territorial capital. They were few in number but high in quality, the nucleus of the force being the Fourth U. S. Infantry, ordered from Pittsburg, under the command of Colonel John P. Boyd. Boyd was a Yankee soldier of fortune. After three years' service in the regular army he resigned his commission and went to India, where he took service under the *Nizam* of Hyderabad. He came back, after a sojourn of nine years, with substantial evidences of the favour of the Indian potentate, and was at once appointed colonel of the Fourth Infantry, Around this force had assembled a considerable body of the Indiana militia with two companies of Kentucky riflemen. These troops Harrison had trained and disciplined with the most painstaking care and they proved themselves fully the equals of any American soldiers who ever fought. They were in no sense the disorderly militiamen, or , trained bands, which had brought the name of militia into such disrepute in the first half of the century. They were soldiers.

Among those who repaired to his standard in answer to his call

187

were a number of men of the highest. consideration. Abraham Owen and Jo: Daviess of Kentucky, Randolph of Indiana, young George Croghan from Louisville, and many others. Daviess was the most noted character. Tales of his extraordinary courage, his wonderful oratorical power, his striking eccentricities, still remain. He was the attorney, by the way, who prosecuted Aaron Burr. When he went to Washington on one occasion, he had a suit made of red broadcloth! "How else," he remarked when he was questioned as to the reason for this marvellous costume, "would anybody know that Jo: Daviess was in town?" Daviess was intensely ambitious of distinction and had evidently determined to let no opportunity of advancing himself escape him in the coming campaign.

The most noted body of militia was Captain Spier Spencer's company of mounted riflemen who were attached to the Fourth regiment of Indiana infantry. The men were uniformed in short coatees of yellow and were known as Spencer's "Yellow Jackets."

As fast as the different bodies assembled at Vincennes they were sent up the Wabash. Boats carried the major portion of supplies up the river until the site of what is now Terre Haute, at the head of navigation, was reached. The force comprised nine companies of regulars, thirteen of Indians and two of Kentucky militia; of which seven companies, aggregating some two hundred and fifty men, were mounted. Here they built a fort to protect the boats which it was necessary to leave behind. The stockade was called Fort Harrison, and was garrisoned by Lieutenant-Colonel Miller, the famous *"I'll try, sir,"* officer of Lundy's Lane. On October 28th, 1811, the army numbering about a thousand men set forth for the Prophet's town, which was situated at the confluence of Tippecanoe Creek and the Wabash. The word Tippecanoe is a corruption of the Indian word *"'Keh-tip-a-quo-wonk,"* meaning the "Great Clearing."

The shortest way to the town would have been by the east bank, but as it was thickly wooded and convenient for Indian ambuscades, Harrison chose to take the longer way around the bend of the river upon the west bank. A few miles brought the troops for the first time to the vast prairies which stretched far westward through Illinois, and the chroniclers report the surprise and admiration with which they regarded the unwonted landscape. They marched rapidly forward until on the 6th of November, 1811, they came to a thick patch of woodland abounding in ravines and extending some miles to the westward of the river. They proceeded through this with the greatest caution,

Harrison again adopting the arrangement and order of march which he had suggested in Wayne's campaign, to guard against ambush and surprise.

In the late afternoon they were met by messengers from the Prophet, who professed to be very much surprised at the proximity of this formidable force. The Prophet's messengers asked for a council. They said that other messengers had been sent down the east bank to intercept the army, which they had expected would come that way. After some discussion Harrison appointed a council for the next morning.

Meanwhile the American soldiers had been marching up the river. Toward five o'clock they had approached within two hundred yards of the Prophet's town. The Indians massed themselves in front of the town, and a battle appeared imminent. Harrison, however, did not think it advisable to attack the fortified town in daylight, so he halted his men. The representations of the Prophet's envoys that Elkswatawa was peaceably inclined and that all differences would be adjusted at the council, induced Harrison to encamp for the night. He did not expect the council to bring about any results, but he intended to hold it, and then attack the town on the following night. The Prophet merely anticipated him by a night. Elkswatawa should have abandoned the town and led his people in flight until the Americans were no longer able to pursue. The Indian plans were not yet ripe for battle, and should war begin in the absence of Tecumseh the chance of savage success would be slight.

The Americans, being ignorant of the country, the Indians were requested to indicate a proper place for an encampment. They pointed out a knoll about a mile and a half to the right. After it had been examined by officers and found suitable, Harrison moved his army there to pass the night.

The bench of land, or *plateau*, was in the form of a narrow triangle, the apex being to the southeast and very acute. It rested upon a deep rivulet called Bennett's Creek, which protected the rear. The base of the triangle on a level with the surrounding country was open to attack. At the back of the hill the land rose steeply some twenty feet above the creek. It sloped gently toward the Prophet's town in front, and faced, after an abrupt descent of ten feet, a stretch of marshy prairie which extended for a long distance. The place was thickly wooded, the ground cumbered with underbrush and fallen timber. There was plenty of wood and water, two prime requisites, and the situation was fairly defensible, especially against regular troops.

The smallness of Harrison's force rendered it impossible for him to occupy the whole of the plateau. He pitched his camp with the rear resting on the creek and the lines were roughly drawn in the form of a trapezoid, following the shape of the hill, but at some little distance from the edge, the front face occupying about seventy-five yards and the perimeter of the entire encampment being about two hundred and fifty.

Commencing with the northwest corner, the troops were posted in the following general order: The Kentuckians and one Indiana company occupied the left flank; one battalion of regulars and one of Indiana militia were posted in the centre of the front line; on the right flank were more Indiana militia, and Spencer's company occupying the point or narrow part of the line. The rear was allotted to the remainder of the militia and the second battalion of regulars which joined the Kentuckians on the northwest corner. The cavalry under Daviess and Park were posted in the rear of the northeast angle. The officers' tents, those of the regular troops, and the baggage train, were placed in the centre of the enclosure. On account of the length to be covered the men were posted in single rank fairly close together, and a thin line of humanity encircled the field.

The night was very cold. Rain fell at intervals, although toward morning the moon shone fitfully from time to time through the drifting clouds. Huge fires were kindled, without which it would not have been possible for the troops to take any rest. A camp guard of over one hundred men under experienced officers, a large quota for so small a body, was carefully posted, and instructions as to what should be done in case of a night attack were promulgated. The men were ordered to lie with their guns loaded and bayonets fixed. Only the regulars had tents, and in order to keep their pieces dry many of the militia wrapped their gun-locks in their coats or blankets and lay uncovered near the fires.

3. THE BATTLE OF TIPPECANOE

Harrison's experience in Indian warfare had taught him that it was a wise precaution to awaken his men early in the morning, so as to be prepared for attacks which the Indians usually delivered shortly before sunrise. He had just risen, therefore, at four o'clock on the morning of the 7th, from a few hours of troubled sleep, and was pulling on his boots preparatory to leaving his tent and giving the order calling the men to attention, when the stillness of the night was broken by the

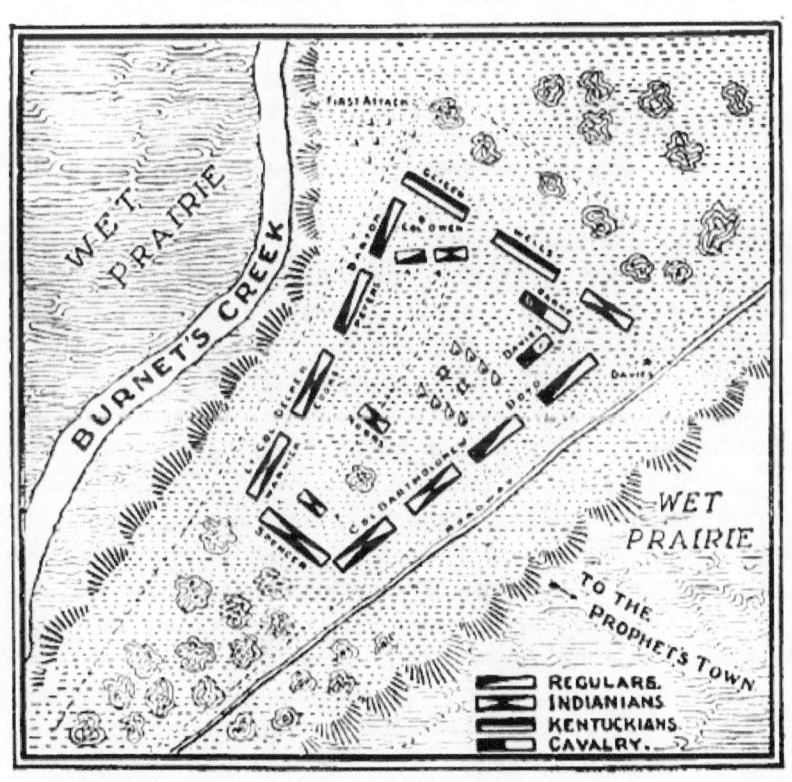

PLAN OF THE BATTLE OF TIPPECANOE.

sound of a rifle shot which came out of the woodland to the north-west. It was instantly followed by a fusillade.

Corporal Stephen Mars of Kentucky, the sentry whose beat extended farthest in the woods to the northwest, had detected dark bodies creeping noiselessly through the underbrush toward his post. He fired upon them instantly and then turned and dashed for the camp, shouting in alarm as he ran. The Indians who had approached thus near the lines with wonderful skill, saw that concealment was at an end. They shot Mars dead before he had gone a dozen paces, and then, shouting their war-cries, rushed upon the regulars and Kentuckians who were posted on either side of that angle. Almost before the startled men, so suddenly awakened, were aware of their situation, the red warriors burst upon them.

Seizing their weapons, after a single discharge of rifle or musket, there being no time for reloading, a desperate hand-to-hand conflict ensued, with rifle butt and bayonet against *tomahawk* and scalping knife. Such was the dash of the Indian attack that the two companies gave ground, as the savages in apparently countless numbers came leaping upon them out of the darkness.

Meanwhile the whole camp had sprung to arms. The men stood in line, peering out into the black dark woods surrounding them, awaiting the next development, which was not long in coming, for presently along the whole front and extending around the right flank the crackle of rifles and muskets was heard, so that the entire camp, save for the space protected by the creek, was simultaneously assailed.

Up in the northwest corner the condition of affairs was indeed critical. In spite of the heroic efforts of the troops, the Indians effected an entrance in the camp, and if they could maintain their position the lines would be taken in the rear while they were attacked in the front, and the result would be annihilation. Major Baen of the regulars was mortally hurt, Captain Geiger of the Kentuckians wounded, and many other officers and men were killed or wounded, and the line was giving away in great confusion. Some of the Indians who had broken through stopped to plunder the tents. It had all happened in a few moments.

Harrison was equal to the emergency, however. He acted with true military promptness. Not stopping for anything he had run from his tent at the first shot. The horses were plunging wildly at their halters in the excitement and confusion. Just as the general reached them, his own horse, a white stallion, broke his halter and escaped in the darkness. Harrison sprang to the back of the next one, which happened to be a dark bay, and to this fortunate circumstance he probably owed his life. His principal *aide*, Major Owen, was mounted upon a white horse, his own. The Indians had marked Harrison's white horse at the meeting of the evening before, and as the general and his *aide* galloped to the northwest corner, the savage marksmen singled out the man on the white horse conspicuous in the firelight. He was shot and instantly killed.

Harrison arrived at the angle just as the regulars and Kentuckians broke. He ordered Peters' regular and Cooke's Indiana militia companies up from the rear, the only face unassailed, formed them across the gap, and charged forward with them with great spirit and success, the shaken troops rallying upon them and reoccupying their old places. Not an Indian who had entered the lines was left alive when the lines were re-established. The first dash had failed, but the Indian fire was kept up with unabated vigour and the camp was furiously assailed everywhere.

Meanwhile Jo: Daviess with the cavalry in the opposite angle was greatly desirous of distinguishing himself. As the fighting continued and the enemy drew closer he sent a messenger to Harrison requesting permission to charge. The general, in the thick of the fray at the time, directed Daviess to be patient, that he would give him opportunity enough to distinguish himself before the battle was over. Patience, however, was not one of Daviess' qualities. He sent a second time, and received the same answer, and finally a third time, whereupon Harrison replied, "Tell Major Daviess he has had my opinion twice. He may now use his own discretion."

Daviess instantly gave the order to charge. Instead of going out in line abreast he led his force through his own lines in single file, and made a rush for the woods. According to some accounts he was on horseback, at any rate he was conspicuous from a white blanket coat which he wore. He was shot through the body before he had gone ten paces, and his men retreated carrying him with them. The Indians attempted a counter-charge, but the dragoons rallied and the attack was easily beaten off.

The plateau was now encircled with fire. The troops standing near the edge were plainly visible to the Indians by the light cast by the remains of the huge fires back of them, while the savages could not be seen by the Americans, who could only fire at the flashes in the darkness. Every assailable point was hotly attacked again and again.

Harrison rode up and down the fines freely exposing himself, his clothing torn by bullets, heartening and cheering the men, throwing a little reserve now here, now there, to re-enforce a weak spot, doing everything that a brave and efficient officer could do to insure success. The steadiness of the militia was marvellous. They stood in the darkness after a time and fought like heroes, for the fires were extinguished by Harrison's orders as soon as the exigency permitted. Men fell on every side, yet there was no thought of retreat or giving back.

After the failure to break the line on the left flank, the attack was concentrated on the narrow side of the right flank. Colonel Bartholomew was wounded, Lieutenant- Colonel Decker was next struck down. Captain Warrick, acting major, was then shot through the body. He was taken to the fire, his wound dressed, and as he was able to move, though his injuries were mortal, he went back to the line and fought with his men until he died.

Spencer's "Yellow Jackets" bore the brunt of the fight at the point. The Indians were in front and on both sides of these brave men. Captain Spencer was shot in the head and severely wounded, but refused to leave his post, and continued to encourage his men. A few moments after he received his first wound he was shot through the thighs and fell to the ground. Still he would not permit himself to be carried to the rear, but was being lifted up to cheer his soldiers, when he was shot in the heart and fell dead where he had fought.

All the field officers of the Indiana militia at this point were killed or wounded, and most of the company officers also. There is a story told that Harrison, riding furiously up to the imperilled point, found the troops under the command of a mere boy, whose face was begrimed with powder and stained with blood from a wound in his forehead.

"Young man," said the general in great anxiety, not recognizing him in such a case, "where is your colonel?"

"Dead, sir," was the answer.

"Your major?"

"Dead, sir."

"Your captain?"

"Dead, sir."

"Who commands the regiment?"

"I do, sir. Ensign Tipton, Fourth Indiana, sir."

The story may well be true; it is certain that the boy went into the campaign a private, and that night of battle made him the captain of his company.

Harrison had one company still in reserve, Robb's Kentucky riflemen. He at once led them to the support of the right flank. They
numbered thirty-five men, and seventeen of them were killed or
wounded before the day broke. The men behaved with the greatest
gallantry. Many of them had never been in action before, yet they
coolly stood to their guns, and when it came to hand-to-hand fighting
they displayed high courage.

Captain Geiger of the Kentuckians narrowly escaped death at the
knife of an Indian who had broken into the camp, whom he killed
with his own hands. The flint of a soldier's piece slipped out of place.
The man deliberately walked over to the remains of the fire in spite of
expostulation, sat down by it and remained until he had fixed his musket, although the bullets fell around him like hail. Other men sprang
upon the Indians crawling toward the line and killed them with knife
or hatchet, or were killed themselves in the struggle.

Two hours the battle raged, but as day broke the regulars and Kentuckians on the left flank led by Major Wells moved out and by a
spirited bayonet charge drove the savages in headlong rout, which
extended all along the line. At six o'clock the fierce little battle was
over.

Harrison's loss in killed and wounded is usually given as one hundred and eighty-eight men, but the returns upon which this statement
is made apparently do not include some of the casualties among the
officers, so that I am of the opinion that there were nearly two hundred casualties out of the one thousand engaged, or about twenty *per
cent.*, a fearful proportion indeed. Daviess died of his wounds during
the day and with the other dead was interred upon the field.

Harrison sent a detachment to burn the Prophet's town, which
was found deserted, and to lay waste the surrounding country. Then
destroying his private baggage and putting the wounded in the baggage-wagons, he retraced his steps to Fort Harrison. The sufferings of
the wounded upon this rough wagon journey were indescribable.

The casualties among the Indians have never been learned with ac-
curacy, but it is likely that they were at least as great as those sustained
by the Americans. The Indians, who were from a number of tribes,
were led by three chiefs named White Loon, Stone Eater, and Win-
nemac. The Prophet, who had, after the manner of his kind, promised
immunity from the American bullets to his followers, had witnessed
the battle from a situation back of the creek; also, after the manner of

his kind, taking care to be well out of range. When he was reproached by the surviving Indians for having misled them with pretended immunities, he stated that his wife had touched the pot in which he had brewed his incantations that night, and the charm had been broken by her profane hand! A child of Adam he, indeed. He was not believed, of course, but there was nothing to be done then.

Alas for the Indians, more than the charm was broken on this occasion, for the whole confederacy, at least so far as the northwest was concerned, went to pieces in the face of the crushing defeat. The many warriors from so many different tribes carried the news everywhere, the Prophet was discredited, and Tecumseh in his absence was deserted by all but his own tribe. The Creek war with its awful massacres and bloody battles ensued in the south, but the spirit of the northern Indians was broken.

When Tecumseh returned and found his careful plans, his far-seeing statesmanship frustrated by the signal ability with which Harrison had taken advantage of his absence and the folly of the Prophet, he was heartbroken, too. The war of 1812 opening soon after, he naturally cast his lot with the British, bringing many of the northwest Indians with him. Appreciating his influence and ability they made him a major-general, and he rendered brilliant and effective service against the Americans in all the campaigns of the war.

Proctor, the English commander, was greatly inferior to the Indian both in military talents and in personal character, and anything that was accomplished by the allies was due to the genius of the savage rather than to the efforts of the Briton. He and Harrison faced each other many times in many hard-fought battles until the end came on the 5th of October, 1813, near the Moravian Town on the River Thames in the Province of Ontario, Canada.

4. The Battle of the Thames

After the stupendous victory of Perry on Lake Erie the British, utterly disheartened, abandoned their positions and fled precipitately to the northwest, closely pursued by Harrison and Governor Shelby of Kentucky, one of the heroes of King's Mountain, thirty-three years before, in command of a fine force of three thousand regulars and Indiana and Kentucky troops, of whom the aged Shelby was not the least ardent—"Old King's Mountain" they called him from his share in the famous victory. They greatly outnumbered the allies, who comprised some seven hundred regulars and about one thousand two hundred Indians under the command of Tecumseh.

Bitterly protesting against flight and earnestly pleading with the British commander to give battle, Tecumseh at last induced him to await the American attack at a place peculiarly well adapted for defence. With the left flank protected by the river Thames, here high banked and unfordable, and his right flank resting upon an almost impassable swamp. Proctor finally resolved to make a stand. Between the river and the large swamp a smaller swamp, or marsh, divided the allies into two parts. The ground was thickly wooded with huge trees with but little undergrowth. Proctor with the British regulars took the left of the line, Tecumseh with his Indians the right.

Harrison, coming upon them late in the afternoon, determined to assault them in regular fashion by advancing his infantry under cover of skirmishers, and after the battle had been joined throwing in his cavalry, of which he had a very fine regiment of Kentuckians, commanded by Colonel Richard Mentor Johnson. But upon learning that the British troops, through some unaccountable blunder, were drawn up in open order, Harrison changed his plan and began the battle by launching a furious cavalry charge upon both sides of the small swamp. At the same time he deployed a portion of his army to the left to attack the Indians, who had extended on his flank in the large swamp. Old General Shelby had charge of this portion of the advance. The cavalry, upon the word, charged with the utmost gallantry on both sides of the small swamp. Colonel Johnson led the attack on the Indians, and his brother and Lieutenant-Colonel on the British. The Johnsons were a family of fighters, for two sons of the lieutenant-colonel, one only a boy, accompanied him in the charge.

After two volleys and some irregular firing, the British, overridden by the impetuous horsemen, who were closely followed by the infantry, threw down their arms and surrendered, Proctor fleeing like the coward he was from the field which he had failed to defend. He was afterward court-martialed and severely censured for his lack of conduct. On the Indian side of the swamp, however, the battle was more fiercely contested. All the loss the American army sustained practically occurred here. The engagement was general for perhaps ten minutes, when Tecumseh was shot and the Indians at last gave way in all directions before the steady advance of the American soldiers. The American loss was about fifteen killed and thirty wounded; the British loss, about eighteen killed, twenty-six wounded, and six hundred prisoners. Thirty- three dead Indians were left on the field, many were wounded but escaped, and their total loss was probably heavy.

Who shot Tecumseh is one of the unsolved and unsolvable mysteries of history. Colonel Johnson, who was wounded no less than five times in the fight, did shoot with a pistol a prominent Indian who had already wounded him and was making toward him to finish him. It was alleged that this Indian was Tecumseh. Johnson, who was afterward Vice-President of the United States, never made the claim himself that it was, although his political partisans did so for him. Volumes have been written to discover the fact, but it remains as far from solution as ever. Of one thing is there assurance, and that is, that the great chief fell in this battle, which was after all scarcely more than a skirmish. There are gruesome stories about his skin being flayed from his body for razor-strops, but they are not well authenticated. Indeed, the identification of his body after the battle is by no means complete. That he died there, however, appears to be certain.

A petty ending to all his great ideas, his brilliant planning, his splendid courage, his noble dream of a Red Men's Republic! He was beyond his time, and beyond his people. So his life was wasted. Let it be said of him that he was a merciful Indian in accordance with his lights, that he permitted no burning of prisoners nor other torturing, that the massacre of the Raisin River was not due to him, and that he observed in large measure what are called the rules of civilized warfare.

It is significant, too, that before this last battle of which the baffled, disappointed man saw the inevitable end, he had communicated to his friends his resolve never to leave the field alive, and he had stripped off his British uniform and gone into the action attired in the savage simplicity of his ancient forefathers.

Harrison, with Perry, who had been present at the battle, and General Shelby and Colonel Johnson were the heroes of the hour. The national significance in our early development of the battle of Tippecanoe, to which the victory of the Thames called renewed attention, has been pointed out. It had an interesting personal significance to the American commander as well, for it undoubtedly called the public attention to Harrison in such a way that, when it was coupled with his brilliant campaigning in the subsequent war, it finally made him the foremost man of the Republic and at last the President of the United States. Men yet live who remember the stirring slogan of his political campaign, which joined his name with that of his running mate in these words: "Old Tippecanoe and Tyler too."

As the industrious and indefatigable Lossing says of the battle:

History, art, and song made that event the theme of pen, pencil, and voice; and when, thirty years afterward, the leader of the fray was a candidate for the Presidency of the United States, he was everywhere known by the familiar title of 'Old Tippecanoe.' His partisans erected log cabins in towns and cities, and in them sang in chorus :

Hurrah for the father of all the great west,
For the Buckeye who followed the plough;
The foeman in terror his valour confessed,
And we'll honour the conqueror now.
His country assailed in the darkest of days,
To her rescue impatient he flew,
The war whoop's fell blast, and the rifle's red blaze,
But awakened Old Tippecanoe.

And Tecumseh's name reappears in history in the monitor which was sunk in Mobile Bay by the Confederate torpedoes off Fort Morgan, and in the cognomen of that great modern warrior, William Tecumseh Sherman.

3

The Massacre on the River Raisin

Woe, and woe, and lamentation!
What a piteous cry was there!
Widows, maidens, mothers, children,
Shrieking, sobbing in despair.

Woe to us, ah, woe Kentucky!
O, our sons, our sons and men!
Surely some have 'scaped the Indian,
Surely some will come again!

Till the oak that fell last winter
Shall uprear its shattered stem—
Wives and mothers of Kentucky—
Ye may look in vain for them!
                    —Adapted from Aytoun.

1. THE ARMY OF THE WEST

In the early part of 1813 tidings of an appalling disaster to our arms came blowing down the winter wind from the far northwest. Although there were no telegraph lines, nor railroads, nor other means of quickly diffusing intelligence, rumours of a bloody battle fought and lost, and succeeded by a ruthless massacre, spread with incredible swiftness in ever-widening circles of apprehension and alarm. The news carried dismay and desolation and anguish to the people of Kentucky. Winchester's detachment had been cut off, it was reported, and every man of them slain. Later and authentic information mitigated the first impression of the calamity, but the tidings were bad enough at best and they needed no exaggeration to send a wave of grief and rage throughout Kentucky primarily and the United States generally.

It is difficult to overestimate the important part played by Kentucky in the War of 1812. Because she was a trans-Allegheny state and most of the campaigns in which her soldiers took part occurred in the north-western territories, their achievements, except in the case of William Henry Harrison, have been somewhat lost sight of. Yet the best blood of the new state responded with spontaneous enthusiasm to the demands of the government; and not only in the regular army of the United States but in the regiments of volunteers with which our greater wars have usually been fought, her citizens displayed an alacrity and self-sacrifice which set the pace and established the mark for older communities.

The best men in the state did not disdain to fill the stations of subalterns, and numbers of them were even found in the ranks. Many of these volunteers were killed or wounded, and the regiments of which they made up the principal quota participated in some of the hardest of the little fights with which the war abounded.

After the pusillanimous surrender of Hull at Detroit, a vigorous effort was inaugurated to recover the lost city and drive the British from the peninsula of Michigan. After various hesitations the supreme command of the force designed for the recapture and invasion of Canada was conferred upon Harrison, who was appointed a major-general in the regular army. His force was assembled in three small divisions, the left being under the command of Brigadier-General James Winchester.

Winchester was a veteran of the Revolution. He had been a lieutenant in the Virginia Continental line at the age of twenty-four. It was his misfortune to be captured early in the Revolutionary War and to spend over four years as a prisoner. Most of the fighting was over when he was released, and as he had enjoyed no opportunity for distinguishing himself, consequently he had not risen above a subordinate rank. He was at this time over sixty years old; a brave, upright, estimable gentleman, with no other qualifications whatever for military command.

Under him was a force of some twelve hundred men, including the Seventeenth U. S. Regular Infantry, under Colonel Wells, who had fought brilliantly at Tippecanoe, the First, Second, and Fifth Kentucky Volunteers, the First Kentucky Riflemen, and some other troops. The soldiers, who had been enlisted in August, were provided only with clothing for summer campaigning, and as the winter approached, they suffered terrible hardships. The winter was one of unusual severity.

Harrison appealed personally to the women of Kentucky, and with patriotic zeal they laboured to provide blankets, overcoats and other clothing for their men in the field, but these supplies had not yet reached Winchester's detachment. Harrison intended to concentrate his men at the Rapids of the Maumee, preparatory to marching on the British head-quarters at Maiden, now Amherstburg, Ontario, Canada; and thither he directed Winchester to repair early in January, to fortify the place and to establish a depot to which would be sent the sorely needed supplies.

The Kentucky troops were not well affected toward Winchester at first. He had been sent out by the National Government to supersede Harrison in the chief command, and a bitter feeling had been engendered thereby. Harrison had found it necessary to appeal to the patriotism of the troops; but Winchester himself, by kindliness of heart, shown in the lax discipline he maintained, had changed the state of affairs, so that he had become personally popular with the men, although their efficiency had not been promoted by his actions.

They were, however, in good spirits at last in spite of hardships and exposures, and were become so zealous that when they were ordered to march to the Maumee Rapids, finding their horses and mules, as ill provided as their masters, unequal to the labour, the men dragged the cannon and supplies over the frozen country, gladly taking hold of the traces and pulling the wagons and guns with their own hands.

Everything connected with the army was in a chaotic state. There were few, if any, trained soldiers among the officials. The war had not yet developed those whose talents enabled them to supplement their lack of experience, and things went on very slowly indeed; as they always do, even in the best of times—as they did in the Spanish-American War, for instance.

2. A Hazardous Expedition

While they were waiting in the cold for the bringing up of the supplies, the arrival of re-enforcements, and the approach of the other detachments of the army, which Harrison was vainly endeavouring to hasten, an appeal for help was brought to Winchester from a little village called Frenchtown, situated on the River Raisin, a few miles above the place where it empties into Lake Erie and where is now the city of Monroe, Michigan.

The settlement was a small one, of some thirty families and as many houses. It was French in its origin and dated back in the previous century. The first settlers had named the stream upon which they had established themselves the *Rivière aux Raisins*, on account of the prevalence of wild grapes which they found there.

The settlement was menaced by a body of Canadians and Indians under the command of Major Reynolds, who had been despatched to seize it as a convenient outpost for watching the Americans, by Colonel Proctor, the British commander in the northwest. Messengers were sent to Winchester's camp asking him to send a detachment to drive away the enemy and protect the citizens from the Indians.

Moved by feelings of humanity, he committed a most serious military blunder. Feelings of humanity seem to find little place in military manoeuvres, unfortunately. Frenchtown was within eighteen miles of Maiden, in which lay a force of five thousand British and Indians. It was about thirty miles from the camp on the Maumee. Winchester divided his small force into two parties, and on the 17th of January, 1814, he sent the first moiety, some six hundred and fifty men, under Colonel Lewis, to dispossess the British and Indians from Frenchtown. He immediately re-enforced him with a small detachment under Colonel Allen, which overtook the advance before the battle the next day.

Winchester's soldiers, whose terms of service were shortly to expire, were clamorous for movement. They did not wish to go home without having struck one blow at least, and through their officers they had strenuously urged upon the feeble general the despatch of the expedition. It does not appear that Winchester made any great resistance to their demand, or that he ever realized his blunder.

The weather was bitter cold, but the ill-clad troops, rejoicing in the prospect of fighting, set forth sturdily upon their hazardous undertaking. They marched rapidly, and after a day and a night approached Frenchtown. They crossed the River Raisin upon the ice, formed up in the woods, seized the town, and drove out the advance guard of the allies, whom they found drawn up in a convenient situation ready to receive them.

There was a spirited little engagement in the afternoon of the 18th, in which the British supported by a howitzer held their own for a time and inflicted a loss of some twelve killed, including one officer, and fifty-five wounded, including three officers, but they were finally driven from successive positions by the Americans. They retreated in good order, and maintained an unbroken front until evening put an end to the battle, which was certainly a victory for the Americans, since they remained in possession of the town and battlefield.

Colonel Lewis, whose conduct had been characterized by courage and skill, withdrew to the town and went into camp. His wounded were gladly cared for in the houses of the French people and his men established themselves in a good defensive position, enjoying through the hospitality of the villagers the first good warm meal they had eaten for a long time. A messenger was at once sent back to Winchester telling of their success, and then they remained quietly in camp within striking distance of the whole British army to wait their general's pleasure.

The houses of the village were mostly surrounded by gardens, the greater part enclosed by "puncheon" fences, which were in effect small stockades of heavy timber, or split logs, between four and five feet high and admirably adapted for defensive warfare. Lewis seems to have knocked out some of the intercepting fences so as to make a clear stockade around the southern part of the town, in which he posted his troops.

The messenger with the news of the success of the detachment raised the greatest enthusiasm in Winchester's camp. His men clamoured to be led forward to the new position. Although there was no strategic importance to be attached to the possession of Frenchtown, and to hold it removed the division from its base of supplies and disorganized the plan of the commander-in-chief, it seemed on the face of it a bold, threatening, forward movement, and as such appealed to the unthinking.

It was, in fact, so rash a movement that it amounted to foolhardiness. If one can forget that Proctor was a coward and an ass, it might be likened to thrusting one's head into a lion's mouth. At any rate, Winchester determined to establish his camp on the Raisin. Leaving some three hundred men at Maumee with instructions to guard the stores until they could be sent for, and also to receive other stores, and despatching a messenger to Harrison with the first news of the little victory and the projected movement, Winchester, accompanied by Colonel Wells and the Seventeenth regulars, marched to Frenchtown. When they got there on the 20th a petty little question of precedence which arose necessitated an arrangement which brought about the ultimate disaster of all of them.

Wells, as a colonel in the regular service, was senior in rank to Lewis and was thus entitled to what is known as the right of the line. On the left of the stockade occupied by Lewis there was another garden enclosure which would have afforded excellent cover for Wells,

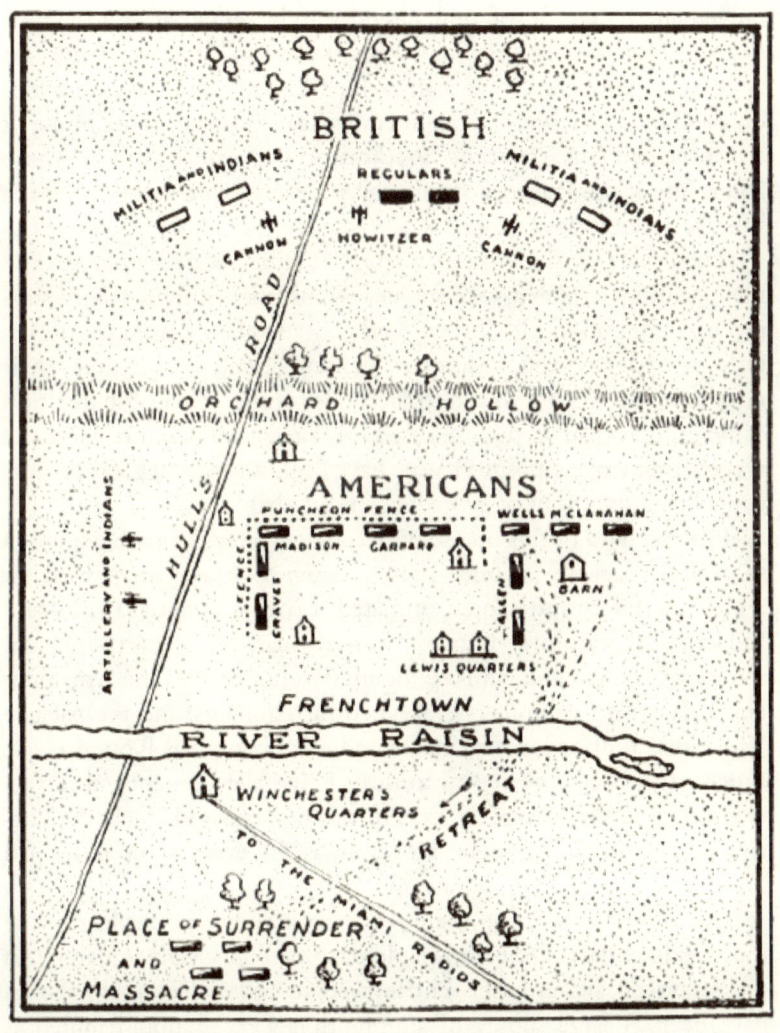

MAP OF FRENCHTOWN AND THE MASSACRE ON THE RAISIN.

but in a spirit of military punctilio he chose to maintain his right to the right of the line, and accordingly encamped his men in the open on the right of Lewis, with no protection whatever. His detached force was therefore a weakness rather than a strength to the army.

Winchester seems to have made no objection to the foolish arrangement. Indeed, it was only intended to be temporary, for the next day, the 21st, the officers pitched upon a suitable location for a fort large enough for the whole army, which they arranged to commence on the 22nd. Winchester established his head-quarters at the house of a man named Navarre, some three-quarters of a mile from the camp and south of the Raisin, a stream seventy yards wide and now frozen solid between its low banks.

There they lay, therefore, some nine hundred and fifty officers and men, without artillery, without provisions, with only a scanty supply of ammunition, ill-clothed, with no adequate commissariat, utterly unsupported and within easy striking distance of six times their number of the enemy. To add to their misfortunes the foolish question of precedence had so disposed them that over one-third of the force was in an untenable position. Wars have been waged and great peoples ruined over questions of precedence more than once.

Proctor, who in this one solitary instance seems to have exhibited some little capacity, at once moved down to attack them with six pieces of artillery and a force estimated at twelve hundred British and Indians, of whom three hundred were regulars of the Forty-first and the Royal Newfoundland Regiments, two hundred of the remainder being Canadian volunteers embodied in regiments, and the balance Wyandotte Indians led by a celebrated chief known as Round Head. Proctor supposed that he was to meet Lewis' detachment only, or he would have taken a larger force. He was ignorant of Winchester's arrival with a re-enforcement. However, as the event showed, he had more than enough for the purpose.

In the American camp there seems to have been a neglect of the most rudimentary duties of a soldier. No scouts were ordered, no pickets placed, and even the sentries were not extended as they should have been. A large supply of ammunition was left undistributed at Winchester's headquarters, although some of the troops had only ten rounds with them.

Colonel Wells and Colonel Lewis finally began to fear that their position would invite attack and made representations to General Winchester snugly ensconced in the Navarre house across the river.

He pooh-poohed their fears and made light of their suggestions, until finally the news was brought by one of the French inhabitants that a large force of British and Indians had left Maiden and were approaching Frenchtown. This was contradicted vehemently by another Frenchman, who bore the historic name of La Salle, who it was afterwards learned was in the pay of the British. Winchester was reassured by La Salle's protestations and accordingly did nothing.

3. THE BATTLE OF FRENCHTOWN

The night of January 21st was intensely cold, the ground was covered with snow, the wind blew fiercely. The poorly clad sentries almost perished during their long vigils, and they naturally kept an indifferent watch. Some of the approaches to the town were left entirely unpicketed. No scouting parties were sent out. The American army lay huddled around its fires, or crowded the huts and houses of the village seeking shelter from the freezing cold of the bitter winter. The whole army passed the night in confident security, and Proctor with his well-clad troops and Indians was enabled to approach near the camp without discovery.

Between four and five o'clock, probably nearer five, while it was yet dark, the drummer-boys began beating the reveille. The echoes of the drums had scarce died away under the black sky when three rifle shots from the nearest sentries, instantly followed by the report of a cannon and the bursting of a bombshell, crashed through the morning air. The discharge was succeeded by the rattling of musketry mingled with the cheers of the British and the yells of the Indians.

The startled Americans sprang to their arms in the gray misty morning, and in their bewilderment opened a fire upon the flashes of light which told of the presence of the enemy. If Proctor had realized the situation he could have rushed the camp and surprised the Americans almost in their sleep. He chose, however, to bombard the pickets with his artillery, and the first gun, with a few random shots from the American pickets upon him as he marched forward in the snowstorm and darkness, followed by the general discharge, apprised the Americans of the advent of the enemy.

Fortunately the darkness prevented much damage from being done on either side by the firing, and it was not until daybreak that the battle became serious. Meanwhile Proctor extended his line, placed two of his guns to the eastward of Lewis' division, and massed a large force of Indians on the exposed flank of Wells' command.

Winchester had arisen when he had heard the sound of firing in the winter morning, hastily dressed and galloped to the front with his staff. There was no want of courage in the old man. He at once took position on the right flank of Wells' troops. As it grew lighter he discovered the mass of Indians menacing this right, the discovery being emphasized by the severe fire which the Indians poured upon the regulars from the cover of the trees with which the country abounded. Then for the first time he seems to have realized the untenable position of the men, and he ordered them to withdraw into the stockade, or, as it is sometimes alleged, to retire and reform behind the houses back of Wells' position.

The greater portion of these troops had never been in action before. As a rule it is only seasoned veterans who can safely be withdrawn from a position in the heat of a fierce action. The little prairie upon which the town stands was now ringing with musketry. The Americans were fighting coolly, although they were suffering great loss. It was evident, however, that the position of Wells' regiment was hopeless. Winchester had to order the retrograde movement or see the flank cut to pieces where it stood.

The regiment started back in good order, but the Indians, mistaking the manoeuvre for a retreat, contrary to their practice broke from cover and rushed upon the Americans. They were two to one at the point of contact, the march became a run, the run engendered a panic, and in a wild, disorganized mass the soldiers streamed past the stockade, through the town and made for the frozen river.

Colonel Lewis in the stockade, seeing the disaster, despatched Colonel Allen's regiment to charge the advancing Indians and give the regulars time to recover. He himself gallantly left the stockade and joined Winchester, Wells, Major McLanahan, and other officers in an heroic effort to stay the wild rout, but all in vain. Allen's men, who charged the Indians bravely, were shattered by a heavy fire, the Indians made a counter-charge in the smoke, the Americans were swept away and at once followed the others in retreat, the savages close on their heels.

Round Head had handled his savages with great skill and he was now reaping the reward of his generalship. The fleeing men were shot down, tomahawked, and scalped in scores. Of the whole lot, only thirty-three escaped. The remainder were overtaken and surrounded south of the Raisin and butchered without mercy. One young officer surrendered himself, and twenty men and the whole number, saving himself, were immediately shot, or tomahawked, and scalped. Colonel Wells and Major McLanahan were killed and most of the other officers as well.

Colonel Allen, desperately wounded, backed up against a tree for support. His offer to surrender was at first accepted, but two Indians made for him with hostile intent. Allen, perceiving their design, determined to sell his life dearly. He cut the first man down and killed him with one terrific blow of the sword. The second man shot him dead. He was one of the finest gentlemen of Kentucky.

General Winchester and Colonel Wells were taken alive. The Indians stripped the poor old general and his surviving officers of their uniforms, so that they nearly perished with cold, and then marched them to Proctor's headquarters. The right wing of the American army had not only been routed but annihilated. The battle, so far as they were concerned, had ceased when they began to retreat. The field was turned into a shambles. The Indians in this part of the affair suffered but little loss.

Meanwhile Proctor had been furiously assailing the stockade. Three times he had launched his regulars and Canadians in force upon it. Although dismayed and appalled by the repulse of the right wing, the Americans under Major Madison, a veteran of the Revolution, in which he had fought under George Rogers Clark, at the age of twelve, and of the Indian Wars under St. Clair and Wayne, put up a fierce defence. Major Graves, the senior officer, having been severely wounded early in the action. Three times they repulsed the British, killing and wounding over half the regulars present. So accurate was their rifle fire that sixteen men were killed or wounded, in quick succession, around the nearest six-pounder of the English, and the service of the gun was abandoned.

The Indians, flushed with their victory, now joined the beleaguering force and poured in a tremendous fire upon the stockade, which was spiritedly returned, and a heavy loss was here inflicted upon the savages.

Proctor finally withdrew his cannon and had about made up his mind to abandon the siege when he resolved to try a stratagem. The frozen, exhausted, old American general was brought to him. Winchester had just witnessed the annihilation of nearly half his force. Proctor assumed a threatening manner and declared that the stockade was practically in the power of the British, and unless it were immediately given up he would abandon it to the Indians, with the result that all the Americans would be massacred. The British commander said that if the matter came to a storm he would be unable to control the Indians. If, however, Winchester would order his men to surrender. Proctor pledged his sacred honour that he would give the prisoners protection from the Indians, treat them as prisoners of war, and allow the officers to retain their side arms and private property.

Winchester, a kind-hearted old man, whose nerves had been greatly shaken by the awful slaughter he had witnessed, for the supposed sake of his men wrote an order directing Major Madison to surrender. Winchester, being a captive, had no right to give an order of any kind, and no obedience would have been required from any man to such an order.

So successful had been the defence of the stockade that when Madison's men saw the flag of truce coming they imagined that it might be a request for a parley to permit the British to secure their dead and wounded and march away, or perhaps even surrender. Though how they could have thought that troops in the open, capable of retreating, would surrender to troops in a stockade is difficult to understand. Madison's men knew that the right wing had been repulsed, but were ignorant that it had been annihilated, and when they received the order, and the news as well, they were appalled.

Through some error Winchester's order for surrender did not specify anything about protection or other conditions. Proctor, who had come himself with the flag of truce, had a fiery interview with the American commander, who refused absolutely to surrender until promised safety for his men from Indian attacks. This Proctor assured him in the most solemn manner; thereupon Madison yielded his position.

He probably would not have done so, but his ammunition was all but exhausted. Had Proctor made another attack this fact would have been developed and the Americans would have been at the mercy of the enemy. As soon as the surrender was announced the Indians, frenzied by the excitement of battle and the number of slain, immediately rushed upon the Americans *tomahawk* and scalping knife in hand. Fortunately the troops still retained their arms and they turned upon the savages with muskets, bayonets, and bowie knives, and taught them a salutary lesson. Proctor had manifested little desire, and had made no attempt to restrain the Indians, but they were so savagely handled that they fled, leaving these Americans severely alone.

There had been about six hours of fighting, during which the

"Proctor ... had a fiery interview with the American commander."

Americans had lost about three hundred and fifty killed. There were some seventy-five severely wounded in addition and about five hundred were made prisoners. Proctor, in deadly anxiety lest Harrison should approach him with his army, immediately put his force in array to march back to the main body at Maiden. The American wounded were left at Frenchtown under the care of two of their surgeons who had survived the slaughter of the battle, in charge of a British major and three interpreters with no force to protect them. Proctor promised to send sledges to fetch them the next day.

4. THE MURDER OF THE WOUNDED

The Indians marched away with Proctor, but it was learned by the inhabitants of the village that they halted six miles from Frenchtown by Proctor's permission for "a jollification"—a war or scalp dance, or some such hellish revel. The night of the 22nd was passed in terrified apprehension by the poor wounded men for whom the surgeons were doing the best they could. On the morning of the 23rd some two hundred of the savages returned to Frenchtown. They were already excited by the liquor they had imbibed and they procured an additional supply by breaking into some of the houses. The wounded prisoners were dragged forth. Those who were unable to walk were stripped, shot, tomahawked, and scalped. Some of them were left in houses which were set on fire and then burned to death.

The lives of about thirty who could manage to drag themselves along were spared, and they were driven in the frightful cold toward the headquarters at Maiden. All who could manage to stagger tried to make the journey; they hobbled along till their strength gave out and were butchered where they fell. Many of the prisoners were not given up to the British, but were retained in bondage by the Indians.

This was the way Proctor kept his promise. These two hundred Indians comprised the escort he had ordered to bring up to Maiden the wounded prisoners who had trusted to his honour. An old report from a Canadian paper, in my possession, has the following comment: "All day throughout the Indians behaved nobly, and the instant the enemy surrendered, their forbearance, as in former actions, was strikingly conspicuous." Wasn't it?

The fate of Captain Hart, the brother-in-law of Henry Clay, was particularly harrowing. Although badly wounded he had begged of Captain Elliott that he might be taken with the other prisoners on the 22nd, and the men of his company offered to carry him. But Elliott

212

pledged his honour that Hart would be safe and that his own private sleigh should be sent for him the next morning. This Elliott had been a whilom personal friend of Hart's and a man who was indebted to Hart's family for many kindnesses before the war. He had charge of the Indian allies and is reputed to have said significantly to some of the wounded who asked for attendants and assistance, "that he would leave them to the Indians, who were *all good doctors!*"

Elliott, of course, broke his promise; his honour was no stronger than Proctor's, and Hart was ruthlessly killed with the rest the next morning. His last words were a prayer to God for strength to meet his fate.

The British loss was twenty-four killed and one hundred and fifty-eight wounded, most of the casualties being from the regular regiments. The Indian loss was probably under fifty. The American loss was between three hundred and ninety and four hundred killed, besides the few wounded whose lives were spared. Thirty-three got away and about five hundred and forty were captured.

Yes, there was sorrow and grief in the tidings to the people of Kentucky. But they were inflamed to furious wrath by the story of the killing by the Indians of the men who had surrendered and of the ruthless butchery of the helpless wounded permitted by Proctor. This affair was known colloquially as "The Massacre of the Raisin," and the war-cry of the Americans, which was heard on many fields and most fiercely at the Battle of the Thames, where Proctor fled like a coward and Tecumseh died like a hero, was, "Remember the Raisin." It is reported that some of the Kentucky borderers flayed the bodies of the Indians, cutting their skins into long razor strops after the Battle of the Thames to "Remember the Raisin."

One of the most damning indictments that has ever been drawn against any civilized nation is that against Great Britain for employing the Indians as allies in this war against the Americans, although in justice to one Indian it may be said, that if Tecumseh had been with Proctor on this occasion it is probable that the massacre might not have occurred.

4

George Croghan and the Defence of Fort Stephenson

1. A Boy in Command of Other Boys

This is a story of a mere boy and a lot of other boys, on the frontier; an account of their heroic but forgotten exploit. It is barely mentioned in the larger histories, and its value is scarcely understood. Important or not, it introduces us to specimens of young American manhood of which we may well be proud.

Strange to say, few people at present have any but the vaguest idea as to who George Croghan was, and fewer still have ever heard of the fight at Fort Stephenson; yet the names of both soldier and battle were once on everybody's lips, and they deserve a high and honourable place in the long and brilliant galaxy of American fights and fighters.

Prior to the War of the Rebellion, by specific acts of Congress, from time to time, some forty-two of our soldiers and sailors were awarded medals for heroic exploits or successful battles. Eleven went to Revolutionary heroes, the French and Tripolitan Wars were credited with one each, the War of 1812 with twenty-seven, and two commanders were so distinguished in the Mexican War. The total number of medals for all causes distributed by act of Congress prior to 1861 was eighty-four.

The War of 1812 brought forth so large a number because every captain who took a ship in the marvellous sea fights of the period, received a medal. Also, in several of these ship and squadron engagements medals were awarded to subordinate officers for distinguished conduct. Therefore, it would be fair to say that possibly not more than twenty-five separate actions in eighty-five years of thrilling history in which six wars were fought have been commemorated by the United

States in this signal way. To digress; but two medals were awarded in the Rebellion (to Grant and Commodore Vanderbilt) and but one since (to Dewey), Now the general medal of honour has taken the place of the old-fashioned Congressional award.

One of the 1812 medals was awarded to George Croghan for his heroic defence of Fort Stephenson, and this little prelude shows the importance of it in our history. I believe Croghan was the youngest man to be so signally honoured.

Croghan was a Kentuckian. The family was one of prominence in early American history. His mother was a sister of the famous George Rogers Clark, and it was in her house near Louisville, where Croghan was born November 15, 1791, that the old Revolutionary hero died. Croghan's father had been a Revolutionary soldier, a major, who had fought with credit during that struggle. His parents were fairly well-to-do, and he received the best education then obtainable, at William and Mary College, Virginia, where he graduated in 1810, at the age of eighteen—a bright youth indeed!

When General William Henry Harrison started on his Indiana campaign to break up the conspiracy of Tecumseh, in 1811, young Croghan, whose predilections were entirely military, accompanied the expedition as a volunteer aid to Colonel Boyd, who commanded the United States troops on this occasion. He distinguished himself at the famous night battle of Tippecanoe, received a coveted appointment in the army, and the War of 1812 found him a captain in the Seventeenth Regiment of United States Infantry. He participated in all of Harrison's early campaigns and he again distinguished himself in a sortie at the famous siege of Fort Meigs, where he did valiant service as Harrison's *aide-de-camp*. He was mentioned in the despatches and rewarded by being promoted major of the Seventeenth Infantry.

After the abandonment of the siege by the British he was sent with a battalion of his regiment, comprising with the officers one hundred and sixty men, to garrison Fort Stephenson. These officers, all youths, most of them junior in years to their boyish commander, have earned a place in history, and their names are here set down: Captain James Hunter, Lieutenants Benjamin Johnston and Cyrus A. Baylor, Ensigns John Meek, Joseph Duncan, and Edmund Shipp; all of the Seventeenth Regulars except Meek, who belonged to the Ninth. With them went Lieutenant Anderson, who, having no command, served valiantly as a volunteer in the ranks.

Fort Stephenson was a ramshackle old stockade, built around a former Indian trader's house at the head of navigation on the San-dusky River, about twenty miles from the Lake Erie shore, in what is now Sandusky County, Ohio. The place was sometimes called Lower Sandusky, and the battle is frequently referred to as the defence of Lower Sandusky. The stockade, which was not in particularly good repair, was made of piles sixteen feet high, and surrounding them was a dry ditch about eight or nine feet wide, and five or six feet deep. The fort, enclosing about an acre of ground, was laid out in the form of a parallelogram, with a blockhouse at the northeast corner and a guardhouse at the southeast. To supplement these Croghan had erected another blockhouse midway on the north wall, from which he could enfilade the ditch. He also strengthened the palisade, and put it in as good a state of repair as possible.

The place had not been designed as a fort. Originally it had only been intended as a defence against Indians. It was situated on low ground near the river, commanded by surrounding hills, and was un-tenable in the face of artillery. It was a depot of supplies of some importance, although the great depot for Ohio was at Upper Sandusky, some twenty miles up the river. There was also a third depot and much valuable government material at Erie, where Perry had been busily engaged in building and outfitting his famous squadron. Fort Stephenson, therefore, was an outpost which stood between the two great depots in which were stored the provisions and munitions of war for all the American armies in the northwest. It was at the apex of a triangle, the base line of which connected Erie and Upper Sandusky. Its fall would leave a way open to attack one or the other of these vitally important places without much difficulty. Harrison with a very inconsiderable force was posted at Seneca Falls, about ten miles away from Fort Stephenson.

In the latter part of July, 1813, General Proctor, with a large force numbering at least three thousand Indians under Tecumseh, and six hundred British regulars, crossed the Lake from Maiden and appeared before Fort Meigs on the Maumee. Finding that he could not tempt the small garrison to a sortie by a clever ruse invented by Tecumseh, he determined to leave the fort for the present, and re-embarking his regular soldiers in gunboats and directing the Indians to follow them along the shore, he made a swift dash at Fort Stephenson. He expected to capture it without difficulty, fall on General Harrison's little force at Seneca Falls, and after defeating it have the government storehouse and in fact the whole of Ohio at his mercy. Harrison, of

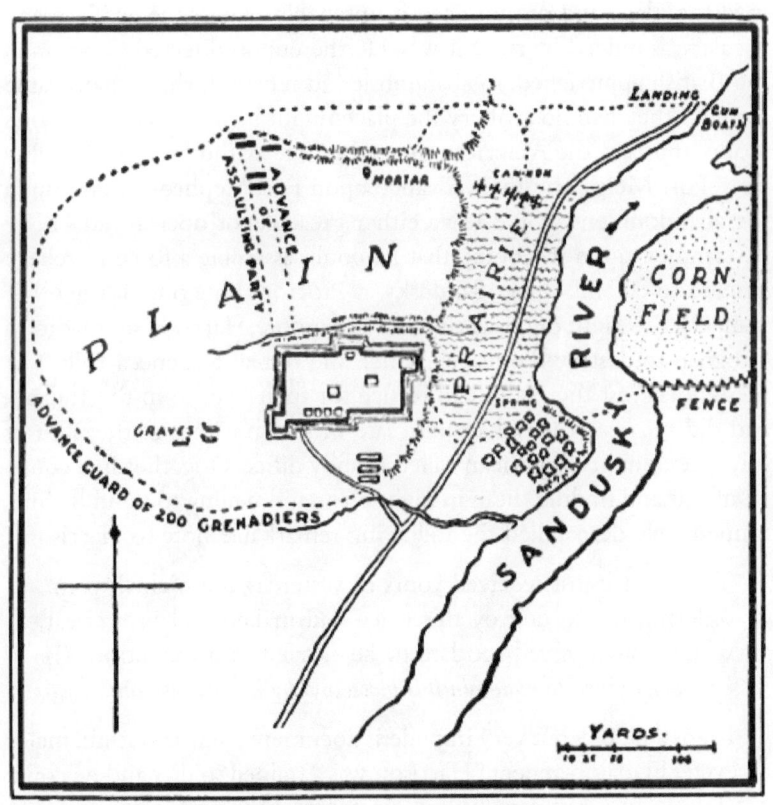

MAP OF FORT STEPHENSON.

course, divined his plan, and the people of the northwest who could remember the bloody massacre at the Raisin River, well knew what to expect from the mercy of Proctor and his braves. It was Croghan who frustrated this brilliant scheme.

2. THE IMPUDENCE OF THE YOUNG CAPTAIN

A few days before the arrival of the British, Harrison had examined the place and pronounced it untenable against the artillery and regulars, as indeed by right it was. He thereupon directed Croghan, if the British approached, to abandon it and retreat. If the Indians came alone, as they had no artillery, the place might be defended. Harrison's scouts apprised the American general of the withdrawal of the allies from Fort Meigs, and their advance upon Fort Stephenson. Although the abandonment would leave either great depot open to attack, he determined upon it, hoping that he could assemble a force to relieve Erie, or to defend Upper Sandusky, as Proctor chose one or the other plan. On the night of the 29th of July, therefore, Harrison sent word to Croghan to destroy the place at once and retreat to Seneca Falls. The messengers lost their way, had to flee for their lives from the Indians, and did not reach Croghan until late in the morning of the 30th of July. The doughty American called his boy officers together in a council of war and finding them in high spirits and willing to stand by him, immediately despatched the following remarkable note to Harrison :

Sir:—I have just received yours of yesterday, ten o'clock p. m., ordering me to destroy this place and make good my retreat, which was received too late to be carried into execution. *We have determined to maintain this place, and by heavens, we can.*

It was a plucky but very impudent document from a youthful major to a veteran major-general! Harrison was a trained soldier and he could not brook for a moment having his orders disobeyed in this manner. He sent a squadron of cavalry with an officer to supersede Croghan and ordered him to report at headquarters at once. The cavalry fought its way down the river through hostile Indians, of whom they managed to kill nearly a score, by the way, and delivered the message. Croghan turned the fort over to Colonel Wells, and repaired at once to headquarters. He explained that the general's orders had been delayed in reaching him and the woods were now filled with Indians. He did not think it prudent under the circumstances to retreat with so large a body of infantry, and he had worded his reply in the bluff way in which

218

he did in the hope and expectation that it would fall into the hands of the enemy. He expressed himself as confident of his ability to hold the post, or at least make the British pay a staggering price for it, and begged to be reinstated in his command and to be given permission to try it. Harrison, who was very fond of the young fellow, generously accepted his explanation, and allowed him to resume his command.

Croghan immediately returned to the fort, relieved Wells, and made vigorous preparation for its defence against the expected attack, which was not long delayed. On the first of August, about noon, the Indians were perceived in large numbers surrounding the fort. Tradition has it that one of them climbed a tall tree overlooking the enclosure, but before he could make any report of what he saw he was shot dead by the unerring rifles of the Kentuckians. Others who made the attempt fared in the same way, and the Indians at last concluded that it would not be safe to reconnoitre in that manner. They gathered in some force on the edge of the clearing finally, but a discharge from a six-pound gun,[1] Croghan's solitary piece of artillery, easily dispersed them.

About four o'clock in the afternoon the British boats appeared at a bend in the river and opened fire upon the fort from the boat guns. The British troops were disembarked about a mile below the fort, and a five and a half inch howitzer was landed and began a cannonade, a fire the garrison received for the most part in silence, although the six-pounder which was mounted in the northeast blockhouse was dragged from port-hole to port-hole to give the impression of force, and fired occasionally. The number of the besiegers was about twelve hundred, of whom seven hundred were Indians. Tecumseh, with two thousand savages, was placed some miles back to menace the troops in Fort Meigs and the camp at Seneca Falls, if either moved to relieve Fort Stephenson, and he took no part in the battle. The odds were heavy enough as it was; twelve hundred with ample artillery, against one hundred and sixty and one gun, led by youths!

As soon as the British landed, Colonel Elliott and Major Chambers, accompanied by Captain Dixen of the Royal Engineers, commanding the Indian auxiliaries, were sent forward with a white flag by General Proctor to demand the surrender of the fort.

Ensign Edmund Shipp, the youngest officer in the post, and he must have been a mere boy indeed, was sent out to discover the pur-

---

1. The soldiers called this cannon "Good Bess," for what reason it is hard to say. Why is it that so many guns, rifles, cannon, etc. , famous in history have been called "Bess" or "Betsy"? What's in that name to make it appropriate, I wonder?

port of the flag; whereupon, after the usual salutations, an interesting conversation took place. Colonel Elliott demanded the "instant surrender of the fort, to spare the effusion of blood, which we cannot do, should we be under the necessity of reducing it by our powerful force of regulars, Indians, and artillery."

"My commandant and the garrison," replied the gallant young Shipp, "are determined to defend the post to the last extremity and bury themselves in its ruins, rather than surrender it to any force whatever."

"Look at the immense body of Indians," urged Dixen, "they cannot be restrained from massacring the whole garrison in the event of our undoubted success."

"Our success is certain," added Chambers promptly.

"Sir," said Elliott, "you appear to be a fine young man. I pity your situation. For God's sake urge the surrender of the fort and prevent the slaughter which must follow resistance should you fall into the hands of the savages."

"It is a pity," continued Dixen beseechingly, "that so fine a young man as your commander is represented to be, should fall into the hands of the savages. Sir, for God's sake surrender and prevent the dreadful massacre that will be caused by your resistance."

"When the fort shall be taken," replied Shipp dauntlessly, entirely unaffected by these terrifying appeals, which only disclosed the incapacity of the British to control their red allies, "there will be none to massacre. It will not be given up while a man is able to resist."

Pretending to be fearful for Shipp's safety. Colonel Elliott thereupon urged him to go back to the fort at once. As the boy officer turned away, an Indian sprang from the bushes and endeavoured to wrest his sword from him and cut him down. It was with great difficulty, which is believed to have been a pretence, that Dixen dragged away the savage and besought Shipp to return with all speed to save his life, as he could not control the Indians! The bluff did not work at all. The young subaltern did not scare a little bit. Croghan was standing on the rampart, watching the scene, and when he perceived the insult to his envoy he shouted:

"Come in, Shipp, and we'll blow 'em all to hell!" Language which it is presumed he did not learn at William and Mary College, but which was singularly appropriate at the time! It was a bold defiance indeed from the one hundred and sixty to the twelve hundred. There was a massacre sure enough, too, as it turned out, but the Americans were not the victims.

3. Desperate Fighting

The bombardment began at once, and continued with more or less vigour all the night, during which the British landed five six-pounders, parking three of them in a battery on a hill covered by trees, about two hundred and fifty yards from the stockade, and disposing of the others to advantage. In the morning they opened a furious fire to which the Americans made little or no reply. During the night, with immense labour, Captain Hunter, the second in command, had succeeded in transporting the six-pound gun to the blockhouse on the north wall. Anticipating an assault upon the northwest corner of the fort upon which the fire of the British had been concentrated during most of the day, the gun had been so placed as to rake the ditch. It was loaded with a half charge of powder, on account of the short range, and a double charge of slugs and bullets. The port-hole was masked and the gun remained hidden.

During the day whenever an Indian or a soldier showed himself outside of cover the Kentuckians took quick and generally successful shots at him, but otherwise the garrison made little response to the continuous cannonading, husbanding their powder, of which their supply was small. They were very busy, however, carrying sacks of flour and bags of sand from the storehouse to support the northwest corner of the stockade, which was being breached and demolished under the heavy battering it was receiving from the British guns. Croghan, of course, had taken his position on the northwest corner.

Everyone was on the alert, however, when about five o'clock in the afternoon a storming party of some three hundred soldiers of the Forty-first Regiment rushed for the northwest corner, while at the same time two hundred grenadiers made a detour through the woods and advanced to attack the south wall. Under cover of a fierce fire from the batteries and from every tree or hill on the high ground, which surrounded the fort, which would serve to conceal an Indian, the attack was delivered. The sky was black with storm clouds at the time, and peals of thunder in heavy detonations mingled with the roaring of the cannon and the rattle of the musketry.

The place was covered with smoke which concealed the main advance until the English were within twenty feet of the fort. The first warning the startled Americans had was the sight of the grim faces of the red-coats shoving through the smoke. A deadly rifle fire

"THE YOUNG SUBALTERN DID NOT SCARE A LITTLE BIT."

which flashed from every port-hole checked them and threw them into confusion.

The hesitation of the British, however, was but momentary. Lieutenant-Colonel Short, their leader, sprang to the head of the column. Waving his sword in the air, he so inspirited them that they once more advanced. They came on with fixed bayonets without firing, in spite of a rapid and continuous discharge from the fort. Although many fell, they did not hesitate even when they reached the edge of the ditch, crying, "Come on, men! We'll give the damned Yankees no quarter!" Short, followed by Major Muir, and Lieutenant Gordon of the Forty-first, and the redoubtable Dixen, leaped into the ditch, and tried to scramble up the other side of it.

The Americans could not depress their rifles sufficiently to reach the men in the ditch, unless they exposed themselves above the stockade, which would be to invite destruction from the fire of the Indians. Short and his men, who had followed him most gallantly, concluded that when they gained the ditch they were safe for the time. Alas, they knew nothing of the masked six-pounder, for at this instant, the port was thrown open and the cannon, effectively served by some Pittsburg volunteers, hurled its deadly charge of bullets and slugs at short range into the British huddled together in the ditch. No less than fifty men were killed, or so seriously wounded by that awful discharge that they could not escape from the death trap, and numbers of others were slightly injured. Colonel Short received a mortal wound and with his last effort raised his handkerchief upon the point of his sword, pleading for mercy, although but a moment since he had threatened to give no quarter. Gordon was instantly killed; Muir, Dixen, and other officers were wounded, but managed to escape.

Appalled by such an awful slaughter and met by a continuous withering fire from the American rifles and muskets, the Englishmen who had not yet entered the ditch hesitated for a moment and, being without a leader, turned and fled, pursued by effective discharges from the six-pounder and dropping on their retreat in scores. On the south wall, where Hunter commanded, the attacking party under Colonel Warburton had fared scarcely any better. On both sides of the fort a long swath of dead or wounded grenadiers, writhing upon the ground in agony, showed the ebb and flow of the disastrous attack.

The retreating British soon gained the safe shelter of the woods, where they were finally re-formed, and the cannonade which had been intermitted at the moment of storm was feebly resumed. Croghan, however, knew that he had nothing more to fear. The assault had been repulsed with fearful loss, the actual fighting occupying scarcely half an hour. He had made good his defiance and had held the fort.

The situation of the wounded men in the ditch was pitiful. The British could make no move to extricate them or succour them. To come out in the open and face those rifles was death to them; and the Americans did not dare to open the gate and go into the ditch for the same reason. The poor soldiers had to lie there and endure their sufferings as best they could through the long night. Croghan was a merciful man and he did what he could for them. Buckets of water—the first thing a wounded man in battle craves—were lowered down to them over the stockade, and a small trench was dug beneath it into the ditch through which those who were able to crawl could come into the American works for help. Some of the more slightly wounded managed to reach their own lines under cover of the darkness.

The loss of the British had been so severe during the action of the two days—between twenty-five and thirty *per cent,* of the five hundred engaged, not including the casualties among the Indians, which were considerable—that Proctor retreated during the night with such precipitancy that he left behind one boatload of stores and munitions of war; and the next morning the triumphant defenders gathered some seventy stand of arms, in addition to those taken from the men who had been swept into eternity in the ditch, which had been abandoned by the British in their hasty flight. The American loss was one poor fellow killed and seven wounded, none severely !

The American supply depots were saved, and the whole state of Ohio was again delivered from the fear of a British conquest, with its attendant savage horrors, by the pluck and devotion of this young man and his gallant little band. As General Harrison said, in his report of the occurrence :

"It will not be the least of General Proctor's mortification to find that he has been baffled by a youth who has just passed his twenty-first year. He is, however, a hero, worthy of his gallant uncle. General George Rogers Clark."

Congress brevetted Croghan a lieutenant-colonel, and, years afterward, presented him with a medal of honour for his splendid and magnificent defence with its far-reaching consequences. Like his great uncle, he had again saved the northwest to the American flag. And the "final defeat of Proctor at the Thames may be traced back to this bloody repulse at Lower Sandusky.

1

David Crockett and the Most Desperate Defence in American History

1. A TYPICAL AMERICAN

> **MY DOG!**
> ANDREW JACKSON.

That is what, in emphatic language entirely consonant with his actions, David Crockett said he would never wear on his collar. And the doughty declaration of individual right following may be taken as indicating what David Crockett really was. It reads well in these days of the Boss and His Slaves—which things are we !

> I am at liberty to vote as my conscience and judgment dictate
> to be right, without the yoke of any party on me, or the driver
> at my heels with the whip in his hands, commanding me to
> 'Gee-whoa-haw' just at his pleasure.

The spelling of the paragraph is not that of its author. In his autobiography, one of the most naive and delightful of books, he takes occasion to defend his orthography by remarking that he despised "the way of spelling contrary to nature!" It may be said, in passing, that many of his most eminent fellow-citizens and contemporaries shared his contempt for the rules of orthography. In that book he speaks of himself with the utmost frankness; as for instance :

> Obscure as I am my name is making a considerable deal of fuss
> in the world. I can't tell why it is, nor in what it is to end. Go

225

where I will everybody seems anxious to get a peep at me; and it would be hard to tell which would have the advantage if I, and the 'Government,'[1] and 'Black Hawk,' and a great eternal big caravan of *wild varments*, were all to be showed at the same time in four different parts of any of the big cities of the nation, I am not so sure that I shouldn't get the most custom of any of the crew!

A modest man was David, it would appear, and a confident author, too; witness this assertion:

I don't know of anything in my book to be criticised by honourable men. Is it my spelling?—that's not my trade. Is it my grammar?—I hadn't time to learn it and make no pretension to it. Is it in the order and arrangement of my book?—I never wrote one before and never read very many; and of course know mighty little about that. Will it be on authorship?—this I claim and I'll hang on to it like a wax plaster!

Evidently he considered grammar of no more account than spelling, and equally evidently the porous plaster had not been invented when he searched for a clinging simile !

There never was the slightest room for misunderstanding where Crockett was concerned. His character was plainness and simplicity itself. He usually hit the mark at which he aimed, whether with a rifle or not, in life, so clearly and plainly that dispute was impossible. Even the "'coon" up the tree upon which he "drew a bead" with his famous weapon, the death-dealing "Betsy," at once recognized the futility of resistance, and, being for the nonce endowed with speech, with the famous remark, "Don't shoot, Colonel, I'll come down," gave up the game. True, Crockett would not be Andrew Jackson's dog, and because he countered some of the President's plans he had to give way—as did nearly everyone else in like circumstances. But nothing less than "Old Hickory"—better "Old Steel"—ever mastered or moved this redoubtable pioneer—unless it was a woman. His was a susceptible heart !

Nowhere but in America would such a career as Crockett's have been possible. With Jackson and Houston he represents a phase of American life, opportunity, and success, peculiar to the time and not to be repeated again. Though he was the least and humblest of the fa-

1. By the "Government" he means—and appropriately enough, too—Andrew Jackson, the book being written while Crockett was in Congress.

mous trio in both achievement and reputation, he was not unworthy of association with them. And upon the score of manly, lovable qualities he stood first of the three. His famous motto, which he earnestly strove to live up to, was of the very best :

Be sure you're right, then go ahead!

Crockett was born at Limestone, Greene County, Tennessee, on the seventeenth of August, 1786. His father was an Irish immigrant who had fought in the Revolution at King's Mountain—a patent of nobility on the frontier, that—and his mother was an American girl (the combination is delightful and promising). His parents were poor but happy—and therefore honest it may be inferred. Young David grew up in the wilds of Tennessee, a tall, sturdy, swarthy lad, with hair black and straight as an Indian's and keen yet merry eyes to match. He took to the forest instinctively, loving it, mastering its hidden lore, knowing its secrets, and little else apparently.

At the age of twelve he was apprenticed to a Dutch teamster, very much against his desire. After an enforced journey of four hundred miles to Virginia he ran away, and not daring to follow the road for fear of pursuit, he plunged into the wilderness and made his way back home after a hazardous and wonderful journey alone through the trackless woods. He was thereafter sent to school, where he spent just four days. Having whipped a larger and older boy who attempted to tyrannize over him, he played truant to avoid punishment, and when detected ran away again.

He spent some three years in teaming and nearly two years with a hatter—singularly inappropriate calling—and then returned home. He found his people in straitened financial circumstances and generously worked a year to cancel two notes amounting to $86 which a neighbour held against the elder Crockett. Thereafter he resolved to go to school. Love sent him there. The young girls of the vicinity scorned him for his ignorance, which of books at any rate was dense, not to say, total. As he said long after:

But it will be a source of astonishment to many who reflect that I am now a member of the American Congress—the most enlightened body of men in the world—that at so advanced an age as the age of fifteen I did not know the first letter in the book!

He continued at school for six months, working two days a week

227

for his board and attending the sessions on the other four. And that completed his education. At the age of fifteen he "struck out" for himself and became a farm labourer, teamster, trapper, hunter, and general frontiersman. After various love affairs more or less serious, in 1809 he married a young Irish girl, with whom he moved westward to Franklin County and began housekeeping with "fifteen dollars' worth of things fixed up pretty grand!" For six years the young couple were very happy. They had plenty to eat, largely the result of Crockett's skill with old "Betsy," enough to wear, the fruit of the young wife's loom, and they exemplified in their lives his saying, "For I reckon we love as hard in the backwoods as any people in the whole creation! "The death of his first wife in 1815 was a sad blow to him and his young children.

In 1813 Crockett served with credit as a scout under Jackson in the Creek War. In 1816 he married again, this time a widow. There were three sets of children who lived together in an amicable if happy-go-lucky way. In 1821 he was elected a magistrate and a colonel of militia, although at the time he says he had never read a newspaper! Such was his popularity that he was successively elected to the State Legislature and then to Congress, where he served two terms; his ignorance, his oddity, his humour, his bravery, and his shrewdness, making him a figure of national prominence. Failing of re-election because of his antagonism to the policy of his whilom friend Jackson, and finding any future political career in Tennessee closed to him, he determined like many southern men of that day to go to Texas, then in the beginning of her efforts for freedom. There he hoped to make his fortune and there he found his end. And truly nothing in his life became him better than the ending of it!

2. THE LONE STAR REPUBLIC

By the treaty of 1819 with Spain the United States relinquished all claim to the western part of Louisiana, so called, lying south of the Red River and west of the Sabine, including the territory now comprised within the present state of Texas, then a part of the vice-royalty of Mexico. In 1821 Mexico revolted from Spain, and in 1822 one Iturbide assumed the government and the Imperial title; his career was brief but stirring, and in 1824 he was deposed and a constitution establishing the Republic of Mexico was adopted. Of this Republic Texas, conjoined to Coahuila, its western neighbour, became one of the states.

The first American colony of any moment had been planted there in 1820 under the leadership of Stephen F. Austin, justly styled "The Father of Texas." Successive immigration from the southern United States during fifteen years had brought the number of white Americans within the quarter million miles of Texas land up to twenty thousand, with a small but steadily increasing number of negro slaves. The Spanish or Mexican population was inconsiderable.

The character of the American immigrants was not uniform. There were many insolvent debtors who had fled from their creditors in the States, broken shopkeepers leaving the letters "G. T. T." (Gone to Texas) chalked upon their doors, not a few adventurers and soldiers of fortune, and as everywhere, some scoundrels, but the general average of the American settlers was remarkably high. The majority were honest, capable, law-abiding, hard-working people of the middle class, the best stock out of which to build a nation. Accustomed to hunting and frontier life, they were bold and hardy, if reckless and impatient of discipline and restraint. All of them, like Crockett, were expert riflemen.

Meanwhile, the Mexican government became the prize of a succession of worthless adventurers, using their opportunities for their own aggrandizement. Finally, in 1833, one Antonio Lopez de Santa Anna seized the Presidential office, abolished the Congress and made himself Dictator. This petty "Napoleon of the West," as he loved to style himself, was as black-hearted a scoundrel as ever schemed himself into power. Born at Jalapa in Mexico in 1795, he had been successively a lieutenant-colonel in the Spanish army, an adherent of Iturbide, a traitor to him, the *diabolus ex machina* of the successive revolutions with their different presidents, dictators, etc.—in short, a sort of subtropic Warwick!

He was not without some of the qualities of a soldier, however, and he certainly knew how to win the confidence of his countrymen again and again, in spite of their frequent repudiations of him, in his long and eventful career. His oppressive hand was at once laid upon Texas, and because the Americans would not tamely submit to be deprived of every political right by a series of drastic measures which actually included the proposed confiscation of their arms—their sole means of defence against Indians and the Mexicans themselves—they revolted. As a matter of fact they were eager to do so.

The position of Mexico on the question of slavery was a great cause of irritation to the Texans. Slavery was prohibited by the Mexican Congress in 1824 and was formally abolished by the legislature, all Mexicans, in Texas-Coahuila, in 1829. The Americans refused to be governed by these enactments and prohibitions and defiantly retained their slaves, even adding to their number by importation. This was flat and open rebellion and was quite sufficient to account for the hostilities that followed. However, Mexico might have cared but little about that matter if the colony had not rebelled against the wretched maladministration of the Mexicans and because the Americans were practically refused even the smallest share of the government, in spite of the constitution. Besides, it is not the habit of Americans to submit to the domination of any alien race whatsoever, especially of the Spanish family. They could not stand the Spaniard in his Mexican, or any other guise—that was enough to account for it.

3. THE MISSION DEL ALAMO

The Texan War of Independence began with a skirmish at Gonzales near the end of October, 1835. A Texan declaration of principles was adopted November 13th, 1835, and the Declaration of Independence on March 2nd of the following year. The battle of Concepcion was won by the Texans on October 28th, 1835, and on December 10th, after a siege and an assault which continued for six days, the city of San Antonio de Bexar, the most considerable town in Texas, was captured, and every Mexican soldier was expelled from the territory. Hard by the town stood the buildings of the Mission of San Antonio de Valero, commonly called the Mission del Alamo, or the Alamo, word signifying cotton-wood tree. The Alamo was founded by the Franciscans in 1703, and after various removals, established in its present location in 1722.

The mission buildings comprised a main *plaza* in the shape of a long parallelogram about fifty by a hundred and fifty yards, with the major axis north and south; the enclosing wall, built of *adobe* bricks, was about eight feet high and three feet thick. On the west side of the *plaza* stood a row of one-storey buildings, and along the middle of the east side for about sixty yards was a two-storey convent eighteen feet wide. To the east of the convent lay a yard about a hundred feet square with walls over three feet thick and about sixteen feet high, further strengthened on the inside by an embankment eight feet high. At the northeast corner of this yard was a sally-port covered by an earth redoubt. At the southeast corner of the yard stood the stone church of the mission, built in the form of a cross, properly orientated; the walls of the church were five feet thick and twenty-two feet high, and the

The Mission del Alamo

building was roofless and dismantled.

A formidable stockade connected the church and the southeast corner of the main *plaza*. Fourteen small pieces of artillery were mounted on the walls, including three in the chancel of the church. Two aqueducts touching the west wall and the church respectively provided a sufficiency of water.

Early in 1836 the commander of this fort, if such the mission may be called, was Lieutenant-Colonel William Barrett Travis, a young lawyer from North Carolina, a tall, manly, red-headed young fighter, then just twenty-eight years of age.[2] Associated with him in the Alamo was Colonel James Bowie of Georgia—he of the sinister knife of the same name. Bowie was senior in age and rank to Travis, but had been disabled by a fall and was then confined to his room by the injury, to which an attack of pleuro-pneumonia was superadded; and he was therefore compelled to yield the command to Travis. Bowie was not too ill to fight, though, as we shall see. Under these two officers were about one hundred and forty officers and men, a totally inadequate force, as it would have required at least one thousand men properly to man the extensive lines of the Alamo.

To this little band early in February, 1836, came a welcome re-enforcement in the shape of David Crockett with twelve of his Tennessee friends and neighbours willing to help Texas to gain her independence and incidentally to join in what they all dearly loved—any kind of a fight! They were all clad in hunting suits, with 'coon-skin caps, and armed with long rifles and Bowie knives! It is significant of the spirit of the man, that Crockett refused to swear allegiance to "any future government of Texas." until the word "republican "had been inserted after the word "future" in the prescribed form of the oath.

4. The Hundred and Eighty against the Five Thousand

On the twenty-third of February, 1836, Santa Anna in person appeared before the fort with the advance of his army and demanded its

---

2. Since the first publication of this sketch, I have received a number of letters from persons prominent in the local history of South Carolina, asserting that Travis' name was William Barr, not Barrett, and that he was a foundling; the name, which should be spelled Bar, being given him, it is alleged, from the fact that he was found one morning tied to the bars of a gate on the farm of a man named Travis, who adopted him and named him accordingly. The Travis lot was situated on the public road between Saluda and Johnston, South Carolina, and my correspondents claim Travis should therefore be credited to that State. This adds a further touch of romance to Travis' story.

surrender. He had led some five thousand men of the Mexican regular army, with many camp followers and women, a forced march of one hundred and eighty leagues from Monclova to San Antonio, across a desert country in the depth of a Texas winter with its extremes of heat and cold and blasting storm. Only after incredible hardships and great losses had the terrible march been completed. That Santa Anna could do this is no small evidence of his capacity as a leader and his ability to inspire his men to heroic action.

His arrival was a complete surprise to the Texans; many of them were scattered through the town at a *fandango* at the time. When the alarm was given they repaired to the Alamo and Travis met the demand for a surrender by a shot from his battery, at the same time hoisting his flag. This was the white, red, and green banner of the Mexican Republic with two stars (Texas-Coahuila) in the centre in place of the familiar eagle and serpent. The lone star flag had not then been adopted.

Santa Anna displayed a red ensign signifying that no quarter would be given, and began erecting batteries with which he opened fire, the Texans replying with good effect. The Mexicans, while greatly outnumbering the garrison, were not yet in sufficient force completely to invest the works, although their numbers were increasing as the different regiments followed the advance guard, and the Texans might easily have escaped. Travis, however, had no thought of retreating—not he. He immediately despatched the following appeal for assistance :

To the people of Texas and all Americans in the World.
Commandancy of The Alamo,
Bexar, February 24, 1836.
Fellow Citizens and Compatriots. "I am besieged by a thousand or more of the Mexicans under Santa Anna. I have sustained a continual bombardment for twenty-four hours and have not lost a man. The enemy have demanded a surrender at discretion; otherwise the garrison is to be put to the sword if the place is taken. I have answered the summons with a cannon shot and our flag still waves proudly from the walls. *I shall never surrender or retreat.* Then, I call upon you, in the name of liberty, of patriotism, and of everything dear to the American character, to come to our aid with all dispatch. The enemy are receiving re-enforcements daily and will no doubt increase to three or four thousand in four or five days. Though this call may be

neglected, I am determined to sustain myself as long as possible and die like a soldier who never forgets what is due to his own honour and that of his country.

Victory or Death!

W. Barrett Travis,

Lieutenant-Colonel, Commanding.

P. S.—The Lord is on our side. When the army appeared in sight we had not three bushels of corn. We have since found in deserted houses eighty or ninety bushels and got into the walls twenty or thirty beeves.

Brave Travis! Other ringing sentences from his subsequent letters are worth quoting :

I shall continue to hold the Alamo until I get relief from my countrymen, or I perish in its defence.

Take care of my little boy, if the country should be saved I may make him a splendid fortune, but if the country should be lost and I should perish, he would have nothing but the proud rec-ollection that he is the son of a man who died for his country.

The thought of that little boy adds a touch of pathos to the story of the dauntless cavalier and his devoted band facing fearful odds "for liberty and honour, God and Texas, victory or death!"'

Travis also despatched messengers invoking assistance from adjacent garrisons. Colonel James Butler Bonham, a young South Carolina volunteer, broke through the Mexican lines and rode post-haste to Colonel Fannin at Goliad, some two hundred miles to the southeast. Fannin promptly started out with three hundred men and four guns, but his ammunition wagons broke down, his transportation failed him, his provisions gave out, he could not get his artillery over the rivers, and he was reluctantly forced to turn back.

He tried in vain to keep Bonham with him. "I will report to Travis or die in the attempt," returned the chivalric Carolinian, who had been a schoolboy friend of Travis, as he started back to the fort. At one o'clock in the morning of March 3rd he succeeded in reaching the fort through the beleaguering army, after a long and dangerous ride in which he literally took his life in his hands. So far as anyone could see he came back to certain death with his friends. Honour to him! Travis had received a valuable re-enforcement of thirty-two heroic fellows from Gonzales, who dashed through the lines on horses, cutting their way into the Alamo at three in the morning of March 1st. Captain J. W. Smith led them and they came cheerfully, although they divined what their fate would be if the place was stormed.

For eleven days the siege continued. The Mexicans lost heavily whenever they came within rifle range; on one occasion they tried to bridge the aqueduct and thirty of them were instantly killed. Sorties were made by the besieged at first, but were soon given over. The bombardment of the works was continuous, but, strange to say, no Texan was killed, although the whole garrison was completely worn out by the strain of ceaseless watching and continual fighting. There is no question but they could have cut their way out and escaped at almost any time, but no one dreamed of such a thing. They were there to stay until the end, whatever it might be.

Santa Anna would undoubtedly get the fort eventually; well, he might have it by paying the price; so they reasoned, but that price would be one, in the words of a later revolutionist, that would "stagger humanity." Knowing Santa Anna, they could have no doubt of his intentions toward them, especially as he had made no secret of his purpose to put them all to death unless they surrendered at discretion. The calm courage with which they faced this appalling certainty is as noteworthy as the high heroism of their last defence.

The last of Santa Anna's army arrived at Bexar on the second of March; he allowed them three days for recuperation and on the fifth held a council of war to decide upon the course to be pursued. The council, like every other, was divided, with a preponderance of opinion in favour of waiting for siege guns to breach or batter down the walls. Santa Anna, however, determined upon an immediate assault, to be delivered at daybreak the next morning. Twenty-five hundred picked men in four columns, commanded respectively by General Cos, who violated his parole thereby, and Colonels Duque, Romero and Morales, were detailed to make the attack. They were provided with scaling ladders, axes, and crowbars, in addition to their weapons; and the cavalry of the army was disposed at strategic points to prevent escape should any of the hundred and eighty defenders succeed in breaking through the assaulting columns. Or, possibly, their function was to cut down any panic-stricken Mexican who might wish to withdraw from before the death-dealing Texas rifles !

Colonel Duque was to lead the main assault on the north side, while a simultaneous attack was to be made on the east and west sides and at the redoubt covering the sally-port from the convent yard. No attack appears to have been contemplated on the stockade on the south wall at first. Accounts of what happened differ widely; it is to be remembered that no American lived to tell the tale, and it is hard to get at the absolute truth from Mexican testimony, and the frightened recollection of two dazed women and two servants. Each narrator must build his own account by considering all the testimony and weighing the evidence. This that follows seems to me to be what happened.

About four o'clock on Sunday morning, March the sixth, the notes of a bugle calling the Mexican troops to arms rang over the quiet plain, across which the first gray light, precursor of the dawn, was already stealing. Bugles all about caught up the shrill refrain, lights appeared in the circling camps, the trampling feet of hurrying men, the commands of the officers, the rattling of arms, the neighing of the horses, all apprised the weary garrison that the moment they had expected was at hand. They were instantly assembled.

What happened as they fell in on the *plaza* before they went to their several stations? Tradition has it that Travis paraded them, briefly addressed them, pointed out their certain fate, as he had sworn never to surrender, and bade any who desired to do so to leave him freely and escape while there was yet time. Not a man availed himself of the permission. "We will stay and die with you," they cried unanimously as they repaired to their stations on the outer wall.

Cool, calm, and resolute, they waited the breaking of the battle storm; undaunted by the prospect, unshaken by the fearful odds before them. America has produced no better soldiers! Even the dozen sick men in the long room of the hospital with Bowie were provided with arms, of which, fortunately, they had a good supply, and they, too, shared the same heroic resolution. Ill and well were equally determined.

It was early morning when all the dispositions were made on both sides, and the day was breaking clear, cool and beautiful, a sweet day indeed in which to die for home and country and liberty, in the great cause of human freedom—so they may have thought as they looked toward the eastward light for the last time. The quiet watchers on the walls presently detected movements in the dark rank of the besiegers. They were coming, then! Music, too, was there. All the bands of the Mexican army stationed with Santa Anna on the battery in front of the *plaza* were playing a ghastly air called "*Deguello*"—cut-throat!— that and the red flag speaking of no quarter pointed out a deadly

236

purpose. Well, the Texans needed none of these things to nerve their arms. Rifles were lifted and sighted, the lock-strings of the carefully pointed cannon were tightened; they could not afford to throw away any shots, there was no hurry, no confusion.

The Mexicans were nearer now. The bugles rang charge, the close ordered ranks broke into a run. From the east, the west, the north, they came, cheering and yelling madly! A shot burst from the *plaza*, the crack of the rifles broke on the air, a fusillade ran along the walls on every side. The cannon roared out, hurling into the faces of the Mexicans bags filled with hideous missiles. The advancing lines hesitated, paused, halted, fled! The first assault was beaten off, the ground was covered with dead and wounded; comparative stillness supervened. Well done, brave Texans, look to your arms again, snatch a cup of water, enjoy your moment of respite, they are coming again!

The east and west columns had been driven to the north. Colonel Duque, gallant soul, re-formed them on his own brigade; there was a small breach in the north wall; he hurled the mass at it, himself in the lead. The Americans ran to the point threatened; again the withering rifle fire. Duque fell, desperately wounded; mortal man could not face that deadly discharge; the soldiers gave way once more—repulsed a second time; would they dare come on again?

Far off on the east side the roar of battle still surged around the redoubt covering the convent yard. How went the battle there, thought the triumphant defenders of the *plaza* as they gazed on their flying foemen? It was a critical moment for the Mexicans. Santa Anna recognized it, and galloped on the field leading a re-enforcement. He noted that the west wall had been denuded of most of its defenders, and with soldierly decision threw his fresh troops against it, leading them in person, some accounts say. Oh, for a thousand brave hearts and true to man the long lines! The hundred and eighty could not be everywhere, the few at the point of impact died, and the Mexicans entered the *plaza*, at last.

At the same time the officers drove the men up to the third assault on the north wall. Under the eye of Santa Anna they advanced for a last desperate attempt. Honour to those Mexicans for their bravery too. In this attack a bullet pierces Travis' brain—the little boy has only the heritage of honoured and heroic name then—he falls dead on the trail of a cannon. Bonham is killed serving a gun, the north wall is taken, the redoubt to the east is gained, the stockade is attacked, other soldiers swarm up to the south wall, break through the gate—

they come in on every side. The Texans are surrounded by fire and steel. Some of them run back while there is yet time and rally in the convent where Bowie lies. Others follow Crockett, now in chief command, to the church to die with him there. The whole Mexican army is upon them now, the nine score against the five thousand at last.

The old convent is divided into little cell-like rooms, each with a door opening into the yard or *plaza*, but with no connection between the rooms. A few Texans hold each chamber, and into each smoke-filled enclosure the infuriated troops pour their gun fire and then rush the rooms, to writhe and struggle over the bloody pavements until all the defenders are killed. No quarter indeed!

What of the invalids in the hospital fighting from their beds? Forty Mexicans fall dead before the door of the long room before they think to bring a cannon and blow the defenders into eternity. Bowie lies alone in his room waiting with grim resolution for what is coming, pain from injuries forgotten, fevered pulse beating higher; his bed is covered with pistols and near his hand lies his trusty knife. A brown fierce face peers in the door, another and another, the room is filled with smoke; yells and curses and groans rise from the floor where a trail of stricken soldiers reaches from the door to the bedside. And one bolder than his fellows lies on Bowie's breast with that awful American knife buried deep in his heart and Bowie has died as he had lived—sword in hand!

The only fight left now is in the churchyard. A little handful, bloody, powder-stained, desperate, are backed up against the wall. It is hand-to-hand work now on both sides, no time to reload, bayonet thrust against rifle- butt in berserker fury. Hope is lost, but they are dying in high fashion, faces to the foe, striking while they have a heartbeat left. "Fire the magazine," says Crockett to Major Evans, the only remaining officer. The man runs toward the church where the powder is stored and is stricken down on the threshold. The Mexicans rush upon Crockett and his remnant. The keen death-dealing "Betsy" has spoken for the last time, the old frontiersman has clasped it by the barrel now. Swinging this iron war-club he stands at bay, disdaining surrender. The Mexicans are piled before him in heaps, but numbers tell; they swarm about him, they leap upon him like hounds upon a great stag, they pull him down, bury their bayonets in his great heart, spurn him, trample upon him, spit upon him—so he makes a fine end!

It is over. Gunner Walker, the last man in arms, is shot and stabbed, tossed aloft on bayonets in fact. The flag is down. No one is left to

"So he makes a fine end!"

defend it longer. Five wounded, helpless prisoners are dragged before Santa Anna and at his command butchered where they lie, or stand, some of the Mexicans officers—to their credit be it said—vainly protesting. Six people who were in the fort at the beginning were left alive by the Mexicans, two women, two children, and two servants, one a negro slave, the other a Mexican.

One hour! One short hour filled with such sublime struggle as has not been witnessed often in the brief compass of sixty minutes. The sun is shining. The *plaza* is filled with light, the light of morning, the light of heroic death, of self-sacrifice absolute; and the day breaks, a day of eternal remembrance. Wherever men live to love the hero, these will not be forgotten. By the defence of that old deserted Spanish House of Prayer, it was consecrated anew to the service of God, through the sufferings of men. Their sacrifice had not been in vain, for the cry that swept Texas to freedom, that drove the Mexican beyond the Rio Grande was

Remember the Alamo!

One scene remains of the splendid story. By Santa Anna's orders the dead Texans, to the number of one hundred and eighty-two, were gathered together and arranged in a huge pyramid, a layer of wood, a layer of dead, and so on, and the torch applied. A not unfitting end. As the dead demigod of Homeric days was laid upon his funeral pyre, as the dead Viking of later time was burned with his ship, so these modern heroes. The wind scattered their ashes on the spot their defence had immortalized and made it forever hallowed ground.

The hundred and eighty had done well, each one had accounted for more than four of the enemy, for the Spanish casualties are estimated as between six hundred and a thousand. And most was in hand-to-hand fighting. The Texan-Americans had done their best and given their all. Honour to their valour and their courage !

On the monument erected at the state capitol at Austin, to commemorate their unparalleled achievement, is graven this significant line:

THERMOPYLÆ HAD ITS MESSENGER OF DEFEAT,
THE ALAMO HAD NONE.

The Worst of Santa Anna's Misdeeds

1. THE DELAY AT FORT DEFIANCE

There are thousands who have read of the siege and defence of the Alamo. The tale of the heroic resistance put forth by the little band of Americans under Travis, Crockett, Bowie and Bonham, who fought until they were exterminated without exception, when Santa Anna stormed the old Mission in San Antonio, is a familiar one. Without in the least measure condoning the action of the Mexicans, there was some degree of justification for it, in that the Americans refused to surrender, and when the place was taken by storm they were naturally put to death by the infuriated soldiery, especially as they disdained to ask for quarter. To ask mercy would have been useless anyway, for other events showed that it would not have been granted. But for the massacre of the men of Fannin's command at La Bahia, or Goliad, there is not the shadow of justification. And their story is not often told outside of Texas and is practically forgotten by the general reader.

In the spring of 1836 the bulk of the Texan forces was stationed at the town of Goliad, or the old Spanish Mission of La Bahia, on the San Antonio River, in the south-western portion of the present state, under the command of Colonel J. W. Fannin, a brave, enthusiastic young southerner, a soldier of fortune in fact, who had proffered his services to the Texans to assist them to gain that independence of Mexico for which they were struggling. Fannin's command comprised nearly five hundred men, all Americans, less than a score being Texans. The men were all volunteers who had come principally from the southern United States, although the recruits were by no means confined to that section; among them were several from Illinois. Texas had spread appeals broadcast throughout the Union, and the response had been prompt.

Old Sam Houston, the commander-in-chief of the Texan army, unfortunately was not allowed to have his way, and differences between him, the President, and the Vice-President, and other authorities, produced the inevitable results of divided counsels and many heads; successive failures. The loss of the Alamo need never have occurred, and the fearful fate meted out to Fannin and his men, as we shall see, was more unendurable to think of because unnecessary.

The Mexicans invaded the country in force. Instead of concentrating the Texan troops and the volunteers, who were men of a very high class indeed, the Texan forces were scattered. Consequently they were beaten in detail and it was not until Houston's masterly strategy had drawn Santa Anna, the Dictator, far into the country, where his force was annihilated and he was captured at San Jacinto, that success attended the American efforts for freedom.

A column of Mexican troops under General Urrea, marching up the coast of the Gulf of Mexico, had overwhelmed several small detachments of Fannin's command, the main body of which was concentrated at Goliad for the purpose, utterly futile, of invading Mexico with a view to capturing Matamoras. Urrea's success with the detachments was complete, though not won without a heavy cost in life, for the Texans resisted manfully and never gave up as a rule until their ammunition was exhausted and they were left without means of defence.

The Mexican Republic had decreed that any foreigners—that is, Americans—captured under arms, or found bearing arms against Mexico, should suffer instant death. Urrea, like all the other Mexican commanders, invariably executed the members of the detachments as fast as he captured them. Once in a while one or two from the different little garrisons escaped to tell the story, but that was all.

When the Alamo was captured and its defenders slaughtered, Houston sent peremptory orders to Fannin to retire to Victoria, where he would be in position to join forces with the commander-in-chief. He instructed him to bury his heavy artillery and destroy or conceal such stores as would impede his rapid movement, and to start immediately.

Some twenty-five miles south of Fannin's post, which he called Fort Defiance, was a little station called Refugio. Learning that there were some unprotected families there, Fannin had despatched Captain King with his company of some twenty-eight men to bring them off. King marched to Refugio and got there just before Urrea, who immediately assaulted him with his advance. The Texans seized the Mission church and defended it gallantly, so that Urrea's efforts to storm were successfully withstood at great cost to the Mexicans.

Meanwhile Fannin waited, delaying his departure and postponing obedience to Houston's orders, for tidings of King. Finally on the arrival of a messenger from Refugio asking for help, he sent Lieutenant-Colonel Ward, his second in command, with one hundred and seventy-five men to Refugio to bring off King and his party. Ward reached the Mission in safety.

Fannin's force was divided into two battalions, a Georgia battalion, of which Ward was the immediate commander, and the Lafayette battalion. King, belonging to the other battalion, foolishly refused to acknowledge Ward's seniority and in the face of the enemy there was a difference between the two commanders, which resulted in King's leaving Refugio with his own men and a few of Ward's.

They were pursued, captured, and shot dead to a man. Ward with the remainder of his command, now defending the Mission, fought off the Mexicans, who, whatever may be said against them, certainly showed dauntless gallantry in assaulting so often and so unsuccessfully fortified positions defended by men whose ability as marksmen had been proven over and over again; but the ammunition of the Americans at last grew low, and finding that he had but a few rounds left, Ward broke through the besieging line in the night, and by keeping closely in the timber and marshes, thus avoiding the effective Mexican cavalry, he made good his escape for the time.

He headed for Victoria, where he supposed he would find Fannin and possibly Houston. Meanwhile Fannin, having weakened his force by some two hundred men, was still waiting at Goliad. Six days actually passed after he received the order to move immediately before he complied with it. He was moved to delay, first, by a desire to help the people at Refugio, and then by his unwillingness to sacrifice King's command, and then by the necessity of hearing from Ward's expedition, so that for the sake of a few families, whom he eventually failed to save, he threw away the precious days and finally involved the whole command in overwhelming disaster. An eye-witness testifies that the order to retreat was received just before the march of Ward's battalion. Fannin's excuse was, of course, his chivalric reluctance to abandon King.

The military exigency was so great that he should have started without a moment's hesitation in obedience to his positive orders. He held the command of by far the most efficient body of men in Texas; if lost they could scarcely be replaced. He was not a professional soldier, however. His military experience had been confined to the battle of Concepcion late in the previous year, in which he had distinguished himself for courage and daring, of which indeed he manifested no lack at this juncture. Finally he received information from one Captain Frazier, who had volunteered to procure it, which convinced him of the folly and futility of waiting any longer for tidings from Refugio and, after wasting Friday in some useless scouting, on the morning of Saturday, the nineteenth day of March, 1836, he moved out from Fort Defiance, first dismantling it, and started to march to Victoria.

Even then he lingered, although the Mexican troops had been reported the day before. Instead of discarding everything but absolute necessities he took with him a great train of artillery and supplies drawn by oxen. The party now numbered about three hundred and fifty men. The day was damp and foggy. Although they started very early in the morning they did not succeed in getting across the ford of the river until after ten o'clock. Then they moved slowly over the open prairie until about noon, when they halted in a little depression of the country which had been burned over and in which, perhaps because it was low and received the drainage, there was an outcrop of fresh grass. They rested here an hour to give the cattle time for a mouthful.

2. THE BATTLE OF THE COLETA

Fannin now sent his only horsemen, some thirty troopers, under the command of Colonel Horton, ahead to reconnoitre. This little band was prevented from rejoining the main body and so escaped capture. Early in the afternoon the oxen were yoked to the wagons and the party started forward again, hoping to reach the heavily wooded banks of a little river, the Coleta, where they would find shelter and water and could make camp for the night. They were about four miles from the river when a body of horse galloped out from the cover of the trees and approached them from the flank.

At first they imagined that the horsemen were their own cavalry, but they were soon undeceived. The troopers were accompanied by infantry, and easily got between them and the river. On either side the Americans the tree clumps extended for some distance, and as they halted and opened fire with a six-pounder on the Mexican cavalry, other troops broke from the woodland referred to and debouched upon the open prairie. A glance backward revealed additional troops following upon their trail. It took but a moment to discover to them that they were fairly surrounded upon an open prairie without wood, or water, or protection.

They happened at the time to be in a depression some six feet below the normal level of the prairie; some little distance off there was a slight elevation raised as many feet above the level. Fannin at once put his force in motion to reach the knoll, but the breaking down of his ammunition wagons forced him to stay where he was. He drew up the three hundred men in a hollow square in the shape of a parallelogram, with the oxen and wagons in the middle, with a few women and children whom he had brought with him. He placed a small piece of artillery, a four or six-pounder, at each corner of the square and then resolutely awaited the attack.

The flag carried by the Georgia battalion, a white field with a single blue star with the words, "Liberty or Death!" was then unfurled. Fortunately the Texans possessed an abundant supply of arms and ammunition. There were two or three weapons to each man, rifles, muskets, and pistols.

The Mexicans made no haste to approach, and Fannin very deliberately completed his preparations, cautioning his men by no means to fire until he gave the word. Between two and three o'clock Urrea, who was in command of the Mexican forces, began the battle. His troops, converging upon the square from all sides, opened fire as they came within range, and under cover of the smoke tried to rush the Americans with the bayonet.

Reserving their fire until the Mexicans were close at hand, the Texans poured in volley after volley, which did frightful execution, and as the Mexicans turned and fled, leaving numbers of dead and dying upon the field, the six-pounders opened fire upon them with good effect.

The Mexicans had no artillery with which to make reply, but with remarkable courage—considering the popular idea of their quality— they re-formed out of range and came on once more, only to be whirled back in another disastrous repulse. Finally Urrea in person led a dashing cavalry charge on the front of the square, at the same time making a demonstration with his infantry on the other sides to prevent Fannin from detaching men to meet the onset of the horse.

The attack was gallantly made, but was no more successful than the first two had been. Although the cannon through rapid firing had become by this time so clogged and so hot as to put them out of ac-

245

tion, there being no water in the square with which to sponge them, the Texans managed by quick and hard lighting to beat back for the third time the Mexicans, who outnumbered them three to one. An eye-witness gives the following account of the field after their first repulse :

> The scene was now dreadful to behold. Killed and maimed men and horses were strewn over the plain; the wounded were rending the air with their distressing moans; while a great number of horses without riders were rushing to and fro back upon the enemy's lines, increasing the confusion among them; they thus became so entangled, the one with the other, that their retreat resembled the headlong flight of a herd of buffaloes, rather than the retreat of a well-drilled, regular army, as they were.

The casualties in the little band had been by no means light, and there were already many wounded in the square. Instances of heroism were many. One young lad named Ripley, who was shot in the thigh, especially distinguished himself. Unable to stand, he was lifted up on a cart, and with a woman to assist him in making a rest for his gun, he watched his opportunity and killed four of the Mexicans in succession by accurate shooting before he was hit a second time in the arm and was unable to take further part in the action.

During the whole of the battle most of the men remained lying down until the successive assaulting columns had nearly reached them, when they would rise and deliver their fire. Fannin and his officers, however, persisted in standing, as the artillerists of necessity had done. Many of them were wounded, including Fannin quite severely in the thigh.

As evening drew on, numbers of Indians, allies to the Mexicans, crept forward through the tall grass, skilfully masking their progress and successfully concealing themselves, until they were close enough to take pot shots at the Texans, who suffered more from this attack than from the previous efforts of the Mexicans.

When it grew dark enough, however, for the, Texans to see the flashes of the Indians' guns, their skilful marksmanship drove the savages out of range. It was as much as a man's life was worth to fire his gun, a Texan bullet always found the flash and the man back of it, so that when darkness came the enemy drew out of range. Out of the three hundred men sixty-seven had been killed or wounded, most of the wounded being seriously hurt.

Their situation was critical. They were surrounded by an over-whelming force of Mexicans. There was no water in the square, and they found by some oversight that no food had been brought along, or the wagons containing it had been abandoned. It was possible for the survivors, staking everything on the attempt, to break through the Mexican lines in an endeavour to reach the river, but to do it they would have to abandon some sixty wounded comrades to the mercy of the conquerors, which was not to be thought of. The matter was debated furiously early in the evening, and it was unanimously de-cided to stay together.

Fannin, whose superb courage redeems his lack of capacity, was confident that as they had beaten the enemy before they could do it again without difficulty, and that if they maintained a bold front the Mexicans would withdraw. The wounded stifled their groans and en-dured their sufferings, therefore, as best they could; while the surgeons, of whom there were several with the party, men of skill and training, did what they could to alleviate their sufferings in the pitch darkness. Everybody else worked in preparing for the attack of the morrow. The area enclosed by the square was much contracted, and the wagons were placed on the outside to form some sort of a protection, a trench was dug and a slight earthwork thrown up behind which the men could await the coming attack.

Nobody slept. The night was chill and damp. The next morn-ing, Sunday, the twentieth of March, Passion Sunday, broke clear and warmer, but the day brought no encouragement to the hungry, thirsty little army. The Mexicans had been heavily re-enforced during the night until they numbered some 1,200 effectives, and they were now provided with artillery overmatching the useless American guns. The battle began at once. The artillery fired grape shot and solid shot, de-molishing the frail American entrenchments and rendering the posi-tion untenable. The Americans replied as well as they could, but their ammunition presently gave out and there was nothing left for them but surrender.

3. THE MASSACRE AT GOLIAD

Fannin was averse to capitulation, but he was over-borne. Indeed it is hard to see what else they could have done but surrender. Ac-cordingly, after passively enduring the enemy's fire for some time, the white flag was raised. After due preliminaries a solemn convention was drawn up in triplicate, duly signed and witnessed, by which the most favourable terms were given the Americans. The officers' side arms and private baggage were to remain in their possession, and the whole party was to be sent back to the United States upon their promise not to bear arms against the Mexican government in future. As solemnly as men could do it, these conditions were expressed and the terms made. The men were to be treated as prisoners of war until they could be sent back, with every right jealously preserved. Upon these terms and no other Fannin surrendered. The Mexicans allege that the surrender was unconditional, but their statement is disputed by every American witness who survived the massacre that followed.

The captured Americans were immediately disarmed and marched back to Goliad, whither they were joined a few days later by eighty recruits who had landed at Matagorda Bay and been captured before they had an opportunity to strike a blow. They were also joined by the survivors of Ward's command who were taken near Victoria. Ward's party had but three rounds of ammunition left per man when they surrendered.

The surgeons, of whom there were eight with the several commands—the Texan cause seems to have appealed powerfully to doctors—were left on the battlefield with the wounded of both sides, who were treated temporarily as well as possible, and two days afterward they were all brought back to Goliad.

General Urrea seems to have acted at first in good faith. In spite of his severe wound, Fannin, in company with a German officer in the Mexican service named Holzinger, and some of his own subordinates, had gone down to Matagorda to charter a steamer or other vessel to take the prisoners to New Orleans.

None being immediately available, however, he returned to Goliad to wait. The men suffered the usual hardships of prisoners of war, but otherwise were not badly treated, except in the case of the wounded.

The loss of the Mexicans in the battle was never ascertained definitely. It must have been, however, between two and three hundred, although the Mexican reports claim much less, for the Texans were remarkably good marksmen, who shot to kill. At any rate, there were at Goliad over one hundred Mexican wounded, most of them so severely as to be utterly incapacitated. The services of the American surgeons were invaluable to these, and the Mexicans at first refused to allow the Texan wounded to be attended to at all until the Mexicans had been looked after, but the doctors stoutly insisted upon treating the cases in the order of their severity, without regard to nationality, and in the end had their way.

Santa Anna, who was campaigning to the eastward, had been apprised of the capture. He instantly despatched an order to the commanding officer at Goliad, in the absence of Urrea, one Colonel Portilla, directing his attention to the proclamation of the government—himself—with regard to foreigners in arms against the Mexican Republic, and peremptorily ordering him to carry out the decree—in other words, to have the prisoners shot at once!

The order reached Portilla on Saturday night, March 27th. It filled him with dismay, and it is only just to the other Mexican officers to say that their commander's dismay and horror were shared by the most of them. But Santa Anna was the Dictator of the miscalled Mexican Republic, and no despot ever ruled more supremely than he. Portilla deliberated for a night upon the subject, and finally concluded that he had no alternative but obedience. He determined, however, to save Miller's men, who had committed no overt act other than landing on the shore, and the surgeons as well, with some others who had been attending to the wounded, eight in all.

He did this largely on the representations of Colonel Garay, one of his subordinates, whose name deserves to be held in kindly remembrance, for he protested vehemently against the order and repudiated all connection with it both before and after the catastrophe.

The eight surgeons, in entire ignorance of the reason for the order, early on the morning of Palm Sunday, March 27th, 1836, were marched to Garay's headquarters and kept there with two other men to whom he had become attached, and to save whom he had risked much. The wife of one of the officers, Senora Alvarez, also secreted several of the Americans.

The prisoners were entirely unconscious of the fearful fate prepared for them. Indeed, although Fannin had not succeeded in getting a ship, they anticipated an early release, and one of the survivors relates that they spent the evening before congregated around one of their number who had saved, or borrowed, a flute, and who played hymns which they sang, ending with "Home, Sweet Home," in which everybody joined. Early in the morning of the fateful Sunday the three hundred prisoners appointed for massacre were divided into three companies of one hundred each. The wounded for the present were left behind.

The men were lined up between two rows of Mexican soldiers fully armed. One party was told that it was to go out to slaughter beeves; another party that it was to be taken to a convenient place for exchange; the third, that it was to be quartered somewhere else, as the place it had occupied was needed for Santa Anna's army which was approaching.

It was a pleasant, sunny, delightful spring morning. Chatting and laughing among themselves and entirely unconscious of any impending disaster or treachery, the three parties set out in different directions. As they marched through the town many pitying glances were cast upon them, and here and there a woman, more tender-hearted than the rest, was heard to murmur, "Poor fellows, poor fellows!" (*Pobrecitos.*) The Texans attached no meaning to these words, however, supposing that they were being commiserated as prisoners, not realizing that it was on account of their approaching murder.

The parties soon separated, but what happened to one happened to all. When they had reached a suitable place outside the town, where each party was hidden from the others, at a sudden command the Mexicans on the left flank, facing about, marched through the open ranks of the prisoners and joined their comrades on the right. The men were ordered to turn their backs upon the soldiers, and sit down, and as, in their bewilderment, most of them did so, the guns of the troops were presented and a volley was poured on the helpless prisoners at contact range.

Nearly the whole of each party fell at the first fire. Some there were, however, who were only slightly wounded, and a few untouched. They made a bold dash instantly to escape. Their efforts in most cases were entirely unavailing, for the cavalry had been ordered out and squads now appeared on the scene running down the fugitives, who were also the targets for rapid firing as the guns were loaded. Most of them were shot down. Out of the whole number some twenty-seven, many of whom were wounded, did make good their escape.

Acts of heroism were numerous.

"Boys," said one young man, "they're going to murder us! Let's die with our faces to the foe!"

Many of them followed his example, refusing to sit down, and faced the Mexican guns, waving their caps and shouting with their last breath,

"Hurrah for Texas!"

With incredible brutality the Mexicans examined the bodies of the fallen and deliberately bayoneted those who yet survived. The hellish work, however, was not yet over. Squads of soldiers went back to the barracks where the wounded Americans lay. They dragged them out on the prairie and threw them upon the ground. Those who could do so struggled to their feet or their knees, but most of them lay helpless on the sod and were shot to death. Ward, a powerful and splendid soldier, died with words of scorn and contempt and bitter reproaches for their treachery on his lips.

Fannin was the last one to be shot. He handed his watch and money to the officer commanding the firing party, asked him not to shoot him in the face and to see that he was suitably buried. Then he struggled to his feet opened the breast of his shirt, and calmly awaited his end. He had no wish to survive after having witnessed the massacre of his men. He was shot in the face, and his body, with those of the others, thrown into a great brush heap which was set on fire with but partial results.

Among the surgeons was one Dr. Bernard from Illinois who has left a description of the situation, of the helpless men in the tents listening to the massacre, even seeing some of the fugitives being shot or bayoneted. Another surgeon was the commander of the Georgia company, the "Red Rovers' Battalion," Dr. Shackelford, who was forced to stand passive in Garay's tent while his own company, composed of the best young men in his neighbourhood, whom he had personally enlisted, and which included his son and two nephews, was shot to death.

The feelings of those who had been saved can scarcely be imagined. Their utter impotence was the worst feature of the situation. Such was the temper of the soldiers, inflamed by the massacre, that they would have killed them out of hand if they could have reached them. The surgeons were eventually saved and with the twenty-seven who escaped and a few others secreted by Madame Alvarez, in all less than forty, were the only survivors of this horrible massacre of quite three hundred and thirty helpless prisoners who had trusted to the solemn word of their captors—men to whom honour was nothing but a name.

When the massacre, coupled with the slaughter at the Alamo, became known, such a wave of horror rushed through Texas and the United States as finally brought about the success of the effort to establish the Lone Star Republic. The Texans at last took fierce vengeance for these butcherings on the bloody field of San Jacinto. It is to be wondered how the officers ever succeeded in restraining the men from executing summary justice upon the bloodthirsty butcher who disgraced the profession of arms and the country over which he ruled

251

by this and other murders and massacres which he ordered without a shadow of justification.

Santa Anna, who loved to style himself the Napoleon of the West, is one of the meanest characters of modern history.

3

Sam Houston and Freedom

1. Some Characteristics of the Man

A remarkable character was General Sam Houston, to whom we were introduced at the Battle of Tohopeka. He was a descendant of a North of Ireland family, coming from the place which may justly boast of the ancestry of such men as Stark of the Revolution, Crockett of the Alamo, and Jackson himself. The Houston family was one of consideration entitled to coat armour in the old country. One of them had been among the redoubtable defenders of Londonderry in 1689. While not belonging to the landed gentry of the Old Dominion, they were large and prosperous farmers.

Houston's father was an officer of the famous brigade of riflemen that Morgan led to Washington's assistance from the right bank of the Potomac. His mother was one of those pioneer women of superb physique, high principles, and strength of mind and courage to match. After the death of her husband, when young Sam, who was born in 1793, was but thirteen years old, she took the family far over the Allegheny Mountains and settled on the borders of the Cherokee Nation in western Tennessee.

Such schooling as the neighbourhood afforded was given Sam. His educational opportunities were meagre, but he made the best of his limited advantages and with such books as the Bible, the *Iliad*, Shakespeare, the *Pilgrim's Progress*, and later when he was commander-in-chief of the Texan army, *Caesar's Commentaries*—in translation, of course, which he studied for the art of war—he gave himself a good grounding. He was a constant student in his way, and in manner and in ability, when he became Governor of Tennessee, President of Texas, Senator of the United States, Governor of Texas, etc., he had no cause to blush when placed by the most distinguished men of his time.

According to some authorities his unwillingness to clerk in a country store, according to others the refusal of his older brothers to permit him to study Latin, caused him to abandon civilization and cast his lot in with the Cherokees, whose territory lay adjacent to his home. He was adopted into the family of one of the sub-chiefs of the tribe, and for a long period he lived a wild, savage life with them. At different intervals during his career he resumed his relations with them, on one occasion taking a wife from among them, who afterward died, leaving no children.

When he was begged to come back, in his grandiloquent way he remarked that he preferred "measuring deer tracks to measuring tape." After several years with the Cherokees, finding himself in debt for some barbaric finery, he returned to civilization and opened a country school at the age of eighteen. His pluck was greater than his attainments, which yet appear to have been sufficient to make the school a success, for it included all the children of the neighbourhood, and he was enabled to raise the tuition fee from six to eight dollars per year, one-third payable in corn at thirty-three and one-half cents per bushel, one-third in cash, and one-third in cotton goods or other kind. He once said, after he had filled almost every elective position except that of President of the United States, that he experienced a higher feeling of dignity and self-satisfaction when he was a schoolmaster than at any period of his life.

Tiring of school-teaching he enlisted in the army as a private and soon won promotion to the rank of ensign. After his early exploits he resigned from the service; one of the reasons therefore being on account of a severe and merited rebuke which he received for appearing before the Secretary of War dressed like a wild Indian! He never liked Calhoun or his Democracy after that day. He was always a dandy in his dress, although at times he affected peculiar and striking costumes which his great height and imposing presence enabled him to wear without inspiring that ridicule which would have attended a similar performance on the part of a less splendid man.

When he was first inaugurated Governor of Tennessee, August 2, 1827, he wore "a tall bell-crowned, medium-brimmed, shining black beaver hat, shining black patent-leather military stock or cravat incased by a standing collar, ruffled shirt, black satin vest, shining black silk pants gathered to the waistband with legs full, same size from seat to ankle, and a gorgeous red-ground, many coloured gown or Indian

"SHE TOOK THE FAMILY FAR OVER
THE ALLEGHENY MOUNTAINS."

hunting shirt, fastened at the waist by a huge red sash covered with fancy bead work, with an immense silver buckle, embroidered silk stockings, and pumps with large silver buckles. Mounted on a superb dapple-gray horse he appeared at the election unannounced, and was the observed of all observers." I should think so!

When he was a United States Senator it was his habit to wear, in addition to the ordinary clothing of a gentleman of the times, an immense Mexican *sombrero* and coloured blanket, or *serape*, and his appearance naturally excited attention in Washington.

While candidate for re-election as Governor of Tennessee, he abandoned his young wife after six weeks of married life, gave over his campaign, and once more sought asylum with the Cherokees. The reason for his action has never been discovered, although he explicitly stated that no reflection upon the character or conduct of the lady in question was implied or expressed by his conduct. Championing the Indians when he came back to civilization, he became involved in a quarrel with Representative Stanberry, whom he publicly caned. For his conduct he was formally censured at the bar of Congress. This quarrel brought him into public notice again. It is shrewdly surmised that he provoked it for that purpose, for he said:

"I was dying out once, and had they taken me before a justice of the peace and fined me ten dollars for assault and battery it would have killed me; but they gave me a national tribunal for a theatre and that set me up again."

Like many men of great physical vigour he was much given to excess. In his last sojourn among the Cherokees, the Indians expressed their contempt for his dissipated habits by naming him the "Big Drunk," but drunk or sober, there was something about him that inspired respect. Whatever he did he was always "Sam Houston." People used to say that he really signed his name "I am Houston." After he was converted, however—and in a large measure before that time, at the instance of his third wife, a woman of the most noble character, who married him to reform him and did so—he entirely stopped drinking and demeaned himself to the end of his life as a sincere and humble Christian of the very highest type. When he got drunk, he got thoroughly drunk, and when he became converted to the Baptist faith, he did it with the same thoroughness; a thorough-going man, indeed.

In one particular he was remarkable among his contemporaries. He had the greatest reluctance to resort to the duel, which was then the usual method of settling differences between gentlemen. He had to endure many sharp remarks and bitter criticisms on this account, his courage was even impugned at times, although we now realize it not only to have been past reproof but actually to have been the very highest courage, as evidenced, for one thing, by those very refusals. Sometimes his wit enabled him to escape. To one gentleman who challenged him, after counselling with his secretary, he informed the gentleman who brought the challenge that his principal was number fourteen on the list, and that he could hold out no hope of meeting him until he had disposed of the other thirteen!

His grandiloquent mind invested the slightest occurrence with majesty. A friend of his gave him a razor, which he received with these words:

> Major Rector, this is apparently a gift of little value, but it is an inestimable testimony of the friendship which has lasted many years, and proved steadfast under the blasts of calumny and injustice. Goodbye. God bless you. When next you see this razor it shall be shaving the President of the Republic, by G—d!

His manner toward ladies was as magnificent as his person, his dress, his oratory. His habitual word of address to them was "lady"; a very courtly, distinguished old fellow was he.

After his supersession as Governor of Texas, because of his unwillingness to allow the state to go out of the Union, when the officers of the Confederacy established a stringent law requiring all men over sixteen years to register and obtain a pass, Houston paid no attention to the order. When he was halted by an officer who demanded his pass, the old man waved him aside in his most Olympian manner, frowning and remarking, "San Jacinto is my pass through Texas." Small wonder that the people loved him.

He had such a sense of humour and the dramatic as few men have ever had. He was one of the best campaigners among thousands of brilliant specimens that America has ever produced. His witty and epigrammatic speech is well illustrated by the following:

A former friend had betrayed him and when the traitor's character was assailed on account of his ingratitude, Houston remarked, "You mustn't be too hard on S———. I always was fond of dogs and S——— has all the virtues of a dog except his fidelity."

This, his characterization of the leader of a certain cause, is one of those brilliant epigrams in which the very truth of history is enshrined: "Ambitious as Lucifer, and cold as a lizard."

He may fairly be called a statesman, he most certainly can be styled an orator, and a little verse which he wrote to a relative illustrates that he was not deficient in the arts and graces, and is worth quoting :

Remember thee? Yes, lovely girl.
While faithful memory holds its seat,
Till this warm heart in dust is laid,
And this wild pulse shall cease to beat,
No matter where my bark is tost
On life's tempestuous, stormy sea,
My anchor gone, my rudder lost.
Still, cousin, I will think of thee.

Houston did everything in his power to prevent the secession of Texas in 1861, but when she left the Union he went with her. We can understand him, Texas was like his own child. He died in reduced circumstances in 1863, his last years embittered by the too evident failure of the Confederacy and the discords which tore his beloved country in twain. But the world is familiar with the events of his strange, romantic and useful career; few men have been so written about, and few men have deserved it more. While he did not rise to the solitary height to which the title of greatness accrues, yet he was one of the most eminent men of his time, and his valuable services are held in undying remembrance. Pass we to the second great day of his life.

2. IN THE SERVICE OF THE TEXAN REPUBLIC

Aroused at last by the pleadings of his better nature he determined to abandon the loose, aimless, lazy, drunken, savage way of life with the Cherokees and go to Texas. It is believed that he went there at the instigation of President Jackson, whose friendship and regard for him never wavered. A man of such prominence could not fail to attract attention in a country like Texas, and he was presently made commander-in-chief of the Texan army. After the capture of the Alamo and the terrible and inhuman massacre at Goliad, Santa Anna deemed that the Texan revolution had been crushed and that the war was practically over. He intended to send back most of his troops to Mexico, but upon the urgent representations of some of his generals he agreed to march them further eastward and complete the subjugation of the country before he did so. Houston with a small body of Texans, numbering less than one thousand, was encamped at the crossing of the

Colorado River near Bastrop, whither he had retired from Gonzales.

It is probable that, in the light of subsequent developments, his force was strong enough on account of its quality successfully to have engaged the whole Mexican army. No one knew or believed this would be so then. The Mexicans were regular soldiers, trained in the latest European methods. They were led by an hitherto successful commander who had succeeded in every battle. The Texans were a body of undrilled, untrained frontiersmen, armed with their own rifles and bowie knives, with no artillery, no bayonets, no camp equipage to speak of. There was but one drum in the whole camp, and Houston did the drumming himself! His reveille was three taps on the drum.

The problem presented itself in this way. If the Texans moved forward to attack Santa Anna he would immediately concentrate his force and Houston would have to engage the whole Mexican power with his little handful of men. If, on the contrary, he retreated, the probabilities were that Santa Anna, disdaining the little Texan army, especially when it was in retreat, would divide his force in order to seize as many points as possible; when, if Houston watched carefully, he might find an opportunity of destroying them in detail. He chose the latter, which was the better course.

3. "The Runaway Scrape"

It was a risky, plan, and the risk lay in this: it is immensely difficult to hold together in retreat an army which has but little organic coherence and is mainly undisciplined and irregular. The men grumbled at being marched back to the eastward, and a panic immediately pervaded the country. Everybody sought to escape from the dreaded Mexican advance. The country was depopulated, and this precipitate flight of the inhabitants passed into history as "The Runaway Scrape."

It was not without hundreds of incidents, tragic and otherwise. One lone woman whose husband was with the army strapped a feather-bed on her solitary pony, tied her three oldest children on it, and plodded on with the baby in her arms. In one of the wagons, an open one, lay a woman with a nine-day-old baby; the mothers of Texas have loved to tell how, one rainy night in the wild flight, they stood about her for hours with blankets held over her to protect her from the storm.

Houston carefully kept his disintegrating army between the fugitives and the Mexicans, and he saw that all the people had left any given section before he took up his daily march. On one occasion he gave over fifty dollars from the military treasure-chest, which only contained two hundred and fifty, to the destitute widow of a defender of the Alamo.

There was the greatest indignation in certain quarters over this retreat and many protests were made. Houston, however, was undeterred by this opposition, which even went so far as to question his courage, and steadily led his men backward over the prairie. When they reached Brazos, he determined upon a continuance of the retreat, and there some of his men broke out in open mutiny. He left several of the most recalcitrant companies to protect the town of San Felipe de Austin at the crossing and marched northward on the west bank of the river.

On the part of the Mexicans it happened as he had imagined. Santa Anna had concentrated his army at the Colorado to meet the Texans, but finding that Houston was in retreat, he had divided his force in three columns and despatched them in different directions, leading the centre column himself, to raid and capture Harrisburg. The Texan army was now reduced to less than seven hundred men. The retreat was conducted under circumstances of the greatest difficulty. Up the valley of the Brazos, over the rain-sodden prairies, the men toiled. Finally some distance up the river, at a place called Groce's Ferry, they found a little steamer called the *Yellowstone*, which they seized and by means of it crossed the river.

Santa Anna, advancing with imperious energy, appeared in force before the Austin defenders, who set fire to the town and promptly did a little retreating on their own account. The Mexicans, by a ruse, inveigled a ferryman from the other side and crossed the Brazos, whereafter Santa Anna, taking no account of Houston to the northward, pushed on to Harrisburg at the head of the centre column.

Meanwhile Houston had been re-enforced by a small body of men, two cannon, six-pounders, called the "Twin Sisters," sent by the citizens of Cincinnati, via Harrisburg, and the Secretary of War. The President at Harrisburg, apprised of Santa Anna's rapid advance, barely escaped before he reached the town. Despatching one of his regiments to the gulf shore to head off the President and his Cabinet, who were fleeing to Galveston, Santa Anna marched on toward Washington. Houston, however, was marching toward the same town. The mutinous Texan companies, persuaded this time of the wisdom of their general, came rushing back and raised his force to about seven hundred and fifty men.

Santa Anna was in the heart of Texas with a force not too great for the Texans to meet with hopes of success and with no possibility of re-enforcement. Houston's strategy had proven his wisdom, and he now prepared to attack the unsuspecting Mexican. The forced march to catch him was a terrible one even to these men inured to all the vicissitudes of frontier life. The rains still continued, and it was with the utmost difficulty that the baggage wagons and artillery could be transported. Houston himself set an example to his soldiers. Dismounting from his horse he put his own shoulder to the wheel, encouraging them in every way, telling them that the opportunity they had craved was at last at hand, making no secret of his hope to strike a blow which would be decisive and result in the freedom of the Republic. On the 18th of April, 1836, the army reached Buffalo Bayou, then swollen bank full and unfordable, opposite the ruins of Harrisburg, which Santa Anna had destroyed.

A celebrated scout named Deaf Smith with Captain Karnes of the regular cavalry met them here with a bag full of captured despatches which confirmed the fact that Santa Anna was with the force which had burned Harrisburg and was marching to New Washington. Houston was overjoyed at the possibility thus of capturing the Mexican commander-in-chief. With him in his possession he would be able to dictate terms of peace. Leaving his baggage wagons with a guard of thirty men he prepared to cross the bayou, taking with him the two cannon and a single ammunition wagon. They found a leaky boat, and upon this and a rude timber raft they succeeded in ferrying over the army.

Houston remained on one bank while the long tedious passage was being made, and Rusk, the Texan Secretary of War, remained on the other. Only by the greatest difficulty was the crossing finally effected. The cavalry horses indeed had to swim the bayou. By nightfall, however, they were all over and on the march toward the junction of Buffalo Bayou with the San Jacinto River, at a place called Lynch's Ferry, where they hoped to head off the Mexicans, who were supposed to be marching toward La Trinidad.

The tired army marched twelve miles that night, stopping for rest at one a. m. on the 20th. Houston allowed his soldiers but a few hours for repose, for before dawn they started again and marched seven miles. A halt was taken for breakfast, but, upon receipt of intelligence that the Mexican army was at hand they left off preparations for the meal and marched post-haste to the ferry, across San Jacinto Bay, a little below the point where the Buffalo joins the river.

They reached the coveted point before the Mexicans, for no sign of the invaders were found. Six men under Captain Hancock, however, had made a valuable capture of a flat boat loaded with flour and filled with Mexicans, who surrendered without firing a shot. That cargo was intended for Santa Anna's army, which, in ignorance of the proximity of the Americans, had been marching for the same spot. It was a most welcome contribution to the American commissariat, for they were almost literally without anything to eat.[1]

Confident that the Mexicans were moving into the trap, they now turned back up the Buffalo for about three quarters of a mile, where Houston posted his army in a strong defensive position in a thick wood on the edge of the bayou. In front of the camp lay a stretch of prairie land broken by three large clumps of trees, known as islands. On the left was the broad arm of San Jacinto Bay, the enclosing marshy shores of which swept around to the south in front of them at a distance of a mile away. The marsh grew wider as it trended to the southwest. Beyond the tree islands lay another clump of trees terminating in the marshland. The country to the southwest was also marshy and impassable. The road up which they had marched to their position led across a deep ravine with very high banks called Vince's Creek. The road crossed this creek on a wooden bridge about eight miles from the battle-ground.

Santa Anna with some twelve hundred of his men was in New Washington when his scouts brought word that the American forces were at hand. A scene of wild confusion and terror ensued, a panic in fact, extending from the general to the soldiery; but as the day wore on and no attack was made the Mexicans recovered their self-control in a measure, and order having been restored, they marched toward Lynch's Ferry to meet the enemy. The Mexican advance came in touch with the Texans on the afternoon of the 20th. Santa Anna's artillery consisted of one nine-pounder. There was a fruitless duel between this gun and the "Twin Sisters," and some cavalry skirmishing, which was not unimportant, in that it gave one Mirabeau B. Lamar, one of the

---

1. There is a legend to the effect that after the battle Houston exhibited an ear of corn to Santa Anna with the question: "Sir, do you ever expect to conquer men who fight for freedom, whose general can march four days with one ear of corn for rations?" The story goes on to say that the men begged the ear from the general, divided its kernels, planted them, and that Texas is full of San Jacinto corn to this day!

romantic characters of the period, an opportunity to distinguish himself under fire by the rescue of a comrade in circumstances of peculiar danger; as a reward for which, he was immediately promoted to the rank of colonel by Houston and given command of the sixty horse which comprised the Texan cavalry !

Aside from this skirmish no attempt was made by either army to bring on a general engagement that day. Houston had his own reasons for not wishing to fight and Santa Anna desired time to bring up a re-enforcement of five hundred men which was near at hand. Houston is reported to have said that his reason for not engaging was that he wanted the Mexicans to bring their whole available force in the vicinity to the field that he might overcome the enemy with one blow and not be compelled to make "two bites at a cherry." At any rate Santa Anna encamped in the woods to the south of the Texans, his right resting on the marshes which extended around his rear from San Jacinto Bay. He refused his left slightly and protected his front by making a flimsy entrenchment of pack saddles, baggage, etc., about five feet high, in the centre of which in an opening he planted his nine-pounder. His cavalry, several hundred in number, he posted on the right.

On the morning of the 21st of April, 1836, five hundred men under General Cos marched up the road from Vince's bridge and joined Santa Anna. Houston gave out that it was not a real re-enforcement but merely part of the army already encamped, marching about to give the impression of an augmented force, but the statement deceived no one. Neither did it diminish the confident courage of the Texans in the slightest degree.

Houston had fully decided upon his course of action. He called Deaf Smith to him and bade him and a companion named Reeves procure two sharp axes and hold themselves in readiness for orders, directing them to keep within close touch during the day. The Texans waited under arms thinking the Mexicans in greater force, in fact outnumbering them over two to one, would attack them. But Santa Anna made no movement to advance and at the request of some of the higher officers Houston called a council of war at noon, the question being whether they should make, or wait, an attack. The two junior officers were in favour of attacking at once. All of the seniors said that it would be madness to attack regular and veteran soldiery with undrilled levies, pointing out that there were but two hundred bayonets in the Texan army, that they had a good strong defensive position

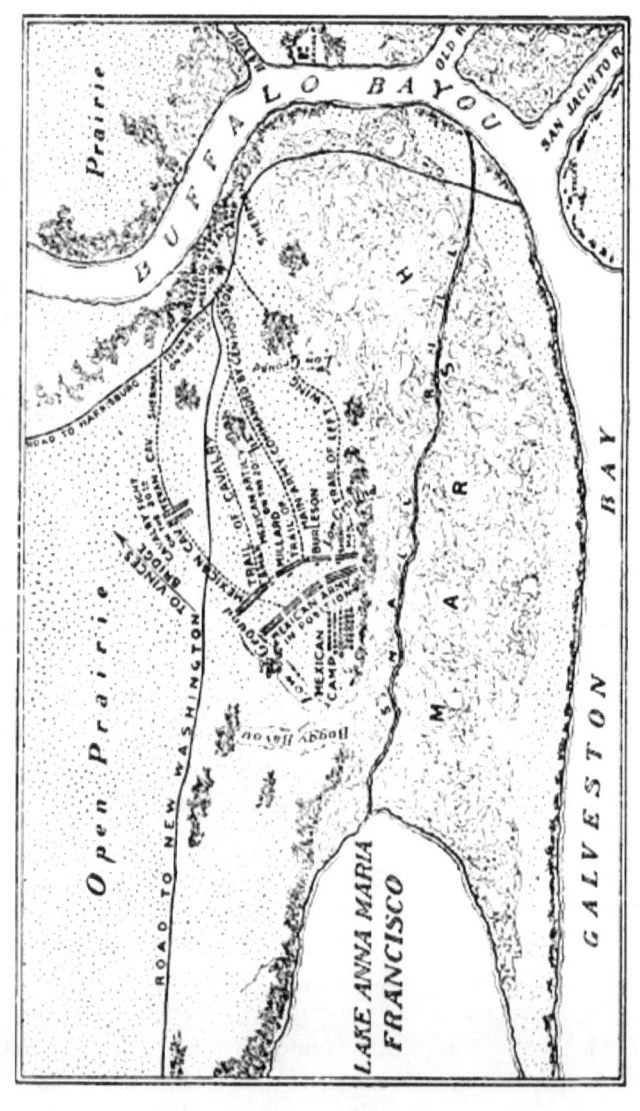

BATTLE OF SAN JACINTO

Lamar, with his handful of horse, had thrown himself upon the Mexican cavalry and routed them.

where they were, and they ought to wait for the Mexicans there.

Houston heard the discussion and received the conclusions in silence. He had already made up his mind, however, for he called Smith and Reeves to him and secretly ordered them to go with all speed and cut down Vince's bridge. In other words, he deliberately destroyed the only practicable means of escape for either army in case of defeat. By his action the battle which ensued was literally fought in an enclosure made by Buffalo Bayou on the north, San Jacinto Bay on the east, the marshes and waste land on the south, and Vince's Creek on the west.

5. THE BATTLE OF SAN JACINTO

At half after three o'clock the men were drawn up on the prairie in front of the camp, their movements being screened from the observation of the Mexicans, who were most careless on this occasion and had apparently posted neither scouts nor sentinels, by the tree islands. Colonel Burleson with the first regiment occupied the centre. Colonel Sherman was on the left with the second regiment, with the two pieces of artillery posted on the right of Colonel Burleson's men. The guns were supported by four companies of infantry under Lieutenant-Colonel Millard. The newly celebrated Lamar, burning to distinguish himself again, occupied the right of the line with his cavalry. Secretary Rusk had general command of the left, while Houston led the centre in person.

At four o'clock Houston gave the order to advance. The band, which consisted of the solitary drum of famous memory, re-enforced by a single fife, struck up a familiar popular air entitled "Will You Come to the Bower?" It was a bright, brilliant, sunny afternoon. The men with their guns a-trail advanced slowly until they passed the timber islands and appeared in view of the surprised Mexicans. Then they broke into a run and darted forward. Houston dashed up and down the lines on horseback, waving his old white hat[2] "and shouting profanely but emphatically, "G—d d—n you, hold your fire!"

When they were within two hundred feet of the Mexican line Deaf Smith tore madly on the field, his panting horse flecked with foam, and shouted in tones that could be heard all along the little line: "You must fight for your lives! Vince's bridge has been cut down!" The purport of this startling message was instantly perceived by the

2. On this day Houston wore "an old black coat, a black velvet vest, a pair of snuff-coloured pantaloons, and dilapidated boots," with his trousers tucked in them. "His only badge of authority during the campaign was a sword with a plated scabbard which he tied to his belt with buckskin thongs."

Texans. Like Cortez, Houston had burned his boats behind him. If they did not conquer, they would be like the army of Sennacherib, "all dead corpses."

The Mexican camp was a picture of consternation and terror. They had never dreamed of the possibility of assault. Santa Anna was asleep, many of the officers were taking their afternoon siesta; the cavalrymen were watering their horses, the company cooks were preparing for the evening meal, the soldiers had laid aside their arms and were playing games. In great astonishment, as they discovered the Texans passing around the tree islands, they ran to their arms, and as Houston's men came on, the Mexicans delivered a wavering volley, which, being aimed too high, did almost no execution. One bullet struck Houston in the ankle, making a bad wound, and several others hit his horse, but nothing could stop the advance. Before the Mexicans could discharge their cannon—it was found loaded when captured—the Americans struck the place.

Quick as had been their advance the "Twin Sisters "had been able to deliver two well-aimed shots which had demolished a large portion of the flimsy barricade. As they reached the rampart the Texans fired point-blank at the huddled Mexicans. The discharge did fearful execution. Before the Spanish could turn and fly, the fierce, furious faces of the Americans burst upon them through the smoke, and with clubbed muskets, a few bayonets, and many bowie knives, began their dreadful work. The cry that ran over the field with ever-increasing volume until it drowned the roar of the guns, had been one filled with menace to Santa Anna and his men.

"Remember the Alamo! Remember Goliad! Remember La Bahia!"

Inspired to fury by the recollection of the cruel, bloodthirsty massacres, which Santa Anna had instigated and in which these men had participated, the Americans swept everything before them by their valour. In fifteen minutes the whole Mexican army was either dead or on the run. Lamar, with his handful of horse, had thrown himself upon the Mexican cavalry and routed them. Horsemen who could do so were galloping headlong down the road toward Vince's bridge pursued by the mounted Americans. The infantry and many officers on the Mexican right plunged into the marshes, vainly seeking safety, only to be slaughtered as they stood enmired.

The Mexican defence, however, was not without some redeeming features. General Castrillon coolly stood in plain view of the Americans on an ammunition box, vainly imploring his flying men to make a stand. When they had retreated at least fifty yards from him, in despair of rallying them, he turned to follow and was shot down by the enemy, several bullets being found in his body after the engagement was over. Colonel Almonte succeeded in rallying some five hundred men in the trees, but was unable to inspire them with any energy, so he surrendered them in a body.

Santa Anna with some others fled at top speed toward Vince's bridge, hotly pursued by Captain Karnes. When the fugitives reached the crossing and found it destroyed they faced about, but the pursuing Texans slaughtered them without mercy. A few, however, Santa Anna among the number, leaped recklessly into the ravine and managed to make good their escape on the other side.

The Mexican army had been completely routed. As an army it had been eliminated from the campaign. Six hundred and thirty dead bodies were left on the field, of whom twenty-four were officers. Two hundred and eight lay wounded and helpless, of whom eighteen were officers. There were seven hundred and thirty prisoners, a few fugitives, and many unknown and unaccounted for, who died in the marshes or rivers attempting to escape. The total Mexican force engaged had been about eighteen hundred. Of Texans there were just seven hundred and eighty-three, of whom eight were killed and twenty-three wounded! It was one of the most crushing and bloody defeats on record.

Though the numbers engaged were small the results were remarkable, for Santa Anna was captured next day by a party of Texans, and with him in possession the war was over, and the independence of Texas accomplished.

Besides the arms and equipments twelve thousand dollars in specie was found in the Mexican treasure-chest. Houston generously gave up his share of plunder to his soldiers. Having set aside a portion for the Texan Navy, the men received on an average about seven dollars and a half apiece, but no reward could have measured up to the standard of their splendid victory; and the Field of the Hyacinth, changed from purple to red by the blood of their enemies, in Thomas H. Benton's poetic figure, is associated with the brightest day in the story of the Lone Star Republic, which then took its place in the constellation of nations.

Houston had again led the charge as he had done years before, and he was the hero of the occasion, although, as he said himself, the "glorious achievement was attributable not to superior force but to the valour of our soldiery and the sanctity of our cause." Certainly I think San Jacinto must be placed high among the memorable conflicts and struggles that have occurred during the evolution of the American people, for it terminated forever any possibility of Spanish dominion in what is now one of the greatest and most important parts of the United States. From that point it is one of the most decisive of our battles.

Old Sam Houston had not read *Caesar's Commentaries* for nothing. His masterly retreat from the enemy inducing him to divide his force, when the composition of the army is considered, was a splendid manoeuvre. He showed that he knew how to carry the shield of Fabius; and when he learned that Santa Anna was alone, with a part of his force at Harrisburg, his forced march to corner him and the brilliant, workmanlike manner in which he planned and fought the battle, his daring in staking all upon the hazard by destroying his only means of retreat, showed that he wielded the sword of Marcellus as well.

While he had no opportunity to distinguish himself on larger fields and with greater force, yet he made the very best possible use of, and secured the greatest possible results from, the means at his command. No one could have done better, few could have done so well. Therefore we may write him down a soldier.

No monument has yet been erected by grateful Texans over his remains, but the state itself, empire as it is in extent, in resources, is forever associated with his name.

LEONAUR

ALSO FROM LEONAUR

AVAILABLE IN SOFTCOVER OR HARDCOVER WITH DUST JACKET

AN APACHE CAMPAIGN IN THE SIERRA MADRE *by John G. Bourke*—An Account of the Expedition in Pursuit of the Chiricahua Apaches in Arizona, 1883.

BILLY DIXON & ADOBE WALLS *by Billy Dixon and Edward Campbell Little*—Scout, Plainsman & Buffalo Hunter, *Life and Adventures of "Billy" Dixon* by Billy Dixon and *The Battle of Adobe Walls* by Edward Campbell Little (*Pearson's Magazine*).

WITH THE CALIFORNIA COLUMN *by George H. Petis*—Against Confederates and Hostile Indians During the American Civil War on the South Western Frontier, *The California Column, Frontier Service During the Rebellion* and *Kit Carson's Fight With the Comanche and Kiowa Indians.*

THRILLING DAYS IN ARMY LIFE *by George Alexander Forsyth*—Experiences of the Beecher's Island Battle 1868, the Apache Campaign of 1882, and the American Civil War.

INDIAN FIGHTS AND FIGHTERS *by Cyrus Townsend Brady*—Indian Fights and Fighters of the American Western Frontier of the 19th Century.

THE NEZ PERCÉ CAMPAIGN, 1877 *by G. O. Shields & Edmond Stephen Meany*—Two Accounts of Chief Joseph and the Defeat of the Nez Percé, *The Battle of Big Hole* by G. O. Shields and *Chief Joseph, the Nez Percé* by Edmond Stephen Meany.

CAPTAIN JEFF OF THE TEXAS RANGERS *by W. J. Maltby*—Fighting Comanche & Kiowa Indians on the South Western Frontier 1863-1874.

SHERIDAN'S TROOPERS ON THE BORDERS *by De Benneville Randolph Keim*—The Winter Campaign of the U. S. Army Against the Indian Tribes of the Southern Plains, 1868-9.

WILD LIFE IN THE FAR WEST *by James Hobbs*—The Adventures of a Hunter, Trapper, Guide, Prospector and Soldier.

THE OLD SANTA FE TRAIL *by Henry Inman*—The Story of a Great Highway.

LIFE IN THE FAR WEST *by George F. Ruxton*—The Experiences of a British Officer in America and Mexico During the 1840's.

ADVENTURES IN MEXICO AND THE ROCKY MOUNTAINS *by George F. Ruxton*—Experiences of Mexico and the South West During the 1840's.

www.ingramcontent.com/pod-product-compliance
Lightning Source LLC
Chambersburg PA
CBHW060344030726
47497CB00003B/591